THE CIVIL WAR IN THE EAST

Related Titles from Potomac Books

The Black Experience in the Civil War South
by Stephen V. Ash

Second Manassas: Longstreet's Attack and the Struggle for Chinn Ridge
by Scott Patchan

THE CIVIL WAR IN THE EAST

STRUGGLE, STALEMATE, AND VICTORY

BROOKS D. SIMPSON

Potomac Books
An imprint of the University of Nebraska Press

The Civil War in the East: Struggle, Stalemate, and Victory, by Brooks D. Simpson, was originally published in hard cover by Praeger, an imprint of ABC-CLIO, LLC, Santa Barbara, CA. Copyright © 2011 by Brooks D. Simpson. Paperback edition by arrangement with ABC-CLIO, LLC, Santa Barbara, CA.

Potomac Books is an imprint of the University of Nebraska Press

Manufactured in the United States of America

First Nebraska paperback printing: 2013

Library of Congress
Cataloging-in-Publication Data
Simpson, Brooks D.
The Civil War in the East: struggle, stalemate, and victory / Brooks D. Simpson. — First edition.
pages cm
Includes bibliographical references and index.
ISBN 978-1-61234-628-1 (pbk.: alk. paper) 1. United States—History—Civil War, 1861–1865—Campaigns. 2. East (U.S.)—History, Military—19th century. I. Title.
E470.2.S556 2013
973.7'3—dc23   2013009591

For Cheryl

CONTENTS

Photo essay follows page 74.

SERIES FOREWORD

"Like Ol' Man River," the distinguished Civil War historian Peter J. Parish wrote in 1998, "Civil War historiography just keeps rolling along. It changes course occasionally, leaving behind bayous of stagnant argument, while it carves out new lines of inquiry and debate."

Since Confederate General Robert E. Lee's men stacked their guns at Appomattox Court House in April 1865, historians and partisans have been fighting a war of words over the causes, battles, results, and broad meaning of the internecine conflict that cost more than 620,000 American lives. Writers have contributed between 50,000 and 60,000 books and pamphlets on the topic. Viewed in terms of defining American freedom and nationalism, western expansion and economic development, the Civil War quite literally launched modern America. "The Civil War," Kentucky poet, novelist, and literary critic Robert Penn Warren explained, "is for the American imagination, the great single event of our history. Without too much wrenching, it may, in fact, be said to be American history."

The books in Praeger's Reflections on the Civil War Era series examine pivotal aspects of the U.S. Civil War. Topics range from examinations of military campaigns and local conditions, to analyses of institutional, intellectual, and social history. Questions of class, gender, and race run through each volume in the series. Authors, veteran experts in their respective fields provide concise, informed, and readable syntheses—fresh looks at familiar topics with new source material and original arguments.

"Like all great conflicts," Parish noted in 1999, "the American Civil War reflected the society and the age in which it was fought." Books in Reflections on the Civil War Era series interpret the war as a salient event in the hammering out and understanding of American identity before, during, and after the secession crisis of 1860–1861. Readers will find the volumes valuable guides as they chart the troubled waters of mid-nineteenth-century American life.

John David Smith
Charles H. Stone Distinguished Professor of American History
The University of North Carolina at Charlotte

ACKNOWLEDGMENTS

My thanks go to Elizabeth Demers and John David Smith, who suggested this project over lunch at San Jose. I appreciate the patience shown by Michael Millman at ABC-CLIO as this project came to fruition. Ethan S. Rafuse went over the manuscript and offered suggestions, while Mark von Hagen helped me to secure the time needed to finish the manuscript.

My father and my sister, Joy, continue to encourage me in my endeavors, for which I can't thank them enough: indeed, it was my father who took me to many of these battlefields in Pennsylvania, Maryland, and Virginia in 1974 after an initial visit to Gettysburg in 1966. Becca, Emily, and Olivia have been patient when their father's been busy and offered welcome relief when it was time to set work aside to do more important things—such as going to hockey games, watching the Yankees, taking them shopping, or playing Halo. Finally, Cheryl's learned more about the Civil War than she ever wanted to know; I trust she has always known how much I love her.

INTRODUCTION

It is fair to ask whether there exists a need for yet another volume on military operations in the Eastern Theater during the American Civil War. Hasn't enough been
written already? What about the countless books on Gettysburg, with doubtless
more to come in a never-ending flow? Don't we have studies of First and Second
Manassas, the Peninsula Campaign, the Shenandoah Valley Campaigns of 1862
and 1864, Antietam, Fredericksburg, Chancellorsville, the Overland Campaign of
1864 and its constituent battles, and Appomattox? At most we presently lack an
overview of the operations around Petersburg and Richmond in 1864–65, and that
may soon well be remedied. Nor are we lacking for biographical studies. What new
can be said about Abraham Lincoln and Jefferson Davis, Ulysses S. Grant and Robert
E. Lee, George B. McClellan and Stonewall Jackson, and a host of other generals?

Oddly enough, it is precisely at such a time that it may prove advantageous to step
back from such focused studies to spend more time surveying matters from a distance.
For all the literature about Civil War military operations and leadership, precious little
has been written about military strategy, particularly in what has become known as the
Eastern Theater (traditionally defined as Virginia, Maryland, Pennsylvania, and the
District of Columbia; occasionally there are allusions to North Carolina and West
Virginia). Yet it is in this theater where the interaction of geography and logistics,

politics and public opinion, battlefront and homefront, and the conduct of military operations and civil-military relations, can be highlighted in sharp relief.[1]

There is something to be said for the notion, popular among some historians, that the Civil War was won by the Union and lost by the Confederacy in the West. After all, it was in the West where the Union forged a successful command team and where Union forces seized key strategic points and gained much ground while strategic stalemate persisted in the East. To be sure, any study of how both the Union and Confederacy conducted military operations cannot escape realizing that events in the East and the West were interconnected, and that theater strategy was part of a larger overall military strategy. Yet time and again contemporary observers measured overall success and failure in large part by what was happening in the East. Abraham Lincoln noted as much in August 1862, when he remarked in the wake of Union set-backs outside Richmond, "it seems unreasonable that a series of successes, extending through half a year, and clearing more than 100,000 square miles of country, should help us so little, while a single defeat should hurt us so much."[2] In 1864, fresh off a series of victories in the West, Ulysses S. Grant came East because he was convinced that it was the place where the commanding general had to be. Those observers who assert the superiority of Confederate military leadership rest their case with emphasis upon the eastern campaigns and the performance of Robert E. Lee and his generals. The same emphasis shapes the enduring impression of Grant's generalship as relying upon attrition made possible by significantly superior resources.

As it turned out, Union triumphs in the West set the stage for eventual Union victory. However, it need not have been that way. Time and again the Confederates hoped to reverse the tide of ill fortune in the West by triumphing in the East. It was in the East where the two capitals were located; it was to the East where many observers, North, South, and abroad, looked to assess the prospects for victory and defeat. If one agrees that the persistence of public will on one hand and a growing sense of war-weariness on the other were crucial to determining the outcome of the conflict, then one cannot minimize the importance of the course of the war in the East to shaping those public impressions. That the Union may have won the war in the West does not mean that it could not have won the war in the East in 1862, in the wake of Gettysburg in 1863, or in the spring of 1864, had things turned out differently. That the Confederacy may have lost the war in the West does not mean that it could not have won it in the East—indeed, the best chance for Confederate victory on the battlefield was probably in the East, and the East may also have been the best place where the Confederacy could have worn out the Union's will to persist and prevail.

This work does not rely upon hitherto unknown primary sources or an extensive rummaging through the mountains of material already available. It does not seek to retell in detail the course of every battle or campaign—books aplenty abound for that purpose. Instead, it takes a fresh look at what's already out there, examines what others may have overlooked, and offers a more integrated interpretation of military operations that demonstrates how politics, public perception, geography, and logistics shaped the course of military operations in the East. The Eastern Theater was a theater of decision (and indecision) precisely because people believed that campaigns could provide decisive results. The presence of the capitals raised the stakes of victory and defeat because of their great symbolic value: in addition, Virginia was crucial to Confederate prospects due to its size, population, and resources. At a time when people viewed war in terms of decisive battles, the anticipation of victory followed by disappointment and persistent strategic stalemate characterized much of the course of the war in the East. Grant's ability to pin Lee against Richmond and Petersburg and to nullify Confederate efforts to reverse the course of events in the summer of 1864 meant that this time there would be no "half-defeat" to negate Union successes elsewhere. Yet it was his inability to take Lee off the board altogether that plunged many northerners into war-weariness that same long hot summer, to the point that Lincoln believed his reelection was in doubt. Perceptions fashioned realities, then as later, when it came to assessing the progress of military operations. Lee's advances across the Potomac in 1862 and 1863 were doomed to be perceived as failures by an anxious public because he failed to deliver a knockout punch, overshadowing any accomplishments achieved during those campaigns. In each case withdrawal across the Potomac in the aftermath of bloody battles appeared to be a defeat. Indeed, for years to come many Americans would cite Gettysburg as the high water mark of the Confederacy, the turning point of the war, when in fact it was no such thing. Had things turned out differently, whatever might have happened at Gettysburg was immaterial: what did happen simply maintained strategic stalemate.

At a time when some authors and readers rest content with the telling and retelling of an epic saga, it is essential to question conventional wisdom, especially when it is not wisdom at all, without giving way to pure and perverse contrarianism. Taking a step back from the battlefield proper may help us understand the ebb and flow of the war in the East much more clearly and place it in proper perspective and context. It allows us to examine more clearly the strategies both sides employed; it also reminds us of the role of public perceptions in shaping military operations. In the process we may learn something useful about the so-called American way of war, then and now.

PROLOGUE

❧

JULY 21, 1861

It was a summer Sunday—a perfect day for a weekend picnic or a drive in the countryside. So thought the people in carriages and on horseback who had made their way down to the grassy fields of northern Virginia and gathered north of a winding stream known to the locals as Bull Run. But those who had made the journey were not seeking peace and quiet. Rather, they were eager to see what many of them believed would be the decisive battle of the American Civil War.

The date, July 21, was no accident. It had been just over three months since President Abraham Lincoln had called for 75,000 volunteers to serve 90 days in military service in the aftermath of the surrender of Fort Sumter to Confederate forces under the command of General Pierre G. T. Beauregard. Those terms of service were close to expiration, and many of the boys in blue (and various other colors—as yet there was no standard uniform) were on the point of going home without ever having seen combat. Since then the president had made calls for men to serve two and three years of service, called Congress into special session on July 4, and declared a blockade of ports controlled by the so-called Confederate States of America, that loose confederation of states that had seceded, one-by-one, since December 1860.

Jefferson Davis had been matching his United States counterpart move-for-move since the Sumter crisis. Anticipating the possibility of military conflict, the

Confederates had raised regiments for a year's service before war had broken out, and the secession of four states had simply added to its manpower pool. In the wake of Virginia's decision to join the Confederacy, the Confederate Congress decided to shift the new nation's capital from Montgomery, Alabama, to Richmond, as a way to fasten the allegiance of the old Dominion and that Congress would convene there on July 20. No sooner had that decision been made than Virginia voters ratified secession; the next day Union troops occupied Alexandria, while, down at Fort Monroe, near the mouth of the James River, Major General Benjamin F. Butler gave everyone a glimpse at what was to come by refusing to turn over three slaves who had escaped into his lines, terming them "contraband of war."[1]

By summer significant Confederate forces stood poised to defend their new republic. One force, under Beauregard, held Manassas Junction, keeping a watchful eye on Union forces assembling around Washington; a second army, commanded by Joseph E. Johnston, was in the Shenandoah Valley, opposing a Union force under the command of Robert Patterson.

In Washington General-in-Chief Winfield Scott drew on his half-century of military experience, strategic expertise, and political and diplomatic instincts to frame a plan of attack. An expedition would seize control of the Mississippi River, while elsewhere Union land and sea forces would contain the Confederacy, isolating it from the outside, and wait until the pressure forced the Confederacy to implode. Surely such a plan would take more than 90 days to implement, however, and it presaged a long if not particularly bloody conflict—thus Scott called for patience. But patience was in short supply that summer. Northerners wanted to fight, the sooner the better. Why allow the service of those brave boys who signed up for 90 days go for naught? "Forward to Richmond! Forward to Richmond! The Rebel Congress must not be allowed to meet there on the 20th of July! By that date the place must be helped by the national army!" So declared the New York *Tribune*. Scott conceded that his plan required resisting such pressure, but he knew that many people "will urge instant and vigorous action, regardless, I fear, of consequences."[2]

It was not as if there had not already been any battles. In western Virginia Union forces under General George B. McClellan were winning a series of minor victories that would do much to secure that portion of the Old Dominion for the Union. Confederates took much more pride in their repulse of several Union columns at Big Bethel, Virginia, on June 10. One look at the casualties (76 Union killed, wounded, and missing versus a single Confederate killed and 8 more wounded) led some enthusiasts to declare that one Rebel could whip ten Yankees, a calculation that overlooked the fact that many of the Federal losses were due to friendly fire in a confused action. Elsewhere, in Missouri, Union forces had gained the upper hand in a critical border state. But it was understandable that everyone looked to northern Virginia for a decisive battle. The Confederates were but a few days' march from

Washington; they were led by the hero of Fort Sumter. Surely they would emerge victorious, even if they were outnumbered.[3]

On July 16, 1861, General Irvin McDowell, in command of the Federal army that had assembled around Washington, directed his men to commence marching. He did so somewhat reluctantly. He knew his men were not ready for combat, and he had reason to suspect he was not, either. After all, no one in American history had commanded a field army some 35,000 strong; most of his subordinates had never before commanded more than a company. Simply donning a uniform adorned with a general's star did not imbue one with military skill. The men needed drilling, training, time to become soldiers. But Lincoln turned a deaf ear to McDowell's reservations. "You are green," he agreed. "But they are green, too. You are all green alike."[4]

As McDowell's men made their way across the dusty Virginia roads on July 16 and 17, Beauregard prepared to receive them. He had learned of McDowell's advance the night it began, courtesy of Rose Greenhow, a spy ensconced in Washington. Deploying his men behind Bull Run, he called for reinforcements. They were already on the way, thanks to Joseph E. Johnston, who mounted his men on railcars headed toward Manassas Junction. They could not come soon enough. On July 18, lead elements of McDowell's army, now occupying Centreville, probed southward toward Blackburn's Ford, where they encountered the waiting Confederates and were repulsed. The next day, as both sides prepared to fight, the first of Johnston's men—a brigade of Virginians led by a former Virginia Military Institute professor named Thomas J. Jackson—reached Manassas Junction. On July 20 Johnston arrived at Beauregard's headquarters. The two generals conferred and decided to advance across Blackburn Ford northwards toward Centreville. Unknown to them, McDowell had decided to move on the Confederates left behind Bull Run. That the Confederate Congress had convened that very day in Richmond suddenly seemed unimportant.[5]

Early on the morning of July 21, as the civilian visitors from Washington arrived, McDowell struck first, fording Bull Run and crossing a stone bridge that spanned the creek. Driving back the Confederate left, the Yankees soon fell victim to their own disorganization. By midday the Confederates had assembled a defensive line along Henry House Hill, just southeast of a crossroads, while reinforcements hurried to extend the Rebel line and stop the Yankee advance. They were helped when Jackson's brigade held firm. A retreating Confederate commander encouraged his men to make a stand by pointing out the brigade commander, who was still wearing his blue uniform jacket from his previous service as a major in the United States Army. "There stands Jackson like a stone wall!" he cried. "Rally behind the Virginians!"

The Confederates fended off a series of piecemeal and uncoordinated attacks: one Union brigade commander, William T. Sherman, sent his regiments up one at a time, thus dissipating any advantage he might have had. The Rebels then rushed forward to capture two artillery batteries that had advanced without adequate infantry support, a move that solidified their hold upon Henry House Hill. Their numbers bolstered by arriving reinforcements, the Confederates counterattacked, driving the Union right flank back (some confusion was due to the fact that both sides had diffi-culty figuring out who was who, given the varied uniform colors, thus allowing some Confederates to come up close before opening fire). The Yankees broke, and scrambled back across the stone bridge. When a Confederate artillery shell over-turned a wagon on a bridge spanning Cub Run to the east, many soldiers panicked, dropping rifles and haversacks as they fled. Bloody, tired, and beaten, the Union sol-diers straggled back to Centreville, and from there on to Washington, making their way past the spectators who were now running or riding for their lives. They left behind cheering Confederates whose enthusiasm barely exceeded their exhaustion.

As the battle drew to a close President Jefferson Davis appeared on the scene. Being a military man, he might have something to contribute to the moment. Should Beauregard or Johnston consider a pursuit? Might they even take a chance on driving all the way to Washington? The moment soon passed, to be revisited in postwar recollections as one of the first "what ifs" to haunt Confederate military his-tory. In truth, the Confederates were also disorganized, making it difficult to mount an effective pursuit. Neither Beauregard nor Johnston was particularly excited to see Davis present, and neither man would enjoy a placid, let alone constructive, relation-ship with the Confederate president.

Back in Washington, Abraham Lincoln was shocked, then saddened by the news of McDowell's defeat. Perhaps both sides had been green, but the Yankee inexper-ience was more costly given that McDowell was on the offensive and required coor-dinated movements to achieve success. Scott condemned himself as a coward: he declared that he should have stood firm in insisting that the army was not yet ready to commence active campaigning.[6] It was now clear that one battle would not win the war. It might take two or three, maybe more.

On both homefronts, it took a while to reach that same realization. Take George Templeton Strong, a New Yorker and supporter of the administration. Having trav-eled to Virginia and Washington in July, he returned to New York as rumors of an offensive in Virginia circulated. "I fear this move is premature," Strong confided to his diary, "forced on General Scott by the newspapers. A serious check on this line would be a great disaster." Two days later he added, "We are all waiting breathlessly for news from the Army of Virginia." That was July 19. Three days later, he reported that the news from the front was good, and the Confederates were falling back upon Manassas Junction. "Thank God for this good news," he reflected. "We shall prob-ably receive a cold-water douche, however, before night in the shape of less comfort-able intelligence." He was right. That evening, he announced that it was now "BLACK MONDAY. We are utterly and disgracefully routed, beaten, whipped by secessionists." The Rebels had brought overwhelming force in the neighborhood of

90,000 men, he reported, to bear upon the hapless McDowell. It looked like another Waterloo to Strong: "Only one great fact stands out unmistakably: total defeat and national disaster on the largest scale." He awaited news that Washington had fallen into rebel hands.[7]

It took only one night's sleep for Strong to offer a reassessment. "We feel a little better today," he announced on July 23. "The army is by no means annihilated. Only a small part of it seems to have been stricken with panic. A gallant fight has been made against enormous odds and at every disadvantage." Although Strong still suspected that General Scott had been pressured into advancing "against his own judgment by outside pressure and popular clamor," the result was not as bad as had first been feared. Strong grumbled over Confederate celebrations of victory and jotted down tales of Rebel atrocities on the field, but life—and the war—would go on.[8]

Meanwhile, in North Carolina, Catherine Edmundston waited for news from Virginia. Riding the railroad on the way to visit a childhood friend, she noted that all the talk was about the impending crisis: "The cars were filled with people who had friends at Manassas & our hearts bled for many of them from the cruel suspense they were in, for rumours of a great battle—vague & contradictory—filled the hearts of wives & children with agony." At Wrightsville she heard news of the battle itself. She recalled that newspaper commentators had been critical of Johnston's movements in the Shenandoah Valley "because they could not understand him . . . but the sequel showed that he knew well what he was about & was in fact a master of strategy." The resulting Federal defeat "degenerated into a rout, the most disgraceful ever known in the annals of war!" Unfortunately, it was not enough. "Could we have followed up the Victory by an immediate march on to Washington it is the opinion of almost all now that we could have dictated terms of Peace—from our own captured Congress Halls—but our troops were greatly exhausted & it did not enter into the heart of man to conceive the extent of their panic." The end had been so close, or so it seemed.[9]

What happened in July 1861 offered a sneak preview of what was to follow in the Eastern Theater. Two armies prepared to clash, each poised to defend its capital while threatening that of the enemy, each seeking the defeat and perhaps the destruction of the opposing army in decisive battle, and each finding out after a pitched battle that the victor was in almost as bad shape as the defeated, and unable to follow up. Two presidents confronted each other, each peering over the shoulders of their generals, each making suggestions, each dealing with dissenters, second-guessers, and opponents, and each impatient for action. Two publics, each looking anxiously for victory, emotions buoyed then dashed by newspaper reports, found themselves inspired and then unnerved by the course of the conflict. So much was expected of a battle at Bull Run, and so little actually happened, although the impression of victory and defeat left by the battle proved durable. The two armies, which in time would evolve into the Union's Army of the Potomac and the Confederacy's Army of Northern Virginia, were both exhausted by the outcome: if the Yankees were too tired to stay, the Rebs were too tired to pursue. That would become the pattern in the East: both sides would seek battle, but battle would achieve little, in part because it proved so hard to follow up on any advantage gained on the field.

Like many of the battles that took place over the next several years, Manassas gained its renown as much from what might have happened or did not happen as what did happen, the tantalizing possibilities not diminished in the slightest by the cold fact that so little actually did happen. For the Union, the battle marked the end of the rush to action caused by the approaching expiration of the terms of service for the 90 day recruits; in its aftermath George B. McClellan would come to Washington to repair the mess, and by the time he left the field in November 1862, he had left a significant imprint on the conduct of the war in the East. The victorious Confederates may have celebrated their temporary triumph, but within days it was obvious that little had actually changed: at most the victory fed Rebel hubris and conceit. There would be significant military action over the course of the remainder of 1861, but it would not happen in Virginia. That colorful tales of what happened on the hills and fields south and west of Bull Run on that hot July day in 1861 persist in the history books despite the overall irrelevance of the battle is testimony to what attracts readers today and how that blinds them to deeper understandings.

In short, Manassas (as the victors called it until August 1862, when it became First Manassas) or Bull Run (as the defeated came to style it) resolved little. Its importance lies in the "what might have beens." The action elevated Thomas J. Jackson to prominence, along with bestowing upon him the nickname of Stonewall; the aftermath saw McClellan taking charge in the East. Perhaps Lincoln learned something about haste, although he would always be sensitive to the pressures of public opinion and some fellow Republicans to act. Within weeks of the battle Davis began to learn that an army did not subsist on gallantry alone, as complaints flowed to Richmond about how the victors were famished and undersupplied. That in turn sparked a debate over whether supply problems deprived the Rebels of a chance to strike a decisive blow by moving directly upon Washington, raising public expectations and disappointments.[10] The reports of imminent victory followed by defeat left many northerners shaken, but only for a short while; down in Dixie, early celebrations gave way to wondering what was to happen next. And yet the hope of decisive battle never quite left many people, whether they were presidents, generals, or the general public. It would be people's anticipation of what might happen, and the ensuing disappointments when reality fell short of their expectations, which characterized how they viewed the war in the East. That narrative proves as gripping today as it was then; it also proves as distorting.

ONE

THE THEATER OF WAR

The Eastern Theater, as it came to be defined by mid-1862, stretched from southern Virginia north to southern Pennsylvania and west from the Atlantic Ocean and Chesapeake Bay to western Virginia. The geographical boundaries of the theater rendered it far smaller than what Civil War historians traditionally call the Western Theater (which, by war's end, came to include the Carolinas as well as Kentucky, Tennessee, Georgia, Alabama, Mississippi, and Louisiana). Most of the battles in the East took place in eastern and central Virginia, along with two major campaigns in Maryland and Pennsylvania. These battles and campaigns have received the lion's share of attention in most military accounts of the war in the East. In contrast, operations along the south Atlantic coast, including the Carolinas, Georgia, and Florida, as well as operations west of the Mississippi River, receive far less coverage.

Many Civil War narratives focus on the battles in the Eastern Theater, Gettysburg being by far the best-known of them. And yet a look at a map that sets forth the progress of the campaigns across the Confederacy between 1861 and 1865 shows that little actually changed in the East, while Union forces occupied or invaded significant portions of the Western Theater. That alone suggests that the triumph of Union arms was rooted in their western successes. Add to that the fact that the general who broke the stalemate in the East and at last brought operations to a decisive close hailed from the West and carried with him a string of impressive victories, and one wonders why the East continues to get so much attention. The imbalance reminds one of treatments of World War I, where there has been far more written about the bloody indecisiveness battles of the Western front than the sweeping offensives in eastern Europe.

Part of the answer, one might conclude, can be found in the drama of battle. Here again Gettysburg claims pride of place. Who can forget the stories about John Buford's delaying action, Little Round Top, and, of course, the wonderfully misnamed Pickett's Charge? Those accounts are simply the best-known of a series of stories in which it seems the tide of battle turned and turned again over three days. The battlefield continues to pull visitors, from first-timers to those who frequent the area, who are captivated by seeing where this drama took place. Yet there's also Antietam, with its cornfield and its sunken road, to say nothing of Burnside's bridge; at Manassas we can see a statue of Jackson standing like a stone wall and walk across the Stone Bridge spanning Bull Run; at Fredericksburg one can stand near the visitor's center and look on with horror and admiration at line after line of Union soldiers assailed Marye's Heights, only to be cut down and driven back by troops deployed behind yet another sunken road; and a dozen miles to the west we can visit the spot where Stonewall's own men shot their commander just as it looked as if victory might be complete at Chancellorsville. Less celebrated but still remembered are the fiery woods of the Wilderness as Grant chomped on his cigar and decided to advance; Spotsylvania's Bloody Angle, where rifle fire cut down a thick tree; and the eerie quiet of Cold Harbor, mute testimony to suicidal assaults. We can read again and again about what happened, and actually see where it happened.

Just to recite these events is to conjure up vivid images in the minds of many people who have an interest in the Civil War. And yet those students of the conflict who have gone beyond that narrative would surely protest that the battles in the West had equally dramatic moments. There's the attempted breakout at Fort Donelson, and the emergence of Unconditional Surrender Grant; the surprise attack at Shiloh and the stand at the Hornet's Nest by Bloody Pond; the rapid movements and the wearing siege that led to victory at Vicksburg; George H. Thomas holding on, steady as a rock, at Chickamauga; the scaling of Lookout Mountain and the incredible charge up Missionary Ridge at Chattanooga; the futility of Kenesaw Mountain and the slugfests around Atlanta; the disaster of Franklin, outstripping both Pickett's Charge and Cold Harbor; and the collapse at Nashville orchestrated by a general under fire from the rear. Surely the battles in the West do not lack for dramatic moments: we just don't hear as much about them.

If it is not sheer drama, what is it? After all, it would be hard to declare that our perception of the relative importance of the two major theaters is a product of a romantic reassessment, because even at the time white northerners and southerners tended to focus on the East. One can see this even in the correspondence of soldiers in general: one comes away from reading many of their letters with the impression that soldiers and officers in the West were more aware of what was going on in the East than the other way around. Part of that had to do with the belief that the stakes were so high given the proximity of Richmond and Washington, given the notion that the taking of the enemy capital was a sure sign of victory (although in past practice that had not always been the case). Some of our emphasis today is doubtless attributable to the fact that after the war, most white southerners tended to celebrate the achievements of Robert E. Lee, his generals (notably Thomas J. "Stonewall" Jackson and James Ewell Brown "Jeb" Stuart) and the Army of Northern Virginia. Much has been written about how Virginians took over the Southern Historical Society Papers in the 1870s and fostered a Virginia-centric account of the war, but the fact is that during the war many white southerners looked to what was going on in Virginia as the best source of hope. Nor can we limit responsibility to white southerners for crafting this Eastern perspective, for white northerners as well tended to emphasize the saga of the Army of the Potomac as it persisted in battling Lee. Down to the present day, we have far more detailed accounts of the Army of the Potomac than we do of its more successful counterparts, the Army of the Cumberland and especially the Army of the Tennessee, the Union's most triumphant field army. The imbalance is especially evident in three mid-twentieth century classic studies. Douglas Southall Freeman crafted a total of seven volumes on Lee and his army; despite his midwestern roots, Bruce Catton chose to celebrate the Army of the Potomac in three volumes. One might well counter that Shelby Foote, sensing this imbalance, gave the West the attention it was due, but even there the romance of the Eastern Theater is evident in his three volumes.

In the end, the attraction of the Eastern Theater, then as now, is due to a combination of its dramatic elements, the location of the opposing capitals, the proximity of the theater to the northeastern press and Europe, the importance of the East economically and politically, and traditional conceptions of warfare that prevailed then and continue to attract us even today. Of these, the most important may be the first and the last named elements. Although today we often view the Civil War as the first modern war or a preview of war in the twentieth century, one has to recall the frame of reference of Americans at the time of the conflict: the wars of the late eighteenth and early nineteenth century, including the Seven Years War, the American Revolution and, perhaps most importantly, the Napoleonic Wars. Moreover, it is the perception of Americans who recalled these conflicts, rather than a dispassionate analysis of the conflicts themselves, that is most revealing. White southerners took much heart from the American Revolution, because it proved that an inferior army could defeat a numerically and materially superior foe: the failure of the British to occupy all of its North American colonies or to subdue them offered the promise that the Union would also fail. So too did the example of Napoleon's failure to establish and maintain dominion over the European continent. Moreover, most Americans thought of war in terms of decisive battles where a stirring assault smashed through an enemy line, or a flanking force surprised an unwary foe and sent the enemy reeling. Every battle was potentially the next Austerlitz or Waterloo. Every battle was potentially decisive: each had its cliffhangers, its critical moments, its climaxes. At least one could believe that, especially with the opposing capitals not so far away.

And yet, in this theater of war, the decisive battle remained elusive. No army was ever quite driven off the field, although there were some seemingly close calls. Even when armies were badly outflanked, they survived: most of the time the two sides simply slugged it out. Battles were almost as damaging to winner as to loser, and sometimes it was difficult to distinguish between the two. One side tended to break off contact, then advanced or withdrew. Whatever advantage that was achieved usually came at such cost that the exhausted victors could not follow it up. Not until 1865 did either side conduct an effective pursuit, and only in the last campaign did a pursuit result in the destruction of the foe. Both sides welcomed the lengthy pause between battles in the first three years of conflict: the longest sustained offensive was Lee's drive northward through Second Manassas and Antietam in 1862. Moreover, until 1864 neither side could hold its advantage for long: neither could prevail in a major battle on enemy soil between June 1862 and December 1863.

In short, the theater of decision was indecisive for much of the war, an area characterized by strategic stalemate. Battles were significant because of what they might have accomplished, what they did not accomplish, and what they prevented. This, ironically, only increased the dramatic potential of the conflict, which might be said to resemble nothing so much as a television soap opera with cliffhangers, recurring themes, intrigue, and plot twists, none of which brings the story much closer to a conclusion. Would Richmond be saved? Was Washington in danger? Would Lincoln change generals? Would the public give up in the wake of defeat? Would the defenders hold the position? Would the attackers break through? Would another general fall at the height of battle, just as victory was within his grasp? What tricks did Lee have up his sleeve? Could anyone stop him? Could he stop Grant? On and on it went, without resolution, for four years. Both sides could derive some satisfaction from that pattern, and so can we as readers. But that should not blind us to the fact that until sometime in late 1864 the Eastern Theater was the scene of strategic stalemate. In the end it was the ability of Ulysses S. Grant to ensure that the Eastern Theater would not become the theater of Confederate decision (as well as his inability to make it the theater of Union decision) that left the decisive blows to be struck elsewhere. There was no glorious battlefield triumph: bloody attrition ground down the Confederacy.

Drama and perception help to explain how people viewed what happened in the Eastern Theater: geography helped to shape how the war was waged. The decision of the Confederate government to shift the new nation's capital from Montgomery to Richmond proved to be the final piece in the puzzle of the region's geography. Both terrain and man-made features played fundamental roles in shaping military operations over the next four years, limiting options, offering opportunities, and imposing conditions on the conduct of military operations.

Both capital cities were located on rivers. The Potomac served as somewhat more of a barrier to military operations than did the James, for it shielded Washington while the James offered a water highway toward Richmond and Petersburg. However, crossing the Potomac proved to be far easier than spanning the James, as generals on both sides discovered. Inland, the rivers tended to run in an east-west direction, except in the Shenandoah Valley: however, they served more as obstacles for attackers to cross (and to overcome the delays involved in crossing) than they served as defensive positions: Lee preferred not to contest river crossings unless the advantage was overwhelmingly clear, as at Fredericksburg. Perhaps the only river to serve as a significant barrier was the Susquehanna River in Pennsylvania. So far as they were navigable, the rivers were double-edged swords for the Confederates given Union control of the water, for the very rivers used to obstruct overland offensives opened routes for amphibious operations.

The rail net reinforced several avenues of invasion. The Orange and Alexandria Railroad ran from Alexandria through Manassas and then southwest through central Virginia to Lynchburg; the Richmond, Fredericksburg, and Potomac Railroad headed due south from Fredericksburg through the Confederate capital and split into three lines at Petersburg. From Manassas and Charlottesville ran two raillines west into the Shenandoah Valley; two more raillines ran east-west, connecting the Orange and Alexandria with the Richmond, Fredericksburg, and Petersburg line. Should Union commanders select an overland route, there were raillines present to move supplies forward; however, those same rail lines were vulnerable to interruption by Confederate raiders. Richmond's links to the heartland were equally vulnerable, especially if Petersburg was endangered. Things were not much better north of the Potomac. Washington was connected by a single railroad that ran north to Baltimore, with a branch going to Annapolis. From Baltimore, the Baltimore and Ohio Railroad ran westward to Harpers Ferry, continued across just south of the Virginia border, then passed through the western tip of Maryland before reentering northwest Virginia and running to the Ohio River.

Thus, due to the size of the armies involved, any overland Union offensive would depend either on retaining control of rail lines or using the Potomac River and Chesapeake Bay to forward supplies to depots along the shore. One could move overland using either approach to supply a movement; one might also undertake a more ambitious movement, using the waterways to move troops up one of the rivers, including the James River itself, which led directly to Richmond. One might also consider offensive movements along the coast of southeast Virginia below Norfolk or North Carolina, but it is worth remembering that as one moved south along the coastline, one also needed to provide for the defense of Washington and the area north of the Potomac. In turn, the Confederates would always find their right flank vulnerable to a waterborne movement; they would have a much better chance of turning back a drive into central Virginia that depended on control of the rail lines for supply.

The Confederates might sit in place and respond to Union offensives, issuing telling counterpunches, and hope the resulting attrition favored their chances. But an invasion of the North always beckoned, and if the risk might be great, so was the reward. Here the lay of the land in the Shenandoah Valley was especially important. The valley ran from southwest to northeast. Union forces going southward found themselves moving almost parallel to Richmond, toward the mountains of southwest Virginia. Confederate forces faced a much brighter prospect. Using the Blue Ridge Mountains as a shield, they could advance towards Harpers Ferry, the Potomac, and points north.

Just as important as the topographical features of the region was the political geography that had been crafted by secession and the placement of the Confederate capital. The proximity of the two capitals to each other made each in turn a tempting target and an essential point to defend: however, there were important differences. Washington appeared vulnerable, especially in the early part of the war, when it was nearly surrounded by Confederate territory. But its strategic importance was mainly symbolic. The seat of government could be moved with minor inconvenience; Washington's major business was government, so its loss, even for a short period of time, would be important primarily in terms of both morale andhow foreign nations viewed the course of the struggle. Richmond was somewhat easier to protect. The best way to get at the Confederate capital was from the rear, either via the James River or by isolating it by severing rail lines southwards. Moreover, the location of the Tredegar Iron Works in the city was important to the Confederate war effort, and to lose that would be damaging; so too was the Shenandoah Valley valuable in terms of the supplies it provided the Confederacy.

The ironworks aside, one could indeed raise questions about why it was so important to defend one's capital. After all, the capital of the United States had been captured before, both during the Revolution (Philadelphia, where the Continental Congress sat) and the War of 1812. In neither case did the fall of the capital inevitably lead to defeat. That was also the case in the Mexican-American War, where the capture of Mexico City in September 1847 did not lead to the total collapse of Mexican resistance. Those examples noted, however, capturing the enemy capital was a traditional measure of military success or failure, especially in European conflicts. Moreover, if people believed it was important, even decisive, then that perception

perception played directly into the political realities of defending one's capital while threatening the other. Confederate strategy really did not envision taking Washington (Jubal Early's 1864 movement to the city's outskirts was more a matter of opportunism than deliberate planning by the Confederate high command). Much could be accomplished merely by threatening the city, including increasing pressure on the Lincoln administration and diverting Union troops earmarked for operations elsewhere. Union strategy always envisioned Richmond as a possible target, although various commanders differed in how they envisioned the relationship between attacking the main Confederate field army and taking Richmond. Sometimes Richmond itself was the target; at other times it proved a means to the end of bringing the Confederates to battle.

With the opposing capitals barely a hundred miles apart and the Chesapeake Bay and tidewater area offering Union generals the same sorts of opportunities sought by Confederate leaders in the Shenandoah Valley, geography shaped military operations in fundamental ways. The very rivers that obstructed Union overland advances offered them the chance to outflank Confederate prepared positions by waterborne movement. If the proximity of the enemy capital proved too tempting to pass up, political leaders and generals on each side feared that a major mishap could lead to an enemy parade down the streets of their own capital city. With such proximity presidents, politicians, and the press peeked over the shoulders of military commanders, some of whom were not reluctant to engage in their own intrigues as they promoted their own fortunes.

Indeed, such proximity—the political geography of the area—shaped the course of events in the East as much as did the physical geography. Both presidents visited battlefields, and Lincoln once came under fire. Davis often called Lee to Richmond to confer, while Lincoln both visited headquarters and directed generals to visit him at Washington. Unlike Davis, who made several western trips, Lincoln never went west. Sometimes presidents talked to subordinates, and Lincoln in particular seemed willing to interview subordinates and to listen as they criticized their military superiors. Commanders on both sides sensed the pressure exerted by their civil superiors. At times Lee did not confide in Davis (or waited until Davis could not stop him), and Joseph Johnston writhed under Davis's gaze. Among the Union commanders, McClellan's discomfort with Lincoln was most evident, but Meade came to complain of contradictory prods and unreasonable expectations. It would not be until 1865 that the top man in the East—Grant—would actually invite the president to headquarters.

Nor were such visits limited to presidents. Cabinet members on both sides paid visits to headquarters, and so did members of Congress and other political luminaries. Especially active was the Joint Committee on the Conduct of the War on the Union side, which appeared interested in second-guessing any commander of the

Army of the Potomac they might distrust politically, questioning generals not deemed to be sufficiently supportive of a policy of earnest war that embraced emancipation, or shielding favorites. Generals, members of Congress, cabinet members, and various advisers communicated frequently, rendering the air thick with intrigue. It was an intensely political environment, and not everyone was prepared to survive it. Every military movement had political consequences: there was always someone promoting a favorite or tearing down a rival. To be sure, politics were present in other military theaters, too, but not in so intimate or constant a fashion. All wars are political, but few as political as this one.

Much the same observation could be made about newspaper coverage. In the West the press could be vocal, especially in Cincinnati and Chicago, as several Union commanders discovered. Nor were generals in the West above currying favor with reporters. Ulysses S. Grant and William S. Rosecrans, for example, showed especial interest in certain newspaper correspondents (as opposed to William T. Sherman, who would have had reporters executed as spies). But there were far more newspapers in the East, especially in New York, and many of the columns of the eastern papers reappeared in western journals. Reporters were known to fabricate stories and exaggerate accounts, and at times the sensationalism characteristic of some war reporting raised unrealistic hopes before cruelly dashing them. Discerning readers learned to cast a skeptical eye on some accounts, even as they tried to keep their hopes or fears in check. That some newspapers were prone to offer outlandish prognostications about what would happen inflated public expectations, sometimes beyond what the generals could meet. Once more, it was the number of papers, the proximity of the cities to the theater of war, and the nature of news competition that together ratcheted up public opinion.

In the end, the war in the East retains primacy in popular perception because people judged the progress of the war as a whole in large part on what was happening in the East.[1] From June 1862 to the end of 1863, the Confederacy in the East enjoyed its best chance to win independence through military victories. Lee's ability to keep Grant at bay in 1864 gave it another chance to win in the aftermath of a Democratic victory in the elections of 1864 (although whether Lincoln's defeat meant Union defeat is a discussion best left for another time). Just as terrain shaped operations, so did political considerations and popular expectations. In the end, it was the failure of the theater (both as a staging place for a drama and as a locale) to produce a decisive result for four years that remained its most outstanding characteristic.

Two

PRESIDENTS AND GENERALS

With the shifting of the Confederate capital from Montgomery to Richmond in the spring of 1861, both Abraham Lincoln and Jefferson Davis began to contemplate strategic options. Generals offered their own ideas: each president would have to decide on which general would implement the plan they chose to pursue. Both presidents would have to wrestle with the pressure of public expectations; both would have to weigh the professional concerns of their military commanders against the clamor to do something; and both would find themselves at odds with their commanders and in the middle of various rivalries.

As Jefferson Davis came to his new office with previous military experience, he presumed that he was already equipped to frame military strategy. Not so Abraham Lincoln, whose experience as a militiaman during the Black Hawk War scarcely qualified him to take on the responsibilities of commander-in-chief. That he had the experienced Winfield Scott at his elbow might seem sufficient to some, but in truth the president was never at a loss for generals, armchair and otherwise, who pressed their advice on him. One officer, Montgomery Meigs, advised Lincoln to mobilize a large army, position it along the Confederate border, and take advantage of whatever opportunities appeared when the Confederates stretched their forces to the breaking point in response; it was too soon to strike deep into the Confederate heartland before the generals, officers, and men alike were ready and able to move.

From Columbus, Ohio, George McClellan offered the novel idea of launching a strike against Richmond from the Ohio River via the Kanawha River, a move that would involve crossing the Appalachian Mountains—an idea from a minor-league Hannibal who no one needed to take too seriously. Such proposals were premature and perhaps half-baked; meanwhile Scott was developing his own notions of how to subdue the Confederacy.[1]

The aging general-in-chief was skeptical about the success of an overland offensive thrust against Richmond. The terrain would assist the defenders; it would be challenging to protect an ever-lengthening supply line; the mere fall of the Confederate capital, he believed, would not mark the end of the conflict. Better to contain the fledging Confederacy, blocking off its contacts from the outside, slowly strangling it while taking care not to provoke its citizens. A man used to combining diplomacy with a show of force (as in the nullification crisis of 1832–33), he may have hoped that what had worked before would work again. The blockade would be a chief weapon in that strategy; so would what Scott believed would be the eventual resurgence of Unionism among many white southerners who were, he asserted, reluctant secessionists. Lincoln shared the latter view, and Secretary of State William H. Seward had grounded his pre-Sumter policy upon that assumption, so Scott understood his audience. Scott advocated one major offensive thrust to secure control of the Mississippi River; control achieved, one could pick and choose among numerous targets of opportunity should white southerners fail to see the writing on the wall.[2]

It was critical to Scott's plan, soon known as the Anaconda plan, that there be no operations undertaken hastily before the new armies were trained and ready to fight —a lesson he had learned during the Mexican-American War. At a time when many people were impatient for the new administration to do something as soon as possible, this was a difficult argument to make. A story soon made the rounds that illustrated the tension. A self-appointed wag told Scott, "General, the country expects *action, action,* sir!" The general growled that "war is a science which is not learned in a day. I have studied it all my life. It requires three things: *time,* money and patience, sir. And sir, the President has promised that I shall have all three!"[3]

It would have come as a surprise to Lincoln to hear that he had made such a promise. He needed to see results sooner rather than later to impress the northern public that he was doing something. Already administration critics from his own party were claiming that the Union's heart was not in this war, that nothing was happening, and that it was time to fight. Some military officers agreed. When Scott presented his approach on June 29, Montgomery Meigs argued that the Union army should take advantage of the proximity of the Confederates and deal a devastating blow instead of plunging into the interior, where logistics would prove a challenge. All this talk about preparation and training meant delay. No one wanted to wait that long.[4]

Then came the disaster at Manassas. The lesson seemed clear; the Union advance was premature. Scott might offer his resignation for failing to insist that nothing be done, but that was at best a grand gesture. Lincoln himself might set forth new priorities in terms of strategic targets and operational plans—maintaining the blockade, reorganizing the forces around Virginia, stabilizing the front in northern Virginia, and then advancing in the west—but he knew that it would take time to meet these objectives.[5] What was needed was a sign that the defeat was nothing more than a bump in the road, a temporary setback. In calling George B. McClellan to Washington, Lincoln showed people that he would not be deterred from trying again. After all, McClellan had been credited for leading Union forces to victory in several small but sharp battles in western Virginia; he possessed the reputation of being one of the bright lights of the Union army; and he looked the part, so much so that he was soon styled "the young Napoleon." His goatee and moustache may have offered a passing resemblance to Napoleon III (and it was true that Union army uniforms bore a striking similarity to their French counterparts), but the very ambiguity of the nickname conjured up images of the icon of military leadership, one promoted by the tendency of McClellan and others to pose with one hand shoved inside their uniform coats.

Drill and discipline were the order of the day in the Union camps. Rid at last of the ninety-day wonders, commanders got down to the serious business of building a professionally-trained army from eager volunteers and restoring the high morale damaged by defeat. McClellan also pondered what to do next. There was no more talk of attacking Richmond from Cincinnati. Oblivious to the fact that his command was defined by the forces around Washington, McClellan on August 2 offered his own vision of proper military strategy. It would be wise to secure control of Missouri, advance south along the Mississippi, and even retake Texas, he advised, but the major blow should be struck in Virginia. Calling for a buildup to 273,000 men, he sought to finish the war with a single battle where victory was certain due to an overwhelming force skillfully deployed: "Shall we crush the rebellion at one blow? Terminate the war in one campaign, or shall we leave it as a legacy for our descendants?" Phrased that way, Lincoln's response was obvious.[6]

Of most advantage to McClellan, however, was the lesson most northerners took from Bull Run: haste led to disaster. "The Bull Run fight had one good result for our side," remarked General William B. Franklin: "It taught our people to be a little patient, and not to expect the army to move next week."[7] McClellan welcomed the lesson. No sooner had he outlined his master plan than he warned that Washington was vulnerable to an enemy offensive, and only when its defenders numbered over 100,000 could he then contemplate taking the offensive. In truth, however, McClellan seemed more intent upon circumventing Winfield Scott than in advancing southward. The man of the hour went around his superior whenever it suited him, declaring "that confounded old Genl always comes in the way—he is a perfect imbecile."[8]

ELSEWHERE IN THE OLD DOMINION, MAY–SEPTEMBER 1861

The focus on Bull Run meant that other military operations in Virginia in the spring and early summer of 1861 were given short shrift. In fact, Union forces had taken advantage of the early months of the war to make inroads elsewhere in the Old Dominion. Although forced to evacuate Norfolk on April 20, Union forces managed to hold onto Fort Monroe at the mouth of the James River, giving them a base from which to commence operations along the coast or advance westward toward Richmond. On May 24, Union soldiers crossed the Potomac and seized Alexandria, although a young charismatic colonel, Elmer Ellsworth, who had done so much to bring the Zouave military craze to the United States, was killed moments after hauling down a secessionist flag waving over a local hotel.

As important as it was to secure these footholds, the most visible Union triumphs were in western Virginia, and it was due to what he had done here, prior to Manassas, that McClellan was now in Washington. He might have fantasized about mounting an advance against Richmond from the Ohio River in the war's early days, but in truth there were valuable assets to be secured in western Virginia, including securing the Baltimore and Ohio Railroad, which cut through the northwestern part of Virginia, and shielding unionists in the western part of the state. The railroad's vulnerability had already been revealed when Thomas J. Jackson had captured some rolling stock near Harpers Ferry. Responding to reports that the Confederates were now targeting other railroad bridges to the west, McClellan sought permission to launch an offensive to secure the railroad as far east as possible. Receiving Scott's approval, McClellan on May 26 ordered an expedition to set forth. Four days later the advance secured Grafton, Virginia, a key point on the rail line. In early June Union forces drove the Confederates away from Philippi, just south of Grafton: the Confederates fled in the face of a Union surprise attack at daybreak, and before long the action was known as the Philippi Races, a source of great pride to the Yankees and great embarrassment to the Confederates. Fortunately for Confederate pride, a week later Union forces advancing westward from Fort Monroe badly botched an attack on a Confederate position at Big Bethel. Although Confederates would point to the wide disparity of losses (suffering a mere eight casualties compared to some ten times that number for the attackers), they did not emphasize that over a quarter of the Union soldiers who fell were hit by friendly fire.[9]

Such minor clashes received much attention at the time, but they were but a minor prelude to the events of mid-July along Bull Run. By that time, however, the Union could claim another triumph in western Virginia. Continuing his deliberate advance eastward, McClellan targeted the Confederate position at Rich Mountain, some twenty miles south of Philippi. He hoped to score a signal victory by flanking the Confederates and cutting off their line of retreat. As he told one of Scott's staff officers, "no prospect of a brilliant victory shall induce me to depart from my intention of gaining success by maneuvering rather than by fighting; I will not throw these men of mine into the teeth of artillery & intrenchments, if it is possible to avoid it"; he pledged "not to move until I know that everything is ready, & then to move with the utmost rapidity & energy"—a lesson he credited to Scott. In light of what was to follow over the next sixteen months, such words were worth a careful reading.[10]

On July 10, lead elements of an advancing Union force under the command of William S. Rosecrans skirmished with their Confederate counterparts. The next day, Rosecrans outflanked the Confederates stationed at Rich Mountain, leaving their commander, Lieutenant Colonel John Pegram, no choice but to surrender: the remaining Confederates at nearby Laurel Hill. Although McClellan failed to carry out the attack he had planned in coordination with Rosecrans's move, he wasted no time in claiming credit for the resulting victory. Within ten days of the battle's end he was on his way to Washington.[11]

Before long, another Confederate general, Robert E. Lee, went to western Virginia to try to recoup what had been lost to McClellan. He found himself hampered by the military inexperience of his two leading subordinates, John B. Floyd and Henry A. Wise, who owed their rank to their political influence. That Floyd and Wise refused to work harmoniously with each other further complicated matters; neither would they work with William W. Loring, a Mexican War veteran whose military experience did not necessarily bring ability. Lee not only failed to regain what the Confederacy had lost, but he also stumbled in his first battle at Cheat Mountain in September, when poor weather and the mistakes of subordinates doomed a plan of attack that may have been too complicated in any case. The Yankees would maintain control of western Virginia, and Lee came under heavy criticism. It looked as if he just might be better suited to desk duty at Richmond as the president's adviser.[12]

In short, too much focus on Manassas, then and later, led observers to overlook the gains achieved by Union arms in Virginia in the spring and summer of 1861. Yet those gains proved valuable in the years to come. Holding on to Fort Monroe and capturing Alexandria gave Union forces important footholds in eastern Virginia, while the campaigns in western Virginia helped protect a critical east-west rail link and helped foster the movement that led to the establishment of West Virginia in 1863. However, most people still turned their attention to the Confederates in northern Virginia and watched as George McClellan trained and drilled a new army built upon the ill-fated regiments that had left Manassas in disgrace. At some point, everyone assumed, someone would take the initiative. But who? And when?

ALL QUIET ALONG THE POTOMAC

For all the emphasis placed on McClellan's inaction in the months following Manassas, the Confederates were also playing a game of wait and see, reacting to Union advances but initiating precious little on their own. Like Lincoln, Jefferson Davis was aware that many people were demanding that Confederate arms do something. "I have felt and feel that time brings many advantages to the enemy, and wish we could strike him in his present condition," Davis admitted, "but it has seemed to me involved in too much probability of failure to render the movement proper with our present means."[13] Joseph Johnston rested content with that conclusion. He was far less pleased with his place on the seniority list of generals when he discovered that he was not at the top of that list. The debate that followed ruined his relationship with Davis. At the same time he discussed with Beauregard and Gustavus W. Smith whether it was a good idea to move closer to Washington with an eye to taking the offensive. At the end of September Davis joined them at Fairfax Court House to consider what might be done. After all, come winter and spring, the one-year enlistment period would expire, just as the Yankees were read to move forward. Now was the time to strike, by crossing the Potomac and swinging east to descend upon Washington. Smith asserted that "success here was success everywhere, defeat here defeat everywhere; . . . this was the point upon which all the available forces of the Confederate States should be concentrated."[14]

Davis was uncomfortable with the risk entailed by the plan put forward by Beauregard and Smith. He also doubted that sufficient reinforcements could be forwarded to improve the odds of success. When the generals failed to tell him from where the needed reinforcements would come, Davis replied that given the present situation it would be better to nip away at the Federals and take advantage of any opportunities that appeared. For the moment, that would be enough.[15]

Davis's approach soon paid dividends. After all, public impatience was evident north as well as south. Parades and reviews were grand sights indeed, but as summer turned into fall some northerners began to wonder whether the phrase "all quiet along the Potomac" was more a complaint that nothing was happening than a reassurance that all was well. "The public spirit is beginning to quail under the depressing influence of our prolonged inaction," muttered Attorney General Edward Bates. McClellan felt the pressure: even as he began mapping out a proposed reconnaissance, he remarked to Lincoln: "Don't let them hurry me, is all I ask."[16]

When McClellan finally decided to move in October, the results were disastrous. The Union commander decided against driving away advanced Confederate elements south of the Potomac near Washington in favor of a blow upstream against a Rebel force stationed at Ball's Bluff, on the south shore of the Potomac, some 40 miles upstream from Washington, near Leesburg. At Ball's Bluff there were places where Union forces could debark and advance. Here was an opportunity to take action, if for no other reason than to satisfy the public hunger. If all went well, Johnston might withdraw rather than face the prospect of being flanked. Leesburg might fall into Union hands.

McClellan issued broad and vague discretionary orders to General Charles P. Stone, the man in charge in the area. Stone decided to launch a probe into the area to test reports of a Confederate camp, and to take advantage of whatever opportunities turned up. Sadly, however, he left the main responsibility for making decisions on the ground to Colonel Edward D. Baker, a personal friend of the president who spoke often of the need to fight and to be brave in combat. Baker mangled his mission, deploying his command in a low-lying area surrounded by ridges and bluffs with his back to the river. It was but child's play for advancing Confederates to silence the artillery before opening up on the trapped Federals. Baker's command scrambled for safety under fire: Baker himself was killed. The defeat was complete, and, at a time when so little was happening, it was guaranteed to draw attention, especially with the death of the popular Baker, a former senator.[17]

What happened at Ball's Bluff would suggest that at least some Union commanders needed more seasoning, and that to take the offensive simply to gratify public opinion and political pressure without any other sound strategic purpose would not do. In the battle's aftermath congressional Republicans decided to exercise more formal oversight of military operations by forming the Joint Committee on the Conduct of the War, an investigating body that would do its fair share of politicizing the assessment of military operations and scrutinizing the performance of generals. Yet the disaster did not quell calls for action: senators still pressured Lincoln to urge his generals forward. The president apprised McClellan of the rising clamor for action, even as he insisted that "you must not fight until you are ready."[18]

The only battle McClellan was ready to fight was against Winfield Scott. He had tired of the old war horse and treated him with scant respect. In turn, Scott had little faith that McClellan was the right man for the moment, let alone for the future: he preferred that Henry W. Halleck, who had quite a reputation as a military theorist, replace him as general in chief. That did not happen. When an exasperated Scott offered his resignation on October 3, Lincoln not only accepted it, but also named McClellan to succeed him as of November 1. The decision simply formalized what had been going on for months, with Lincoln working directly with McClellan, leaving Scott out of the loop—a pattern of circumventing commanding generals on the part of both the president and subordinate commanders that would persist for years to come. Dismissing Lincoln's concern that the burden of overall command might prove too heavy, McClellan declared, "I can do it all."[19]

In short, it looked at first glance as if the lesson of Bull Run had been learned. There would be no hasty advance. It took time to train an army capable of undertaking offensive operations. The impatience of politicians and the public would have to be tolerated and endured. And yet the fallout from Ball's Bluff served to remind anyone who happened to be paying attention that the prosecution of the war would not be left to the generals alone. Even as winter approached, observers wondered whether anything would happen. One would have to look somewhere other than along the Potomac for a more encouraging answer.

OPPORTUNITY FORGOTTEN: THE CAROLINAS

Traditionally, studies of the Eastern Theater include Virginia as the sole Confederate state under study. That in itself is something of a tribute to the obsession many Civil War historians have with the war in Virginia and the retelling of stories about the campaigns of the Army of Northern Virginia and the Army of the Potomac. Yet it need not have been that way. In April 1861, long before there was talk of an Anaconda Plan, Lincoln had shared with his private secretary John Hay, what was on his mind as to how to proceed. He would "fill Fortress Monroe with men and stores; blockade the ports effectually; provide for the entire safety of the Capitol; keep them quietly employed in this way, and then go down to Charleston and pay her the little debt we are owing her."[20]

Through the spring and early summer of 1861, Lincoln did not act upon that impulse. Retaining possession of Fort Monroe was indeed critical, but the Union did little to exploit it following the setback at Big Bethel. Among the planners in Washington little thought was given to the idea that a waterborne approach against Richmond and points south might pay off, although discussions along those lines commenced in late June.[21]

That changed in July 1861. In the wake of the disaster at Manassas, Ambrose Burnside, who had led a brigade in that clash, submitted a plan to strike along the North Carolina coast. So did Benjamin Butler. Before long, military operations began in earnest along the Atlantic coast. In September Butler and Commodore Silas Stringham combined forces to take Fort Hatteras in North Carolina, opening Albemarle Sound to the Union. At the end of October 1861, Flag Officer Samuel Francis DuPont gathered a small fleet, including transports, and prepared to move some 12,000 men under Thomas W. Sherman from Hampton Roads southward along the Atlantic coast. The expedition's target was Port Royal, South Carolina, located between Charleston and Savannah. The Confederates had erected a brace of substandard forts that fell easily in the face of a naval bombardment, and Sherman's command debarked to take possession. Union forces were not prepared to do more than that at the moment, and the lack of preparation to exploit the opportunity presented proved fatal.[22]

As Union forces prepared to take Port Royal, Jefferson Davis responded to the threat posed by the enemy movement by ordering Robert E. Lee (fresh from his disappointing performance in western Virginia) to take charge of the coastal defenses. It proved quite a challenge. No sooner had Lee arrived on the scene than he decided that the scattering of Confederate detachments into bite-sized morsels would not do: better to consolidate forces inland to protect the railroad linking Charleston and Savannah, and make use of the railroad to move defenders where needed to counter any Union advances. He ordered waterways obstructed to block Union gunboats and commenced building field fortifications to maximize the strength of the manpower assigned to the area. Of special importance in the last respect was construction of fortifications at Charleston and Savannah that served to protect those cities from Union offensives from the sea.[23]

Lee had to secure the cooperation of governors Francis Pickens of South Carolina, John Milton of Florida, and Joseph E. Brown of Georgia. Many soldiers were anticipating the end of their year of military service; many recruits were reluctant to be sent out of their native state. Nevertheless, the general achieved his objective. Aside from a movement toward Savannah in February 1862, Union forces seemed content to secure their gains of the previous year. A long-planned expedition to capture Fernandina, Florida, to support blockade operations proved a temporary gain that was abandoned within months. Although Union general T. W. Sherman drafted plans to capture Savannah and Charleston, nothing happened. Indeed, what might have been the start of a series of drives into the Confederate interior had become a way to support blockade operations: it was no accident that the names of the two naval squadrons in the area, the North and South Atlantic Blockading Squadrons, betrayed their mission.[24]

For a while, it appeared that the case might be different in North Carolina. Burnside recruited a force especially earmarked for his coastal enterprise, drawing mainly from New York and New England for recruits; he also began to arrange for the construction of troop transports. In November Rush Hawkins, colonel of the colorful 9th New York, a regiment decked out in distinctive Zouave dress, suggested that North Carolina offered a promising target. Having been a part of the Hatteras expedition, he appeared to have first-hand knowledge of the matter, or so Lincoln and his new general-in-chief, McClellan, concluded. Hawkins reported that the citizens along the coast at Pamlico Sound, including Roanoke Island and Beaufort, harbored pro-Union sentiments, and if the Union army established a foothold in the area, it might raise troops and threaten to do even more. The idea got the administration's stamp of approval, with Burnside heading the army contingent while Flag Officer Lewis M. Goldsborough was to direct naval operations. McClellan enthusiastically endorsed the project.[25]

Not until the first week of January 1862 did the expedition get underway. A month later, having been delayed by rough seas and difficulties in making one's way past the shoals and sandbars, the vessels deposited the bluecoats on Tar Heel soil. Burnside's men carried the day in a sharp clash at Roanoke on February 8, and during the next few weeks poked and prodded about. In March Burnside took New Bern, and, as Confederates hustled about to contain the Yankee advance, he called for reinforcements. Some came, but not nearly enough to launch a full-scale offensive into the North Carolina interior, although Goldsboro and Raleigh were not too far away, and their possession would have snapped a critical rail link between Virginia and the Confederate heartland. Burnside's men settled instead for fighting a series of small engagements along the coast. Even then, their presence alarmed the Confederates at Norfolk, contributing to the decision to abandon that city in May.[26]

Yet nothing more happened. Reinforcements that might have made a difference in North Carolina were sent instead to McClellan's Army of the Potomac, making its way toward Richmond. Disease ravaged Burnside's men, rendering an offensive impossible. Indeed, it appears that even as Burnside was on the move against New Bern, McClellan was seeking reinforcements from him. Eventually Burnside would take his corps northward.[27]

What did he leave behind? More, one might argue, than is suggested in most overviews of the war. A reminder of the area's potential came in February 1863, when Lee had to send two divisions under James Longstreet to southeast Virginia when it looked as if the Yankees were reviving a coastal strategy. Usually, however, the Confederate commander pressed his civil superiors to detach forces defending the coast to reinforce his army, for it became increasingly evident that the Union commanders would not attempt to advance into the interior. Thus, unlike the Western Theater, where Confederates on the defensive found themselves stretching their limited forces to the breaking point to cover a lengthy front line, Lee could concentrate forces on anticipation of dealing out a few blows of his own.

If Union commanders failed to exploit their early gains in North Carolina, they proved equally unable to take advantage of their lodgment between Charleston and Savannah. Upon arriving in March 1862, General David Hunter proved eager to take the offensive. The following month, siege artillery pounded into submission Fort Pulaski, located just south of the border between South Carolina and Georgia. That achieved, Savannah was sealed off from the sea. Rather than attempt to take the city itself, Hunter (after an ill-fated effort to abolish slavery in his command by military fiat) turned his attention to Charleston. In June he dispatched two divisions to James Island, south of the opening to Charleston harbor, and then advanced on Charleston. Confederate defenders took position along a fortified position outside Secessionville, less than six miles due south of Charleston, and on June 16 repulsed a Union assault. Hunter fumed that the commander on the scene, Henry W. Benham, disobeyed orders in attacking. The defeat virtually ended efforts to take Charleston in 1862.[28]

Union strategy missed an opportunity in 1861 and 1862 by not taking advantage of footholds along the Carolina coast. To be sure, the continued presence of Union forces on the coast compelled the Confederates to detach some units to keep a watchful eye over them, and the areas secured proved useful in enforcing the blockade of Confederate ports. But Union planners, with one exception, would not incorporate these areas into planning for operations in the Eastern Theater for the remainder of the war. There would be efforts to take Charleston, but they amounted to naught, and were not conceived in conjunction with other operations. Only Ulysses S. Grant would raise the idea of renewing offensive operations in North Carolina as part of planning strategy in the East, and that plan met with disapproval in Washington. It would be left to forces drawn from various points, mainly the West, to swept through the Carolinas in the winter and spring of 1865 by land and by sea.

WINTER OF DISCONTENT

George B. McClellan, enjoying his new position as general in chief and content with his relationship with Lincoln, believed that the president need not know his plans for action. He snubbed his civilian superior, most famously when he came home, bypassed the parlor where the chief executive patiently waited, then sent down word that he had gone to bed. When the general absented himself from a meeting with several governors, the president excused the misstep, adding, "I will hold McClellan's horse if he will only bring us success."[29]

Still, even Lincoln was growing impatient with McClellan's inaction. On December 1, 1861, he forwarded a suggested plan of campaign whereby one force would advance over land toward Manassas while another waterborne force threatened the confederates' rear. McClellan set aside the offering, explaining that he was working on an even more daring and impressive plan—without offering details. In fact, McClellan's plan simply took Lincoln's proposal a step further, placing primarily reliance on moving the Army of the Potomac via the Potomac and Chesapeake to the banks of the Rappahannock River at Urbanna. From there he could move southward toward Richmond, having outmaneuvered Johnston.[30]

It would have been wise for the general to have confided in the president, for Lincoln was coming under renewed pressure from Republicans for action. The Joint Committee on the Conduct of the War was raising embarrassing questions about Ball's Bluff; it looked bad when Lincoln confessed his ignorance of McClellan's plans. Nor did it help when McClellan fell so sick that people feared for his life.

By year's end Lincoln had waited long enough. He began telegraphing his generals in the west to prod them into action. On a visit to Montgomery Meigs's office, he exclaimed to the quartermaster general: "General, what shall I do? The people are impatient; Chase has no money and he tells me he can raise no more; the General of the Army has typhoid fever. The bottom is out of the tub. What shall I do?" Lincoln decided to meet with several of McClellan's generals. If McClellan had no plans for the army, the president declared that he would like to "borrow it."[31]

News of these meetings roused McClellan from his sickbed. However, in a meeting with Lincoln, several cabinet members, and several generals, he would not reveal the details of his plan, although he promised the president that he had a definite date in mind for an advance into Kentucky. That bought McClellan some time, but when he remained silent, the president, urged on by his new secretary of war, Edwin M. Stanton, decided to act, and he did so decisively. On January 27, 1862, he issued General War Order No. 1, directing that military operations commence no later than the anniversary of George Washington's birthday the following month. Four days later he issued Special War Order No. 1, which mandated a movement on Manassas by the Army of the Potomac.[32]

Neither of these orders reflected a sensible response to the current situation. Both were sure to aggravate McClellan while indicating to the rest of the world that the Union command system was in shambles. The orders made a bad situation worse, and exposed everyone for the amateurs they were. When McClellan objected, Lincoln asked for a comparison of the merits of their respective plans in Virginia, suggesting that victory was more certain, less costly, and less risky under his plan. The general in chief stood by his proposal, offering a rather detailed explanation of his reasoning. While that debate continued, it appeared as if nothing was happening in the Eastern Theater. An effort to span the Potomac by pontoon bridges preparatory to an advance on Winchester in the Shenandoah Valley (where Stonewall Jackson waited) collapsed when it was discovered that the pontoon boats were too large to fit through the locks on the Chesapeake and Ohio Canal. "Everything seems to fail," the president told one of his secretaries. "The general impression is daily gaining ground that we do not intend to do anything. . . . I am grievously disappointed—almost in despair."[33]

Northerners were indeed getting restless at the lack of action. Maria Daly observed from New York City that "still the rebel army of the Potomac threatens Washington, and still hopes to take it, whilst our three hundred thousand soldiers lie opposite them, idle and well-fed, with full pay, their families supported by public charity, their officers spending their time in reveling, flirting, and drinking. . . . No one seems to feel the danger in which we stand, or to realize that we are a bankrupt and ruined nation, should this continue longer." But not everyone was so impatient. George Templeton Strong remarked: "The newspapers are goading McClellan, as they goaded Scott and McDowell last July. Heaven defend us from another premature advance and another Bull, or Bull-calf, run back again!"[34]

The inactivity stood in stark contrast to action in the West, where February saw the invasion of Tennessee, the taking of Forts Henry and Donelson (the latter featuring the surrender of some 13,000 Confederates), and the occupation of Nashville.

That much of this activity was due to neither McClellan nor his commanders in the West, Henry W. Halleck and Don Carlos Buell, but to the initiative shown by a brigadier named Ulysses S. Grant did not escape notice in Washington, for it was Grant alone who received a promotion for his success. While Washington celebrated, Lincoln, mourning the death of his son Willie, continued to contemplate what to do about his general in chief's inactivity. Sharing his frustration with McClellan's chief of staff, the president remarked, "The general impression is daily gaining ground that the Gen. does not intend to do anything."[35]

Fortunately for McClellan, the Confederates remained equally inactive. In February Jefferson Davis sought to address one conflict between two of his generals by ordering Pierre G. T. Beauregard west, leaving Joseph E. Johnston in uncontested control of affairs in Virginia. Immediately Johnston reorganized his command, but he was not prepared to advance. Indeed, he did not particularly care for his position in northern Virginia around Centreville, northeast of Bull Run, and began to urge pulling back across the Rappahannock, where he believed he could establish a better defensive position and parry any effort by McClellan to move his army by water and thus outflank the Centreville position. Davis called Johnston to Richmond, where the two men discussed what to do in front of the cabinet. Seven hours later no consensus had been reached. Johnston thought he had made his case to pull southward when practicable as the weather improved; Davis thought that such a withdrawal would come when it was necessary and not before. Like McClellan, Johnston soon had cause to believe that leaks from the meeting were spreading everywhere, causing him to accelerate his timetable.[36]

In the wake of the meeting Davis had reason to wonder what Johnston might do, and he may have reflected upon how unsatisfactory their correspondence continued to be. It did not help that there were signs of growing friction between Johnston and Secretary of War Judah Benjamin over a multitude of seemingly minor administrative matters. Davis sought assistance. On March 3, he called Robert E. Lee away from the south Atlantic coast to serve as his military adviser. He had intended to name Lee general-in-chief, but rejected that idea after the Confederate Congress fashioned legislation providing for the post that curtailed Davis's own powers.[37]

Lee arrived in Richmond just as action got underway in Virginia. On March 8, the ironclad CSS *Virginia* left Norfolk Naval Yard and made its way out into Hampton Roads, where it destroyed one Union frigate, accepted the surrender of a second, and forced two more vessels to run aground. If such a vessel would continue to have its way unmolested, McClellan's waterborne invasion would also run aground. Rumor had it that the vessel might even make its way north to the Potomac, although in fact the *Virginia* was not seaworthy. The next day, the *Virginia* steamed forth again, but this time it encountered a rather strange-looking vessel, sometimes described as a cheesebox on a raft. It was the Union's newest ironclad, the USS *Monitor*, which had hurried down from the Brooklyn Naval Yard just in time to stave off another disaster. After several hours of indecisive combat, the *Virginia* retreated back to Norfolk. That same evening Joseph E. Johnston decided to abandon his position at Manassas and Centreville. He pulled his army back south of the Rappahannock, much to the shock and chagrin of Davis, who had believed that the presence of the *Virginia* might permit him to reinforce Johnston where he was.[38]

Things were not much better in Washington. By the beginning of March, Lincoln had lost patience with McClellan, and the general was equally frustrated with the president and his advisers. Having pressed McClellan to move, Lincoln now raised objections to any advance that did not satisfactorily protect Washington. McClellan offered to lay his plans before his twelve division commanders for a vote: his plan prevailed by a vote of eight to four. No one seemed aware that voting on the relative merits of two plans was an interesting way of going about military planning, and of course it tended to subvert the chain of command, and identified dissenters and supporters for both camps. Nor was Lincoln initially willing to accept the verdict. It did not help when the president, bending to pressure from members of the Joint Committee on the Conduct of the War, issued orders organizing the Army of the Potomac into four corps, three of which would be commanded by a general who had voted against McClellan's plan. On the verge of moving upon Manassas, McClellan found the order disconcerting, especially as he was not pleased with the president's selections as corps commanders. Moreover, he had just decided that it would be best if his army used the lower Chesapeake as the best area to launch his spring offensive. News of the *Virginia*'s appearance put that on hold for the moment. By the time McClellan himself arrived at Centreville and Manassas Junction on March 11, Johnston was long gone. Compounding the Union commander's embarrassment was the news that in yet a third order the president had decided to strip McClellan of his position as general-in-chief. The following day McClellan, after inquiring whether the *Monitor* could keep the *Virginia* in check, chose Fort Monroe as the point where his army would debark.[39]

Lincoln was willing to approve the new plan provided that McClellan provided for a sufficient force to shield Washington against attack. Far from being embarrassed by Johnston's evacuation, McClellan believed that history would "record it as the brightest passage of my life that I accomplished so much at so small a cost." He believed Lincoln was "my strongest friend." That assumption was soon to be tested.[40]

TO THE PENINSULA

On March 17, McClellan's army began boarding transports headed for Fort Monroe. The general had assured the president that he was leaving behind a force sufficient to handle any threat against Washington. Other than signs that Stonewall

Jackson was growing restless in the Shenandoah Valley, there seemed to be little cause for concern. McClellan had left detailed instructions on how to defend northern Virginia. At last the major movement everyone had been looking for seemed to be getting underway.[41]

At first things moved smoothly. McClellan was pleased to have prevailed when it came to the plan of campaign, and in any case the long winter was giving way to spring. Even the news that on March 23 Jackson had attacked at Kernstown, just a few miles south of Winchester, did not seem to bother him. After all, Jackson had been outnumbered by a force nearly three times his number, suffered more casualties, and had withdrawn. Upon hearing of the clash, McClellan directed Nathaniel P. Banks to drive Jackson south through the valley before resuming his responsibility of guarding northern Virginia. A week later, he learned that Lincoln was detaching a division earmarked for McClellan's army for service in western Virginia. Although he regretted the news, McClellan told Lincoln that he understood the president's reasoning: "I cheerfully acquiesce in your decision without any mental reservation." By April 2 McClellan had joined his men at Fort Monroe. He was ready to advance, assuring his wife, "The grass will not grow under my feet."[42]

Unfortunately, Abraham Lincoln did not share McClellan's confidence, especially when it came to Jackson's presence in the Shenandoah Valley. He wanted to make sure that McClellan had indeed left behind enough men to render the capital safe from attack. McClellan clearly underestimated this concern. He had hurried away from Washington in part to avoid meeting with Lincoln and Secretary of War Edwin M. Stanton one more time, leaving only a document explaining how he had provided for Washington's defense. That may have been understandable, but it was not wise, because by the time Stanton, supported by a cadre of staff officers and other military advisers, had finished with McClellan's information, he had concluded that Washington remained vulnerable because McClellan had not left behind enough men earmarked for its defense, and so informed Lincoln.[43]

A sense of panic was not limited to north of the Potomac. Reports had reached Richmond that McClellan's command was embarking on transports with their destination unknown. Perhaps they would head to Fort Monroe; perhaps they were headed toward North Carolina to exploit recent gains. Anticipating the latter, Davis ordered Lee to repair to North Carolina, but within days it was clear that for the moment, at least, McClellan had chosen Fort Monroe. Meanwhile Davis, Lee, and Johnston discussed whether Johnston should abandon his position south of the Rappahannock and head toward Richmond or points south. Davis and Lee seemed inclined that Johnston should hold his position for the moment, whereas Johnston was in favor of shifting southward sooner rather than later.[44]

This confusion might well have proven costly had McClellan, having arrived at Fort Monroe, pushed forward, determined to test the Confederate defenses at

Yorktown. However, John B. Magruder, in charge of the Rebel defences, did all he could to magnify the size of his comparatively small force, marching units back and forth, bugles blaring and drums beating, with officers calling out imaginary regiments—a performance befitting Magruder's theatrical streak, and all for the benefit of an audience of one: George B. McClellan. It worked. Earlier predictions of a quick victory gave way to McClellan's assessment that the Confederates "are in large force along our front and, apparently, intend making a determined resistance." Only reinforcements—or McDowell's corps in northern Virginia, which had been previously promised to him—could turn the tide. An impatient Lincoln wired McClellan, "I think you better break the enemies' line . . . at once"; McClellan grumbled to his wife that he "was very much tempted to reply that he had better come & do it himself."[45]

Lincoln and McClellan also argued over the size of the force McClellan had left to protect Washington. Concerned by continued Confederate activity in the Shenandoah Valley, the president now believed that the general had misrepresented what he had left behind. McClellan insisted that he had left more than 55,000 men in the area, counting the forces in the Valley and Manassas Junction as well as elsewhere in his calculations. Lincoln calculated differently, and used those calculations to justify retaining control of Irvin McDowell's sizeable corps. McClellan characterized the decision as "the most infamous thing that history has recorded." Over the next few months the president and the general engaged in a tug-of-war over McDowell's force.[46]

Believing that he was under strength, McClellan decided to embark upon siege operations. Meanwhile, he continued to quibble with Lincoln about the size of the force under his command. Greatly dissatisfied, Lincoln set forth his case as to why he had held back reinforcements, and then pressed McClellan to do something: "I think it the precise time for you to strike a blow. By delay the enemy will relatively gain upon you—that is, he will gain faster, by fortifications and reinforcements, than you can by reinforcements alone." Nor was this the president solely urging action. "And, once more let me tell you, it is indispensable to you that you strike a blow. I am powerless to help this." The president had pointed out that shifting where the campaign would be waged "was only shifting, and not surmounting, a difficulty—that we would find the same enemy, and the same, or equal, intrenchments, at either place. The country will not fail to note—is now noting—that the present hesitation to move upon an intrenched enemy, is but the story of Manassas repeated." In short, "you must act."[47]

McClellan maintained that when he did act, it would be at the right time and with great results. "I am confident of success, not only of success but of brilliant success," he told Lincoln. "I think that a defeat here substantially breaks up the rebel cause."[48] Doubtless he was pleased that at last he had been able to pry loose a division from McDowell's corps, with the promise of another one to follow when Washington was deemed secure. But there was no need for him to risk defeat when he was confident that, given enough time, he could guarantee success.

That was precisely what concerned his opponents. By mid-April reports reached Richmond that McDowell was moving southward toward Richmond. Confederate forces at Fredericksburg were supposed to keep the Yankees in check or at least dispute their advance. Lee contacted Jackson. Would it be possible to attack Banks in the Valley? If it could be done, it might relieve the pressure on Fredericksburg, especially as the Confederate commander there had already abandoned the city after burning the bridges spanning the Rappahannock. Left unmentioned was the idea that checking McDowell might also cause Joseph Johnston to cease withdrawing westward toward Richmond.[49]

Lee's request came at a time when the Confederacy was reeling under a series of setbacks. Union forces had claimed victory in the West at Shiloh and Island No. 10; a Union flotilla was pounding away at a brace of Confederate forts defending New Orleans; to the south, Fort Pulaski had fallen. President Davis had just signed legislation instituting conscription in order to build up Confederate manpower. If McDowell joined McClellan, that might prove enough to ensure Richmond's fall. At a meeting in Richmond Johnston had argued that he must either fall back to defend Richmond, abandoning Yorktown in the process, or drive northward to Washington while Magruder held on for dear life at Yorktown. Lee preferred staying at Yorktown for as long as possible to buy time to build a bigger and better army while he could oversee the building of fortifications along the James River nearer Richmond, including Drewry's Bluff, less than a dozen miles due south of Richmond.[50]

Unfortunately for Lee, time was growing short. McClellan seemed on the verge of finally attacking Yorktown. Johnston had no intention of waiting until that happened. He worried that McClellan would use the James to outflank him and send a force to Richmond. He argued that once McClellan finally moved forward in earnest at Yorktown, his position was doomed. He even advocated strikes northward to catch the Yankees off guard: "We are engaged in a species of warfare at which we can never win."[51] On May 4, just as McClellan was putting the final touches to a massive assault, the Confederates evacuated Yorktown. The next day Union forces tangled with a Rebel rear guard at Williamsburg. The way to Richmond seemed open.

As the Rebels left, Lincoln came to pay a visit. The president had been growing impatient for action, and however pleased he might have been by the news of recent successes, he wanted more. He soon had cause to reconsider his estimate of McClellan's abilities. While he had been visiting the troops at Fort Monroe, Lincoln helped direct Union forces to take Norfolk, on the opposite bank of the James River, a move that caused the destruction of the irksome CSS *Virginia*. Now the James was open all the way to Richmond, or so it seemed. That it had been left to the president, assisted by two cabinet members (Secretary of War Edwin M. Stanton and especially Secretary of the Treasury Salmon P. Chase) to direct a military operation down to the detail of selecting landing sites for Union troop transports and having the president himself conduct a nighttime reconnaissance along the beach to demonstrate that a landing was feasible, raised questions about whether professionally-trained military officers were such masters of their craft. No one considered that the Confederates had been planning to abandon Norfolk.[52]

For the next ten days Johnston slowly pulled back and McClellan slowly advanced. The Union commander wanted to supply his men from the York River, although that would eventually mean that any army approaching Richmond from the east would also be supplied by a single rail line. That would facilitate linking up with McDowell's force as it advanced down from Fredericksburg; it also meant that McClellan would not exploit the James River as the Confederates had feared. At the same time, McClellan sought permission to reorganize his command to displace some of the corps commanders imposed upon him by Lincoln, for he was furious with their performance at Williamsburg, where he believed their incompetence had cost him a chance at a bigger victory, and in fact had risked defeat. Here he met within partial success because nine days later the Army of the Potomac was reshaped into six corps from its previous total of four, with McClellan favorites Fitz John Porter and William B. Franklin taking charge of the V and VI Corps, respectively. Lincoln acceded to this new arrangement only after inquiring of McClellan whether the three corps commanders with him (McDowell being detached) were obeying orders. McClellan, it seemed, had been relying on Porter and Franklin as divisional commanders to do much of the work he deemed important. The two men also wrestled over McClellan's decision to remove General Charles S. Hamilton from his division command, as Lincoln came under fire from Hamilton's political supporters.[53]

It did not take McClellan long to press anew for reinforcements. He estimated the Confederates before him to be as much as twice his army of between 70,000 and 80,000 effectives. "It would be unwise to count upon anything but a stubborn and desperate defense," he told Stanton, adding, "Those who entertain the opinion that the Rebels will abandon Richmond without a struggle, are, in my judgment, badly advised, and do not comprehend their situation, which is one requiring desperate measures." Lincoln understood his request, but held fast to his determination to keep McDowell and other forces protecting Washington in place. He was willing to allow McDowell to proceed southward to Richmond, provided he continue to protect Washington—a difficult assignment, to say the least—and it was left to McDowell to point out that it would be unwise for the president to issue orders that might conflict with those prepared by his immediate military superior, McClellan.[54]

If Lincoln and McClellan were squabbling, so were Davis and Johnston. By May 12 the Army of Northern Virginia was a mere 25 miles east of Richmond. Davis and Lee worried that a Federal flotilla might make its way up the James to shell

Richmond itself. Indeed, on May 15 Confederate artillerists at Drewry's Bluff fought off five Union vessels, including the fabled *Monitor,* which no longer had to keep an eye on the *Virginia.* Even a blow by Jackson in the Valley—he had repulsed a Union attack on May 8 at McDowell—failed to raise spirits in Richmond, for it was overshadowed by the loss of Norfolk and the setbacks at Yorktown and Williamsburg. It looked as if McClellan was unstoppable (especially if Johnston continued to withdraw). One sign of confidence in the Union high command was that it took Jackson's victory at McDowell in stride. On May 17 Lincoln authorized McDowell's corps, now over 40,000 strong, to march south and link up with McClellan, who had reorganized his own command to his liking.[55]

Lee was not willing to give in just yet. On May 16 he wrote Jackson, suggesting that aggressive action against Union forces near the Shenandoah Valley might yet stay reinforcements intended for McClellan. "Whatever movements you make against Banks do it speedily," he advised, "and, if successful, drive him back toward the Potomac, and create the impression as far as practicable that you design threatening that line."[56]

JACKSON STRIKES AGAIN AND JOE JOHNSTON GOES DOWN

Stonewall Jackson had read Lee's mind. Even before he received Lee's missive he had been planning to strike once more in the Shenandoah Valley. Marching northward against a Union force commanded by Nathaniel P. Banks, Jackson's 16,000 men ran over a Federal detachment at Front Royal on May 23 and sought to cut Banks's lines of communication and supply. Banks rushed to escape the trap. On May 25 Jackson routed him at Winchester. As the defeated Yankees made their way to Harpers Ferry, it looked as if the Rebels had prevailed again.[57]

In a way, they did. Lincoln ordered McDowell to abandon his march southward to reinforce McClellan. The president hoped to set in motion a series of movements that would result in converging columns trapping Jackson. John C. Frémont would move from the south to close off the Confederate route of retreat southward, and McDowell would march westward toward the valley to seal off the mountain gaps. To McClellan the president wired, "I think the time is near when you must either attack Richmond or give up the job and come to the defense of Washington." McClellan understood the movement for what it was: "The object of enemy's movement is probably to prevent reinforcements being sent me." He promised he would attack Richmond soon; he was not going to give up just now.[58]

Lincoln's response to Jackson's activities in the Shenandoah Valley remains a source of controversy. By acting as he did, the president deprived McClellan of reinforcements, giving a general always complaining about political interference, executive incompetency, and a shortage of manpower yet another reason to protest and procrastinate. And yet one can wonder whether McClellan was ready to act on his word. After all, he had promised to attack before. Moreover, if Lincoln's plan succeeded, the result could only enhance McClellan's military prospects. At a time when the Confederates outside Richmond were skillfully slowing down Union advances, the chance to strike a telling blow against another Confederate force had some appeal. With Jackson off the board, the reduction of Richmond would be only a matter of time.

What Lincoln overlooked was that in order for his plan to work, several Union generals—Banks, Frémont, and McDowell—would have to work together. McDowell expressed doubts that this would happen. "I beg to say," he informed the president, "that cooperation between General Frémont and myself . . . is not to be counted upon, even if it is not a practical impossibility." He was "entirely beyond helping distance of General Banks; no celerity or vigor will avail so far as he is concerned." During the next several days the president learned just how hard it was to have everyone on the same page. Telegram after telegram to various generals prodded and questioned, each betraying a slowly increasing exasperation with the failure of military men to realize the opportunity Lincoln believed lay before them. The president did not consider that his generals in the field might find things more difficult to accomplish than they might appear to be simply by looking at a map.[59]

If Lincoln was growing impatient with his generals, Jefferson Davis was at wit's end with Joseph Johnston. Ever since the beginning of May, the Confederates had retreated and retreated, falling back whenever pressed in the slightest. If the pattern continued, Johnston might well retreat through Richmond itself, or so it seemed: Johnston was already making inquiries about where he would rally his army should it come to that. It was alarming enough when Union gunboats approached Richmond in mid-May, only to be turned back by Confederate cannon at Fort Darling at Drewry's Bluff, just south of the city. Davis paid frequent visits to Johnston's headquarters, accompanied by his military adviser, Robert E. Lee. Neither Davis nor Johnston enjoyed the resulting encounters, and the president began losing faith in his general: "I know not what to expect when so many failures are to be remembered."[60]

It took great self-restraint for Davis not to intervene more forcefully with Johnston. He explained that "when we entrusted a command to a general, we must expect him, with all the facts before him, to know what is best to be done; that it would not be safe to undertake to control military operations by advice from the capital." That did not stop him from offering a few suggestions, however, on how to counter the approaching Yankees. Nevertheless, he added, "my design is to suggest not to direct, recognizing the impossibility of any one to decide in advance."[61]

Johnston continued his retrograde movements, until by May 18 he was within sight of the Confederate capital. That news angered a surprised Davis, who snapped that if Johnston would not give battle, he'd find someone who would. For his part, Johnston kept his plans to himself, despite increasing pressure from Davis and Lee to uncover his intentions.[62] By the end of May Johnston thought he saw the perfect opportunity to attack. In anticipation of linking up with McDowell in line with orders from Washington, McClellan had kept several infantry corps north of the Chickahominy River—which in most places was not so much a river as a swampy morass. That left two corps south of the river, ripe targets for a Confederate assault, which could be launched free of concern about what Union gunboats might do, as they were out of range along the James. Unfortunately for Johnston, the delayed offensive was mangled in a series of traffic jams, uncoordinated blows, and horrendous weather, negating what early success it enjoyed. Johnston himself was seriously wounded. Davis looked for a replacement.

The battle of Fair Oaks (or Seven Pines, as it is also known) proved to be Johnston's only effort to check McClellan's advance. It failed to achieve that objective. It now looked as if the Army of the Potomac was closing in on its objective: the capture of the Confederate capital. Certainly McClellan thought so. In congratulating his troops, he declared, "The final battle is at hand. . . . I ask of you now one last crowning effort. The enemy has staked his all on the issue of the coming battle. Let us meet and crush him here in the very centre of the rebellion."[63]

THREE

⤬

AUDACITY AND ANXIETY

As May 1862 drew to a close, it looked as if matters in Virginia were reaching a climax. Indeed, taking everything into consideration, Union victory might not be far off. After all, Union armies in the West had won a series of victories, from Mill Springs to Forts Henry, and Donelson to Shiloh, Island No. 10, and, as of May 30, the fall of Corinth, Mississippi. Now, in the aftermath of Seven Pines, it looked as if it was only a matter of time before George B. McClellan captured Richmond. That in itself might not end the war, but if the Confederacy continued to suffer setback after setback, defeat after defeat, it would be increasingly difficult to see how white southerners would persist in their quest for independence. Given that the Lincoln administration had yet to launch a full-scale attack upon slavery, there might yet be time to come back into the Union on the old terms.

All that remained between McClellan and Richmond was the Army of Northern Virginia, and that army needed a new commander in the aftermath of the wounding of Joseph Johnston. Fortunately for Jefferson Davis, he did not have to look far or long for a replacement, because the man who was giving him military advice seemed a sound choice for the job. Thus it was that Robert E. Lee formally took command of the Army of Northern Virginia on June 1, 1862. In a general order announcing his appointment, he expressed confidence "that every man has resolved to maintain the ancient fame of the Army of Northern Virginia." Others might have argued that this army had yet to make its name.[1]

Although Lee had served in the field in western Virginia and the Carolinas, he had not exercised direct command of an army until June 1862. Not everyone held him in high esteem, an impression reinforced by his failure to win in 1861 and an impression that perhaps he, like Johnston, was wedded to the defense—a misinterpretation of his decision to defend the Carolinas as he did. Confederate artillerist Edward Porter Alexander later recalled that he had wondered out loud whether the new general had "the audacity that is going to be required in the command of this army to meet the odds which will be brought against it?" After all, the only way to avoid defeat was by attacking the enemy—"bounce him & whip him somewhere before he is ready for us, and that needs audacity in our commander. Has General Lee that audacity?" Not to fear, one of Alexander's fellow officers, Captain Joseph C. Ives, declared: "If there is one man in either army. . . . who is, head & shoulders, far above every other. . . . in audacity [,] that man is General Lee. . . . Lee is audacity personified."[2]

Lee's strategic outlook was simple. The Confederates could not simply remain on the defensive, nor should they hope to draw the war out. Remaining near Richmond simply placed the Confederate capitol in danger, and it meant that Confederate civilians elsewhere would have to suffer under enemy occupation. To wait for McClellan to move would prove a disaster. "McClellan will make this a battle of posts," he told Jefferson Davis days after assuming command. "He will take position from position, under cover of his heavy guns, & we cannot get at him without storming his works, which with our new troops would be extremely hazardous." Thus Lee knew had to find some way to pry McClellan away from Richmond. At the same time, he knew he could not wage a war of conquest, because he simply did not have the resources to do so. So he would have to take the offensive when possible, keeping the enemy off-balance, make the best use he could out of limited resources, and wage war in such a way as to foster war-weariness in the North. One way to do this was to threaten Washington; Lee realized that Lincoln was very protective of his own capital.[3]

Should Lee drive McClellan away from Richmond, he did not plan to stop there. An advance northward would help him protect his sources of supplies, especially the railroads and the Shenandoah. It would bring Confederate Virginians back within friendly lines. He could threaten Washington, causing Lincoln to shift his efforts toward defending his capitol, and by retaining the initiative force his foe to spread out his forces to defend vulnerable areas, allowing Lee to concentrate and attack in a situation where he might secure local parity or superiority.

From the War Department, clerk John B. Jones cheered the news of Lee's elevation "as the harbinger of bright fortune." But not everyone thought that a change in generals meant a change in strategy. Hearing of Lee's assumption of command, Mary Chesnut complained that he was "king of spades. They are all once more digging for dear life. Our chiefs contrive to dampen and destroy the enthusiasm of all who go near them. So much intrenching and falling back destroys the morale of any army. This everlasting retreating, it kills the hearts of the men."[4]

McClellan did not respect Lee, finding him "too cautious & weak under grave responsibility—personally brave & energetic to a fault, he yet is wanting in moral firmness when pressed by heavy responsibility & is likely to be timid & irresolute in action."[5] Nor did the Confederates at first see their new commander as much of a godsend, for Lee immediately ordered his men to prepare elaborate fieldworks. Understandably the men thought that they were in for more of the same sort of defensive warfare. In fact, Lee directed that fieldworks be prepared so that he could thin out the forces defending Richmond without losing defensive strength. That would enable him to gather together enough men to launch an attack on his own. Moreover, Davis trusted Lee as he did not trust Johnston, and in turn Lee was more skillful in his relations with his civil superior.

Even as Lee settled into his new command, events in the Shenandoah Valley compelled attention. In the aftermath of his victory at Winchester, Jackson contemplated what to do next. Initially he pressed northward towards Harpers Ferry. Then, learning of the approach of Union forces, he scurried southward again to evade being trapped. By early June, he had made his way back to the vicinity of Harrisonburg, only to discover that two Union columns, headed by Frémont and James Shields, were still closing in on him. On June 8 Confederate division commander Richard Ewell fended off Frémont at Cross Keys, southeast of Harrisonburg. The following day Jackson directed the majority of his command to strike Shields at nearby Port Republic. The Confederates not only managed to avoid being crushed but had beaten back their attackers. Jackson had helped delay McDowell's march toward McClellan, and in the end McDowell would never join his commander on Richmond's outskirts.[6]

As Jackson outmarched and outfought his foe, Lee pondered the wisdom of reinforcing him preparatory to an invasion across the Potomac, musing to Davis that "it would change the character of the war." It soon became evident, however, that whatever forces Jackson would receive would have to come from Lee, because affairs in the Carolinas continued to demand attention. Within days, however, Lee pondered an equally daring move. Jackson would come to Richmond to join forces with Lee preparatory to striking a blow at McClellan. In order to familiarize himself with McClellan's situation and perhaps fling some dust into his eyes, he ordered cavalryman James Ewell Brown Stuart to swing around to the Union rear. Stuart could gather forage and supplies while threatening McClellan's wagon train. The cavalryman gathered much useful information about McClellan's situation, confirming Lee's belief that McClellan's right flank was vulnerable. A well-aimed blow might threaten the Union line of supply, forcing McClellan to abandon his fortified lines and fight in the open. The next step was to attack. On June 16 Lee urged Jackson to join him as soon as possible; he shifted troops from North Carolina to Petersburg in response to news that Burnside's command would leave North Carolina to join McClellan.[7]

In fact, McClellan was in a dangerous position, if Lee moved quickly. The Union commander had directed Fitz John Porter's corps to remain north of the Chickahominy River in order to form a junction with what was assumed to be McDowell's advance southward from Fredericksburg. Meanwhile his supplies continued to move up the York River and then by rail to the front. However, when McDowell did not advance, and Stuart circled his army, McClellan realized that Porter's right flank was vulnerable (recent rains had flooded the Chickahominy, raising the possibility that Porter might be cut off) and that his supply line was not secure. He was already pondering a shift of base to the James. Still, McClellan sounded as if he was preparing to move forward, although by now wags might snicker that such was always the case. But whatever might be done had to be done carefully, for as he noted, "I must not risk the slightest risk of disaster, for if anything happened to this army our cause would be lost."[8]

It looked as if the climax of the conflict was fast approaching. In Philadelphia, Sidney George Fisher complained, "I cannot pretend to keep the run of these military operations. I think the war virtually over, tho how soon we may peace is doubtful. All interest now centers at Richmond, where the rebels say a great battle is to be fought."[9]

THE SEVEN DAYS

Ironically, it was an advance by Union troops that opened a week's worth of fighting east of Richmond. That brief contact paled in contrast with what was to follow. On June 26 three Confederate divisions smashed into Porter's corps. Had Jackson arrived in timely fashion behind Porter's right, the Yankees could have found themselves in serious trouble. Instead, Porter was able to beat back the attacks, but that night he pulled his command back to Gaines' Mill, located just north of the Chickahominy. That move promised to cut McClellan's supply line reaching back to the York River, confirming to the Union commander that it was time to change base to the James River. The Confederates concentrated on Porter's position the next day, managing at last to dislodge the defenders but failing to prevent Porter from withdrawing south across the Chickahominy. That delay bought much-needed time for McClellan to change his base of supplies.[10]

Back at headquarters, McClellan complained mightily about his situation. Learning that Jackson was north of Richmond, he wired Washington that he anticipated being attacked by perhaps 200,000 men. "I shall have to contend against vastly superior odds if these reports be true. But this Army will do all in the power of men to hold their position & repulse any attack." That could be excused, but what followed was more troubling. "I regret my great inferiority in numbers but feel that I am in no way responsible for it as I have not failed to represent repeatedly the necessity of reinforcements, that this was the decisive point, & that all the available means of the Govt should be concentrated here. . . . I feel that there is no use in my again asking for reinforcements." The implication—that the administration bore the blame—caused Lincoln to snap. "I give you all I can," he replied, "and act on the presumption that you will do the best you can with what you have, while you continue, ungenerously I think, to assume that I could give you more if I would." It remains difficult to determine exactly what McClellan was thinking. If he really believed that the Confederate force totaled 200,000 men, then he would have been outnumbered by over two to one. Yet within hours of forwarding that estimate, he wired that if he had another good division—which at the time would have numbered at most 7,000 men—"I could laugh at Jackson."[11]

As McClellan fended off Lee's advances, he battled with Lincoln and Stanton over reinforcements. Some of his telegrams smacked of the melodramatic. Others, including one which included the comment, "Hope for the best & I will not deceive the hopes you formerly placed in me," suggest that he was torn between feeling sorry for himself and taking another shot at the administration. Still others predicted victory, including one that declared, "I almost begin to think we are invincible." The next day he declared, "Had I twenty thousand fresh & good troops we would be sure of a splendid victory." A day later came the comment, "I have lost this battle because my force was too small. I again repeat that I am not responsible for this & I say it with the earnestness of a General who feels in his heart the loss of every brave man who has been needlessly sacrificed today." Perhaps he was exhausted; perhaps he had not fully recovered from a bout of illness in early June. Nevertheless, these comments were erratic and unwise. Such extreme fluctuations in outlook could not but create confusion. Moreover, it remains difficult to understand how McClellan could both maintain that he was so vastly outnumbered and assert that with ten thousand fresh troops, "I could gain the victory tomorrow." And, of course, McClellan crossed the line when he declared, "If I save this Army now I tell you plainly that I owe no thanks to you or any other persons in Washington—you have done your best to sacrifice this Army." A telegraph operator omitted those damning lines before forwarding the message to Stanton.[12]

Over the next several days, as McClellan shifted his supply base from the York to the James River, the Army of the Potomac conducted an able fighting withdrawal. At one point McClellan appears to have contemplated striking due east at Richmond itself, but this moment of aggressive intent passed. After all, McClellan reasoned, if the big battle of the war was to take place in Virginia, he had to ensure that victory would be his; a defeat might lose the entire war. Despite the fact that his men were more than holding their own, McClellan sounded desperate, as if he was just managing to stave off complete disaster. More calls for reinforcements followed, even though it would have been difficult for any sizable force to reach the James for a week. That reality did not deter McClellan, who believed that with 50,000 more men he could retrieve what had been lost.[13]

Back in Washington McClellan's telegrams created a sense of panic that the president tried to allay. Lincoln believed that the Confederate evacuation of Corinth had allowed the enemy to concentrate at Richmond: "In fact there will soon be no substantial rebel force any where else." Better to continue the advance elsewhere, while protecting Washington. Eventually, a reinforced McClellan "will take Richmond, without endangering any other place which we now hold—and will substantially end the war." In short, what happened on the James River did not need to result in military disaster for the Union cause, if it was seen in the context of the entire field of Union strategy. With this in mind, he contemplated a call for new recruits, but worried that it might be seen as an act of desperation, "so hard is it to have a thing understood as it really is." Perhaps it would not appear this way if the call was to be made in response to a request from the governors. So it happened, and on July 1, Lincoln called for 300,000 volunteers.[14]

Even as he made this call, Lincoln had to explain to McClellan that he could not produce reinforcements instantly. He explained that at present he had barely enough to protect Washington. The idea of sending forward 50,000 men immediately he pronounced "absurd." Reflecting on McClellan's obsession with shifting responsibility for his retreat, Lincoln observed: "If in your frequent mention of responsibility, you have the impression that I blame you for not doing more than you can, please be relieved of such impression. I only beg that in like manner, you will not ask impossibilities of me."[15]

The fact was that even if reinforcements were available, they could not have arrived in time to change the outcome of the campaign. Instead, in battle after battle, the Confederates mismanaged their attacks, and the Yankees stood their ground or withdrew in good order. At one point, while his men were holding off Confederate attackers at Glendale, McClellan met with a naval commander to pick out a new base, then decided to spend the rest of the afternoon aboard the USS *Galena* instead of returning to the front, a decision for which he would long be ridiculed. By month's end both the withdrawal and the change of base were nearly complete, as the Army of the Potomac deployed defensively at Malvern Hill, just north of the James. The position chosen was a most admirable one, with open fields of fire for artillery, located within support of the gunboats, and with both flanks protected by terrain. Nevertheless, on July 1 Lee hurled his army against the Union line. Once more the attack was botched and uncoordinated; this time the result was a bloody setback. Over the next few days each side parried for position, but the main fighting was over. Union losses were in the neighborhood of 16,000 men killed, wounded, and missing, whereas the Confederates suffered some 20,000 casualties, over 20 percent of Lee's total force. Although McClellan persisted in believing that he was badly outnumbered, the truth has become a subject of recent discussion. At one time, most studies suggested that McClellan had the edge in numbers of total forces, although not all his men saw action. More recent studies of the campaign conclude that Lee may have had a slight edge in manpower; however, these studies do not offer the numbers McClellan did in his assessment of the strength of opposing forces.[16]

For Lee, the campaign proved both frustrating and educational. Jackson had not performed well, arriving late to the scene several times in the critical opening days of the campaign. Nor did other generals perform as well as they might, although men such as John Bell Hood took advantage of their opportunities to show what they could do. Lee learned that perhaps his orders had been too detailed, too precise, and that he needed to give his subordinates some leeway. But the Confederate commander believed that McClellan could have been destroyed had things gone better. Not everyone shared his disappointment. As John B. Jones confided to his diary, "What genius! What audacity in Lee!" Surely he was no Joseph E. Johnston.[17]

After surveying McClellan's position, Lee declined to renew offensive operations; he would not move within range of the Union gunboats on the James after what had happened at Malvern Hill. Cheered by the lack of Confederate activity, McClellan assured Lincoln that "my position is very strong & daily becoming more so—if not attacked today I shall laugh at them." The president did not share his general's sense of humor. Indeed, he thought it was time to pay McClellan a visit. McClellan took the opportunity to press his views about the conduct of the war upon his civil superior. "The time has come when the Government must determine upon a civil and military policy, covering the whole ground of our national trouble," he declared. The conflict "should be conducted upon the highest principles known to Christian Civilization. It should not be a War looking to the subjugation of the people of any state, in any event. It should not be, at all, a War upon population; but against armed forces and political organizations. Neither confiscation of property, political executions of persons, territorial organization of states or forcible abolition of slavery should be contemplated for a moment." That said, even McClellan conceded that as a matter of "military necessity" the federal government might seize slaves from masters (provided it compensate those masters), although he thought such measures might be most appropriate in those slave states still in the Union. But that was as far as McClellan was willing to go: "A declaration of radical views, especially upon slavery, will rapidly disintegrate our present Armies."[18]

Many historians have criticized McClellan's efforts to present his notions about how the war was to be conducted. However, he was far from the only general to hold forth on these topics, and he was far from the only general to share his opinion with Lincoln. Moreover, he was not alone in offering the opinion that escalating the conflict might complicate the chances for reunion. "The war is getting to be a fearful thing and there is less confidence expressed as to its fortunate termination," observed one Philadelphian. "The southern people seem inflamed by the most bitter hatred of the North. How then can the Union be restored?"[19] The problem with McClellan's plea for conciliation was that his military strategy had not brought the victory needed to make his vision a reality, and for that he had to accept at least some of the responsibility. On the other hand, given Lincoln's growing distrust of his general, perhaps it was time for a change.

The Seven Days proved to be pivotal in showing how both sides approached the Eastern Theater. McClellan's failure to take Richmond brought an end to talk of a quick victory highlighted by the capture of the enemy capital. Many Republicans had been pressing for the very measures McClellan feared would result in a drawn out, bitter conflict. At the same time, his continual calls for reinforcements led Lincoln to strip forces away from operations in the Carolinas, most notably Burnside's IX Corps, which headed north via water to Fort Monroe, thus abandoning any thoughts of an offensive thrust from North Carolina.

For Lee victory proved almost problematic. True, he had driven McClellan away from Richmond's outskirts, but so long as the Army of the Potomac rested along the James River, a mere twenty miles from Richmond, Lee had to keep an eye on it. At first he also feared that Burnside might make his way from North Carolina to Petersburg, and he wondered whether McClellan might have the same target in mind. With Jackson no longer in the Shenandoah Valley, Union forces in northern Virginia could be consolidated into a single force that might threaten Richmond from the north. "Our success has not been so great or complete as we could have desired," he told his wife.[20]

LEE SUPPRESSES POPE

Even as McClellan and Lee commenced their battle for the fate of Richmond, Lincoln was working to impose his understanding of strategy upon the Eastern Theater. On June 26 he issued orders creating the Army of Virginia, bringing together the forces that had been keeping an eye on Jackson in the Shenandoah Valley as well as Irvin McDowell's corps. That the army was charged with the protection of Washington, advancing toward Charlottesville, and assisting McClellan before Richmond at the same time suggested just how muddled strategic thinking had become.[21]

Moreover, Lincoln had chosen a new general to lead this army. He had known John Pope before the war, and had watched approvingly as Pope scored military success along the Mississippi River with the capture of Island Number 10. Pope had then participated in the siege and taking of Corinth, where he had gotten along with Henry W. Halleck. Coming east in June, Pope said just the things many Republicans had been waiting to hear about a more earnest prosecution of the war. If in his Harrison's Landing letter McClellan had made the case once more for the need to wage a limited war in order to ease the path toward reunion, Pope was calling for escalation (and did so while criticizing McClellan in testimony before the Joint Committee on the Conduct of the War some twenty-four hours after McClellan composed his letter). Those views were expressed in the first orders he issued upon taking over his new command. One could set aside the bravado contained in his declaration that "I have come to you from the West, where we have always seen the backs of our enemies, from an army whose business it has been to seek the adversary and to beat him where he was found." Within days, however, Pope issued a series of orders that called upon his men to live off the land, cracked down on enemy civilians, promised to deport any civilian who failed to take an oath of allegiance, and took measures to hold civilians accountable for the actions of guerrilla or irregular forces. The measures marked an escalation of the war effort, and several of the measures also looked toward a war of movement where armies lived off the land instead of being tautly tethered to a supply base. The directives sparked outrage in the Confederacy, but they were in harmony with the new notion of taking off the kid gloves, a notion that prevailed among many Union commanders, if not McClellan.[22]

The idea to form a new army in north central Virginia had originated before the Seven Days, and Pope had arrived in Washington just before the opening of that campaign. Understandably, however, people linked Pope's arrival with McClellan's defeat. Reports that Pope had advised Lincoln as the president read McClellan's telegrams during the Seven Days augured poorly for future harmony between the two generals. In truth, Pope's original mission was to keep an eye on Confederate activities in the Valley (word had not yet reached Washington of Jackson's sudden movement to Richmond) and draw Confederates toward him in order to assist McClellan's efforts. Circumstances soon dictated a different course, because for the next six weeks after Malvern Hill the Union high command contemplated what to do next in Virginia.[23]

Robert E. Lee was also pondering what to do next. He had not destroyed McClellan's army, and although he had reduced the immediate threat to Richmond, it seemed but a momentary respite. After all, McClellan on the James was actually in a more secure position than he was on the York, and he could move westward along either bank and threaten Richmond directly (on the north bank) or advance towards Petersburg along the south bank. Before long Lee learned of Pope's promotion and Lincoln's call for more men, a sign of redoubled resolve. News that Burnside's corps was arriving in Virginia increased the odds against him. Yet, so long as McClellan remained on the James River, there was little Lee could do without leaving Richmond vulnerable. If Pope and

McClellan advanced, Lee would find himself in a difficult position, for there would be no Jackson in the Shenandoah, and Pope's force would be far larger than the corps that McDowell had at Fredericksburg poised to join McClellan months before. To be sure, Lee was awaiting reinforcements of his own, drawn from the Carolinas. Through month's end, however, he was convinced that McClellan would renew his efforts against Richmond from his base on the James.[24]

It did not help Lee's temper when he read Pope's orders. A hard edge crept into his discussions of the new Union commander. He termed Pope a "miscreant" and pointed to his instructions concerning the treatment of civilian populations as reason enough for him "to be suppressed." However, for the moment the most Lee could do was to detach Jackson to keep an eye on Pope. Even that was not an optimal choice. Jackson complained that he was not strong enough to take Pope on himself, but Lee worried that if he reinforced Jackson, his weakened force might prove vulnerable to another offensive by McClellan. Certainly, as he told Davis, Pope "ought to be suppressed if possible," but it was the qualifying clause that was important. At best, Lee believed, Jackson might strike out at Pope before returning to Richmond. Through the first week of August he determined to remain in place. A show of force by McClellan's command followed by reports that Union forces might be on the south bank of the James, from where they could approach Petersburg, convinced him that it was "too hazardous to diminish the forces here, until something more is ascertained."[25]

It had taken the Union high command some time to figure out its next move, in part because of changes in the chain of command in Washington. On July 11, 1862, Lincoln named Henry W. Halleck general-in-chief. The new position was recognition for all the successes that had happened under Halleck's command in the West. He counted among his supporters Winfield Scott, with whom Lincoln had conferred in June, and John Pope. Renowned as a student of military science, Halleck seemed to possess sufficient qualifications to supervise the Union war effort.[26]

Appearances proved deceiving. Halleck might observe and he might advise, but he lacked the desire to order army commanders to get things done. His explanation was that the commander on the scene knew best what to do. As a result, before too long he served more as a link between army commanders, Stanton, and Lincoln and as a military adviser than as a general-in-chief. After all, during his time in the West he spent more time playing army politics than he did in the field. He bickered with McClellan (then his superior officer) and Don Carlos Buell over who needed to do what and who should be in charge in that theater. He proved more adept at plotting behind Ulysses S. Grant's back than at driving the enemy away, and he was adept at taking credit for the accomplishments of subordinates.

McClellan cared little for Halleck when he was general-in-chief, and he would care even less to have Halleck as his superior officer—he called it "a slap in the face." The two men would find it hard to work together. That became evident when

Halleck, accompanied by Ambrose Burnside, decided to pay McClellan a visit to determine what to do next with the Army of the Potomac. Once more McClellan made the case that he was badly outnumbered and needed reinforcements before he could take the offensive. He was not nearly so clear when it came to outlining a plan of campaign, although he indicated that perhaps it was time to think about crossing the James and approaching Richmond from the south after taking Petersburg. Halleck presented Lincoln's preference: McClellan needed to withdraw from the James, unite with Pope, and approach Lee and Richmond from the north using an overland approach, which was now clearly the one preferred by the president. At best, Halleck added, McClellan might receive some reinforcements before advancing, but Pope would not be joining him.[27]

McClellan should have rested satisfied with that option, but he overplayed his hand. Lee, he believed, had upwards of 200,000 men (in truth, Lee had less than half that number), and McClellan needed at least 30,000 men to augment his present command of 90,000. Had he simply taken what Halleck was willing to give him, he might have been allowed to try his luck once more along the James. No sooner had Halleck returned to Washington, however, than he received a dispatch from McClellan pleading for reinforcements, some 35,000 from the commands of Burnside and David Hunter (which would have stripped the Atlantic coast clean of Union manpower) plus another 15,000 to 20,000 from the West to help him take Richmond. A call for 50,000 or more men was simply out of the question, reasoned Halleck. It made no difference that Burnside had turned down command of the Army of the Potomac, information that did not long remain a secret to McClellan.[28]

McClellan's request for reinforcements had followed an exchange with Lincoln nearly two weeks earlier concerning reinforcements. The president had telegraphed him that by his estimates McClellan should have 160,000, and that in any case some 45,000 men appeared to be unaccounted for. McClellan patiently explained that one's effective force was always much less than one's paper strength, and that while by his own counting he had some 144,407 men present and absent, only 88,665 were present for duty. He estimated that some 40,000 were absent (a number not so far from Lincoln's estimate), and that if these men returned to him he would not need reinforcements. As he told his wife, however, "I was amused at a couple of telegrams yesterday urging me to the offensive as if I were unwilling to take it myself! It is so easy for people to give advice—it costs nothing! But it is a little more difficult for poor me to create men & means, & to wipe out by mere wishes the forces of the enemy."[29]

Lincoln had already expressed his frustration with trying to reinforce McClellan. The general never seemed satisfied with what he had at hand and was always calling for more men. Yet, when Lincoln provided men, their numbers melted away. The president once compared it to shoveling fleas across a barnyard. Would the same erosion in numbers happen if the army was moved to northern Virginia, where the supply lines would be shorter, the distance to transport men far less, and the area presumably healthier?[30]

McClellan's request brought matters to a head. Halleck on August 3 informed him that he was to transport the Army of the Potomac back to Aquia Creek, near Fredericksburg. McClellan vigorously protested: "Here, directly in front of this Army, is the heart of the rebellion; it is here that all our resources should be collected to strike the blow which will determine the fate of this nation. . . . Here is the true defense of Washington; it is here on the banks of the James that the fate of the Union should be decided."[31] For several days McClellan hoped that somehow he would be allowed to stay in place, but at last he gave way, after proving unable to spark combat that might have caused Halleck to reconsider his order.

If Halleck's decision to recall McClellan's army is open to question, so was his decision to keep McClellan in command. Even McClellan anticipated the possibility of removal, and obviously Halleck had sounded out Burnside about taking over. Simply put, Lee could not leave the Richmond area with the forces under his command so long as the Army of the Potomac remained along the James River. That question could be discussed independently of the matter of McClellan's retaining his command. As McClellan realized, it would take him longer to transfer his command to Aquia Creek than it would take Lee to march north, join with Jackson, and take the offensive against Pope. In short, while people criticized McClellan's performance, it appeared no one was willing to take his place, including Halleck and Burnside.

Lee would not know of this decision for some time, although news of Burnside's corps being transported to Aquia Creek offered him some evidence as to what would happen next. Nevertheless, he wanted Jackson to deal with Pope. In turn, Pope had just issued orders to press southward toward Gordonsville in order to threaten the railroads in the area. On August 9 Jackson clashed with a portion of Pope's command, under the command of old foe Nathaniel P. Banks, at Cedar Mountain, about ten miles southwest of Culpeper. The Confederates had the best of a bloody brawl, but, learning that the remainder of Pope's army was not far off, Jackson pulled back. Although initially Pope claimed victory, he declined to continue his advance on Gordonsville.[32]

By the time he heard of Cedar Mountain, Robert E. Lee was also discovering that McClellan was indeed departing from the James River. It was time to join Jackson and "suppress" Pope before McClellan could unite with him. That achieved, perhaps a move across the Potomac might be next. He hurried divisions northward, leaving a small force to shield Richmond. Eager to shift the theater of war to northern Virginia, Lee looked to relieve the tidewater of the stress of war while he enjoyed the freedom of maneuver that was compromised by having to protect Richmond.[33]

On August 15 Lee arrived at Gordonsville and conferred with James Longstreet and Jackson as to what to do next. For the moment it looked as if a rapid move against Pope's left might trap the Union general between the Rappahannock and Rapidan rivers, severing communications with Fredericksburg, but that opportunity faded away when Pope, having obtained a copy of Lee's plans, withdrew north of the Rappahannock. Frustrated, Lee next decided to circle around Pope's right, hoping that Jackson would reach Manassas Junction in the Union rear, where Pope had established a supply depot. Using the Bull Run Mountain range as a shield, Jackson marched through Throughfare Gap and reached the supply depot on August 27. Pope pulled back once more, but he was cheered by the news that the lead elements of McClellan's army had landed and were making their way to reinforce him.

Jackson finally decided that it was time to bring Pope to battle and pin him in position west of Bull Run, away from the Union reinforcements that could concentrate at Centreville. He deployed his men along an unfinished railroad cut a short distance west of the Manassas battlefield and on August 28 attracted the attention of a Union column marching along a nearby turnpike. Over the next two days, Pope brought what force he could to bear on Jackson's position, but the Confederates held their ground against repeated assaults. Meanwhile, Longstreet came up from the west against the Union left flank. Although lead elements of his command engaged Union forces in combat on August 29, Pope did not appear to realize the import of Longstreet's arrival. His target remained Jackson, and he believed that one more day of attacks would allow him to prevail.

Pope continued to hammer away at Jackson's position throughout the afternoon of August 30, committing additional divisions to the assault and ignoring signs of activity to the west. By mid-afternoon, a single artillery battery and a lone undersized infantry brigade composed of two Zouave regiments, the 5th and 10th New York, protected the Union left. Arrayed against them were the nearly 30,000 men of Longstreet's command, which came crashing down, overrunning the two regiments and making their way for Union headquarters. Quickly Pope shifted enough men to blunt the attack, which found the terrain rough going around Chinn Ridge, and the Yankee stand at Henry House Hill staved off complete disaster. As night fell Pope began pulling back toward Centreville, much as McDowell had the previous year.

Lee had scored a major victory, but he wanted more. He sent Jackson toward Fairfax Court House, hoping to outflank the Yankees again, this time on the right flank. However, in another fierce action at Chantilly, some four miles northeast of Centreville, Union forces checked the Confederates once more, as the main body of Pope's army continued to retreat, encountering the remainder of McClellan's army around Washington.

Second Manassas was a telling Confederate triumph. Outnumbered, Lee had driven Pope from the field, inflicting some 14,000 losses at a cost of 8,500 casualties. Yet the outcome should also have served as a cautionary tale to those who dreamed of winning the decisive battle. Rarely in the Civil War did a general have such an opportunity to launch such a devastating attack as Lee had at Second Manassas, and yet, when all was said and done, he had not destroyed his foe. If one could not achieve a climactic victory under such conditions, could one ever achieve it?

THE MARYLAND CAMPAIGN

Thwarted in his effort to destroy the Union army at Second Manassas, Robert E. Lee decided to carry the war across the Potomac. His reasoning was simple. He believed the presence of a Confederate force in Maryland would encourage secession-ist and pro-Confederate sentiment. The news that a Confederate army was north of the Potomac might impress European leaders as they considered whether to offer to mediate between the Union and the Confederacy, and perhaps even intervene. That same sight could but dishearten northern public opinion just as the congressional midterm elections approached.

All that may have been true, and yet one must also consider that Lee's alternatives were far less enticing. Simply to stand in place and allow McClellan to reorganize the forces under his command would sacrifice whatever advantage he had gained during the last several months and restore the situation to year's beginning. Pressing forward toward Washington was out of the question. The Federal capital was shielded by fortifications, and there remained a sizable force to defeat. Withdrawal into a better position would forfeit the morale boost resulting from victory at Second Manassas. Although it would be misleading to say that the decision to invade Maryland was Lee's only choice, it was his best choice. If it involved risk, it also promised the possibility of reward.

All that remained was to convince Jefferson Davis. "The present seems to be the most propitious time since the commencement of the war for the Confederate Army to enter Maryland," Lee wrote Davis on September 3. The Union forces about Washington were demoralized and disorganized; now was the time to move. Over the next two days Lee continued to build his case and urged that he be sent more supplies. He did not wait for an answer; his men began crossing the Potomac on September 5.[34]

As his army entered Maryland, Lee issued a proclamation to its citizens, declaring that "the people of the South have long wished to aid you in throwing off this foreign yoke, to enable you again to enjoy the inalienable rights of freemen, and restore independence and sovereignty to your State." The same day he wrote Davis that it seemed to be the best time for the Confederacy "to propose with propriety . . . the recognition of our independence" by the United States. With an eye to the upcoming elections he believed that if the Lincoln administration rejected the proposal, it would bear the burden of continuing a war with no end in sight. Lee was becoming quite a politician, advising Davis in much the same way that McClellan and Pope had advised Lincoln.[35]

Lee's confidence was due in part to his belief that the Union forces were in no condition to move. Indeed, there was confusion at Washington for several days. Halleck proved utterly useless as general-in-chief, breaking under the strain. Pope was so busy charging disloyalty among his own generals from McClellan's Army of the Potomac that it was not clear whether he would regain his focus in time to deal with Lee. That left McClellan as once more the man of the moment. In the immediate aftermath of Second Manassas, Lincoln placed McClellan in charge of the capital defenses. Several cabinet members objected. Conceding that McClellan had the "slows," Lincoln reminded everyone that he still retained the trust of the army and would excel at reorganizing it and restoring its morale. That in Lincoln's mind McClellan had treated Pope badly, even callously, in remarking that perhaps Pope should be left "to get out of his scrape" had to be set aside. For the moment, he observed, "We must use what tools we have."[36]

Lincoln soon recovered from his despair. In fact, the president saw a great opportunity for Union forces. "We must hurt this enemy before it gets away," he told a private secretary.[37] The only question that remained was who would lead that army into the field. Pope? Ambrose Burnside, perhaps? In the end, it would be left to McClellan to forge elements from several commands into an army and take off after Lee. Within days McClellan had done just that, moving out on the very day Lee reported to Davis that there was no sign of any such movement.

Perhaps Lee was too preoccupied with his plans to pay much heed to McClellan; for once he took his foe for granted. The Confederate commander, somewhat perturbed that Union forces in the Shenandoah Valley had simply not fled before his advance but instead had gathered at and near Harpers Ferry, commenced planning an ambitious offensive, whereby he would split his army into several columns, move to the northwest, and swoop down on Harpers Ferry and its garrison. That done, he could resume his campaign, his line of supply southward unobstructed. He would use South Mountain to shield his command from McClellan's advance, holding the passes with relatively small forces. The stakes were evident—so evident, indeed, that within days of each other the opposing presidents proposed to join their commanders in the field. Lee had to dissuade Davis from joining him, citing the dangers involved, while Halleck advised against Lincoln visiting McClellan in like circumstances.[38]

The mere notion of a Confederate army roaming through Maryland drove many northerners to despair. "I feel ashamed of being an American now," moaned one New Yorker. "To think that we should be conquered by the bare feet and rags of the South, fed from our wagons, supplied from our caissons!" Even as he cast a critical eye at McClellan, George Templeton Strong remarked that "it is idle to criticize his practice until we can name some stronger and better man to put in his place."[39]

Lee's campaign began to unravel within a short time of his issuing orders setting forth the advance on Harpers Ferry, for a copy of the orders went astray and ended up in Union hands. McClellan joyously declared that he now had in his hands "a paper with which if I cannot whip Bobbie Lee I will be willing to go home." Discovering his misfortune, Lee nevertheless decided to go forward with his plan, trusting that his men could delay the Yankees at the mountain passes. They did—barely— as McClellan's men pressed forward on September 14, winning a series of battles along South Mountain. That appeared impressive enough for McClellan, who estimated Lee's strength at 120,000 men—nearly three times its actual size. Hearing of the fall of Harpers Ferry the next day, Lee decided to form a line of defense along Antietam Creek, east of Sharpsburg, Maryland, a short distance from the Potomac. He hoped that enough of his men would make it in time from Harpers Ferry to make a battle of it. Given enough time, if the army reunited, he might even press northward to Hagerstown. It was a daring decision, but Lee counted upon McClellan to be deliberate, even cautious. For his part, McClellan sensed opportunity, but he knew that the cost of failure might be disaster, and he believed he was outnumbered. Better to be sure.

Both sides moved infantry, artillery, and cavalry into position on September 16. Much of Lee's army was now up, absent A. P. Hill's division, which had to wrestle with completing affairs connected with the surrender, including processing some 12,000 prisoners. The following morning, McClellan launched the first of a series of attacks, starting on his right and moving southward toward his left, unable to coordinate his assaults and unwilling to commit his reserve, the V Corps, in part because he did not want to risk their defeat. Lee's men clung on for dear life, launching counterattacks here and there before being forced back. In the afternoon Ambrose Burnside's corps stormed a stone bridge, overran the small Confederate force guarding it, and advanced westward toward Sharpsburg and the roads leading toward the Potomac. Hill's division arrived just in time to drive back this final effort, and the bloodiest day of the Civil War ended.[40]

The losses were shocking. McClellan, some 75,000 strong, lost about 12,500 men, while Lee lost just over a third of his 40,000 men. Yet the Confederate commander decided to stay in place and dare a renewal of the battle on September 18. None came, in part because McClellan's army was seriously damaged, and in part because the sight of the battlefield was so sickening that many Union officers had no stomach to add to the carnage. Remaining in place might have also been an attempt by Lee to mold public perception of what had happened, for by staying in place, he demonstrated that he had not been driven from the field. Nevertheless, he could not long remain. The next day Lee withdrew, crossing the Potomac, and fended off what constituted a Union pursuit at Shepherdstown, Virginia.[41]

It is a matter of some debate as to who really won or lost the Antietam campaign. Lee returned to Virginia with his goals of gaining foreign recognition and arousing pro-Confederate sentiment unfulfilled. He had fought a series of sharp engagements, climaxing in the bloodiest single day of combat in the conflict, and barely held on to survive. Yet one might also recall the damage done at Harpers Ferry. Factoring the gains made there, Lee had cause to believe that he had not done nearly so badly. Indeed, for a few days he contemplated crossing the Potomac once more, but eventually he conceded it was time to rest and refit, especially as McClellan was showing no sign of renewing operations.

For McClellan the results were equally mixed. He had done an admirable job of pulling the various Union elements together after the debacle at Second Manassas and had succeeded in forging an effective fighting force. He had disrupted Lee's invasion plan, nearly shattered his army, and forced a Confederate withdrawal southward. As division commander George G. Meade observed, "Now, if there is any common sense in the country, it ought to let us have time to reorganize and get into shape our new lines, and then advance with such overwhelming numbers that resistance on the part of the enemy would be useless." And yet one came away from the campaign sensing a missed opportunity made all the more painful by the fact that it had been such a near-run thing. Initial reports, after all, had been so promising. "The wheel of fortune has turned around once more and the rebels seem to be caught in their own trap," New Yorker Maria Daly noted. "The Potomac has risen and cut off their retreat. . . . Jackson and Lee are surrounded and will make a desperate resistance. . . . victory must be ours."[42]

And yet in the end it was appearances that mattered most in a war where public support was crucial. Although a careful observer might point out that Lee defied McClellan to attack again on September 18, the fact remained that Lee had invaded, McClellan had advanced and attacked, and Lee had withdrawn. That seemed to resemble a Union victory of some sort, at least to the northern public, and Lincoln seized upon this impression to issue the preliminary Emancipation Proclamation five days after the battle. If half-defeats in Virginia looked like disasters, then a half-victory could be made to appear as a major triumph. The president did not expect to recoup immediate political advantage, and if anything the proclamation aroused more opposition than support among those Democrats and conservative Republicans, who dreaded transforming the war to save the union into the war to free at least some of the slaves. But, just as Lincoln dared not issue such a document in the wake of defeat lest it seem he was desperate in the eyes of the public, he could seize upon Antietam to declare that the war might well enter a new stage if the Confederates did not reconsider their course. To be sure, the revolutionary thrust of the proclamation was blunted by Lincoln's willingness to allow white Southerners to escape its consequences by reestablishing loyal governments, and the president would use the occasion of his annual message in December 1862 to make one last plea for colonization, but even so it was revolutionary enough for the moment and promised to escalate the conflict.

McCLELLAN DEPARTS

Pleased as he might be by the news of Antietam, Abraham Lincoln was disappointed that the battle did not produce the "complete" success broadcast by McClellan. He could not fathom why McClellan did not commit more men to the fray or why he failed to pursue Lee vigorously. It was almost as if McClellan did not want to win. Rumors floated back to Washington that perhaps this was no accident. The brother of one staff officer reportedly claimed that there was a "game" afoot whereby "neither army should get much advantage over the other," so that both sides would settle their differences through a negotiated settlement that would preserve slavery. Lincoln promptly dismissed the staff officer in question, declaring "that if there was a 'game'.... to have our army not take advantage of the enemy when it could, it was his object to break up that game."[43]

It was time, Lincoln decided, to pay McClellan another visit. He arrived at army headquarters on October 1, and conferred with McClellan for a few days. The general thought that Lincoln came to urge him to advance, snarling, "These people don't know what an army requires & therefore act stupidly." The president waited until he returned to Washington before pressing in earnest. When McClellan demurred, Lincoln snapped back, "Are you not over-cautious when you assume that you can not do what the enemy is constantly doing? Should you not claim to be at least his equal in prowess, and act upon the claim?" It was time to move. Should Lee counter by marching northward again, so much the better, for McClellan would "have nothing to do but to follow him, and ruin him." It was time to fight: "if we never try, we shall never succeed. . . . We should not so operate as to merely drive him away. As we must beat him somewhere, or fail finally, we can do it, if at all, easier near us, than far away. If we cannot beat the enemy where he how is, we never can, he again being within the intrenchments of Richmond." Lincoln concluded, "It is all easy if our troops march as well as the enemy; and it is unmanly to say they can not do it."[44]

Lincoln was running out of patience with McClellan for the last time. He dismissed McClellan's complaints that his army was undersupplied, despite evidence that this time the general had a point. It did not help that Jeb Stuart took the opportunity to ride around McClellan's army once more: Lincoln directed Halleck to tell McClellan that "if the enemy had more occupation south of the river, his cavalry would not be so likely to make raids north of it." Finally, when McClellan complained about the condition of the mounts in a Massachusetts cavalry regiment, Lincoln took it upon himself to ask in pointed fashion, "Will you pardon me for asking what the horses of your army have done since the battle of Antietam that fatigue anything?"[45]

At the heart of the disagreement was Lincoln's growing frustration with McClellan's failure not only to move but also to bring Lee to battle. To one group of visitors he exploded in exasperation that neither the generals nor the public at large had the stomach for fighting. "The fact is," he exclaimed, "the people haven't yet made up their minds that we are at war with the South. They have got the idea into their heads that we are going to get out of this fix, somehow, by strategy! That's the word—strategy! General McClellan thinks he is going to whip the rebels by strategy; and the army has got the same notion." This was all wrong, the president observed: "They have no idea that the war is to be carried on and put through by hard, tough fighting, that will hurt somebody; and no headway is going to be made while this delusion lasts."[46]

That, McClellan might have said, was exactly what was wrong with the president's perception of warfare. It was too simple, too direct, too innocent of the complicated matters that beset a military commander. War was more than a mere wrestling match where two headstrong armies simply collided and had it out: it was a matter best reserved to the professionals, who possessed the knowledge, expertise, and training to do the job right. The war was to be won be strategy, namely by superior military strategy, and McClellan was prepared to do it, provided he was allowed to do it his way. The president had meddled with his campaign against Richmond; he had recalled McClellan to salvage what was left after Second Bull Run; now it was time to refit and prepare for another campaign, and that would take time.

The Lincoln-McClellan relationship had turned counterproductive. Distrusting the general, Lincoln badgered him and limited his freedom of action. In turn, McClellan complained of civilian meddling motivated by political concerns as justifying his deliberate planning. In the aftermath of the Maryland campaign, it took time to refit and resupply the Army of the Potomac, as well as to reorganize what had been in truth a motley collection of commands thrown together in the aftermath of Second Manassas. Yet it appeared that Lee had no such problems in wrestling with his challenges.[47] With winter drawing near, the time for campaigning seemed to be running out.

In mid-October, Lee thought that McClellan might advance south into the Shenandoah Valley. He welcomed the idea, but the thrust southward proved but a probe. Finally, on October 26, McClellan began crossing the Potomac in strength. Lee split his command, leaving Jackson in the valley while shifting Longstreet east of the Blue Ridge Mountains to Culpeper. He then went to Richmond to seek reinforcements from southeast Virginia and North Carolina, evidence that he no longer thought these areas were ripe targets for Union offensives. At last, when McClellan did not move rapidly enough to interpose his army between Lee and Richmond, as Lincoln thought he should, the president decided he'd had enough. The day after voters went to the polls in the November elections, orders went out from Washington relieving McClellan of command. To one advisor the president explained, "I said I would remove him if he let Lee's army get away from him, and I must do so. He has got the 'slows,' Mr. Blair." His replacement would be Ambrose E. Burnside. Hearing of the change, Lee turned to Longstreet and remarked: "We always understood each other so well. I fear they may continue to make these changes till they find some one whom I don't understand."[48]

In just over six months the situation in Virginia had radically changed. No longer were Union forces within earshot of Richmond's church bells; no longer would George B. McClellan be in charge of an army. As the Union idol of yesterday faded away, the emergence of a Confederate command team headed by Robert E. Lee marked the high point of military leadership for the Army of Northern Virginia. It was not just that Lee knew how to utilize the skills of Jackson, Longstreet, and Stuart to best advantage, it was also that he had managed to construct a positive relationship with Jefferson Davis that papered over their real differences as to the proper strategy to follow in the East.[49]

The campaigns of 1862 proved decisive in shaping how both the Union and Confederate high command approached strategic issues. They also illustrated a continuing division between leaders as to the proper objective of campaigns in the Eastern Theater, even as operations during that year tended to reduce the definition of that theater to a far smaller geographical area than one might have conceived at year's beginning. The campaigns would leave a legacy that would not be challenged for over a year.

With Robert E. Lee's emergence as commander of the Army of Northern Virginia, the Confederacy no longer looked simply to remain on the defensive in Virginia interrupted by the occasional counterpunch. Lee realized that even if he could repel Union offensives, the war would drag on, and Confederate resources would dwindle. He needed to take the offensive whenever he could, both on the battlefield and operationally, in an effort to force a decision and to wage the sort of war which would spark Confederate morale and bring despair to the North. Yet the results of his offensive in 1862 demonstrated that several assumptions Confederates might have held were deeply flawed. Lee realized that the Confederacy should not look to European intervention to turn the tide—Great Britain would not intervene until its leadership was already convinced that the Confederacy would be victorious, and France would follow Britain's lead. Even then, it was increasingly unlikely that the British would actually risk war with the United States, given how such a conflict would damage a most prosperous trading relationship. Nor would there be an uprising in the border states for the Confederacy: Maryland and Kentucky remained with the Union, and Lincoln's decision to issue the preliminary Emancipation Proclamation suggested that he no longer worried that a blow against slavery might sever some of the remaining slave states.

For the Union, 1862 saw a narrowing of strategic options and confusion over how to conceive of strategy in the theater. At the beginning of the year, it looked as if operations along the Atlantic coast might well offer multiple opportunities to penetrate the Confederate interior. Instead, Union forces remained content to hold onto their coastal positions, and by the middle of the year Burnside and his corps were on their way to oppose Lee. Thus came to an end (for the time being) of the notion of cutting Richmond off from the Confederate heartland. The Confederate high command could dispatch regiments elsewhere, secure in the knowledge that there would be little to worry about from the Yankees along the James, although the Union held on in force to Fort Monroe and Norfolk.

The debate over Union military operations in the East boiled down to whether Richmond or Confederate forces should be the major objective of Union military operations. While several Union commanders remained convinced of Richmond's strategic value, Lincoln urged them to strike at Confederate armies by advancing overland in such a way as to shield Washington from attack. Indeed, the president began to believe that it would be easier to defeat the Confederates near Washington than near Richmond. The closer the Confederates were to Washington, the easier it would be for the Army of the Potomac to be supplied, while it would be the Army of Northern Virginia that would have to protect its logistical links. While the Confederates could defend themselves behind fortifications at Richmond, they would not enjoy such advantages in northern Virginia, and if they chose to cross the Potomac, perhaps they could be stranded on its northern bank. Thus Lee's invasion of Maryland represented a lost opportunity for Union victory. Lincoln would never again look with much favor upon a movement against Richmond via the James River, in part because of the logistical challenge and in part because to endorse such a move would appear to concede to McClellan the superiority of that general's strategic insight.

Thus Union military planners began to frame the debate over how to proceed in the east in terms of attacking Richmond or attacking Lee, almost as if these two objectives were mutually exclusive. This was a mistake. If the Confederates lost Richmond, Lee would be hard pressed to remain in Virginia. The loss of the Confederate capital would be costly politically and economically, and would have a serious logistical impact upon Confederate military operations. One of the best ways to rid Lee of the initiative would be to threaten Richmond. It is hard to see how Lee could have moved northward in August 1862, had McClellan remained along the James River, with at least a sufficient force to draw the attention of the Confederates: McClellan's thinking about a possible movement against Petersburg was worth considering, even if Lincoln and Halleck had lost faith in McClellan's ability to conduct offensive operations. Better to replace the general than transfer the army, especially as it was not clear how McClellan and John Pope would have been able to work together (as events demonstrated, it would have been a terrible relationship). There were plenty of ways to use the threat of a blow against Richmond to force Lee's hand and to retain the initiative in the hands of Union commanders. Focusing on Lee allowed the Confederate commander to keep Richmond lightly guarded, and allowed him to respond as he chose to Union initiatives.

Highlighting the relationship between Richmond and Lee's army in no way constitutes a defense of George B. McClellan's performance as commander of the

Army of the Potomac, although it does counter the mainstream desire to side with Lincoln and denigrate McClellan in all ways possible. The problem with McClellan was different. He wanted things his own way, something generals rarely realize. He would not move until he was ready, and he would not accept the notion of risk in military operations. His last chance to succeed on the battlefield during the Peninsula campaign vanished the moment Lee replaced Johnston. Throughout the year Lincoln lost faith in him, to the point that by the fall of 1862 there was no basis of good faith communications between the president and the general whose horse he had once been willing to hold. In truth, the forces under McClellan's command needed to rest and be refitted after the Maryland campaign, but Lincoln no longer had any faith in McClellan, and thus McClellan never had a chance to see whether his last plan of campaign bore any promise before his replacement in the aftermath of the fall elections.

Much has been made of how McClellan's approach toward waging war and toward his civil superiors pervaded the Army of the Potomac long after he bid his men farewell. For the next several years, certain generals would wax nostalgic over Little Mac as they expressed their contempt for Lincoln, Stanton, Halleck, and politics in general. Even as generals of all political perspectives and professional backgrounds worked their strings with political contacts, the professionals among them complained about political interference and patronage and wished that war could be left to trained military men. At the same time, Lincoln continued to use McClellan as a reference point in accessing the performance of his successors in the Eastern Theater, nearly always to the disparagement of his generals. The president continued to meddle in command relationships, soliciting the opinions of intriguing subordinates always eager to score points against their military superiors. It would not be until 1864 that much of this would come to an end. In the meantime much blood would be spilled, many lives would be lost, and little would change.

FOUR

⮞⮜⮞⮜

BLOOD ALONG THE RAPPAHANNOCK

George B. McClellan's removal from command of the Army of the Potomac appeared to signal that the war in the East had entered a new stage. The Army of the Potomac, stationed in northern Virginia, was poised for the sort of overland offensive favored by Abraham Lincoln, and it would be commanded by a general whose loyalty to the president was unquestioned. True, the Army of Northern Virginia was regaining strength in the aftermath of Antietam, but Ambrose Burnside appeared ready to take on Robert E. Lee. Moreover, with the midterm elections over, Union army operations would be freed of the pressures of the election clock. The time appeared ideal to act.

Fast forward thirteen months, and one would notice that far too little had changed. The Army of the Potomac was now located just a dozen miles southwest of where it had been, and the Army of Northern Virginia, having abandoned Culpeper to the Yankees, was now bivouacked south of the Rappahannock-Rapidan river network. Both armies were somewhat smaller than they had been a year earlier, although that was partly due to detachments elsewhere. The Union army would soon have to replace men who had declined to reenlist once their three years would be up in the spring of 1864. Several generals had disappeared from the scene. Neither one of the men who had been Lee's corps commanders in November 1862 were present in Virginia at the end of 1863, and the Army of the Potomac was now directed by George G. Meade (who had headed a division back in November 1862), with new corps commanders in place. Many other faces were missing as well, the results of over a year's worth of campaigning featuring three major battles in which close to 100,000 men were killed, wounded, or missing (to say nothing of the losses incurred in numerous minor engagements). All in all, however, things had changed but little in terms of the overall strategic situation in Virginia.[1]

Comparing the situation in November 1862 with December 1863 suggests that for all the bloodshed in three terrific battles—Fredericksburg, Chancellorsville, and Gettysburg—little had been accomplished. At most the ratio of attrition due to these battles favored the Union in the long run. Neither side seemed able to secure a decisive victory on enemy soil; neither side seemed able to exploit the opportunities offered by victory. And yet there were those who saw as much in the fall of 1862, including Union general Alpheus S. Williams. "I have no faith in a campaign in Virginia from this or any other overland route," he wrote in the wake of McClellan's removal. "The topographical features of the country, the miserable state of the country roads, the necessity of heavily guarding such a long and exposed line of communication must render success with a politic and shrewd enemy almost impossible. They have done and are still doing what I anticipated, falling back on their supplies and reserves, and thus extending our lines and weakening our force as we move towards the interior." He added that when the Confederates had invaded Maryland, circumstances were reversed. "Their numbers were reduced, and they were sadly straitened for subsistence." To Williams the conclusion was obvious: "The history of war proves that an united people can in the end overwhelm any superior invading force, if acting purely on the defensive." That was bad enough, but as Williams reviewed the scene, he cited another cause for skepticism. "My idea is that the cursed policy of this war has its origin at Washington. Old fogyism has ruled in every department. Trepidation for the safety of the Capital seems to have paralyzed all faculties or preparation and promptness."[2]

For the Confederacy, it was essential to keep the war away from Richmond. Purely defensive operations promised a grinding war of attrition in which the superior numbers of Union forces would eventually prove decisive. Nor could Lee allow the enemy to approach Richmond from the east; he remained concerned that some commander would renew McClellan's waterborne advance. He was torn between choosing to contest the invaders in central Virginia or to strike northwards once more. "The enemy's strength will . . . decrease the further he removes from his base," Lee observed in November, and I hope an opportunity will offer us to strike a successful blow." For the moment he awaited a Union advance, hoping to "baffle" it "until I can get him separated that I can strike at him to advantage."[3] In short, the Confederates would await the right opportunity to strike back, defeating the enemy in detail by concentrating against a vulnerable portion of the invader's force.

FREDERICKSBURG

No sooner had Ambrose E. Burnside taken over command of the Army of the Potomac than he began planning a new campaign. He proposed that his army sweep eastward to Fredericksburg, thereby circling past Lee's right, and crossing the Rappahannock there. If the Yankees moved quickly enough, Lee would find himself in trouble, with the Army of the Potomac nearer to Richmond than were the Confederates. Burnside would locate his supply line, not on the railline so vulnerable to Confederate raiders in central Virginia (the Orange and Alexandria Railroad), but along the lower Potomac River and a supply depot at Aquia Creek, where a rail line running southward to Richmond (the Richmond, Fredericksburg, and Potomac Railroad) would be much easier to protect.

Henry W. Halleck did not care for this plan. Anything that spoke of supplying the army by water smacked of McClellan. Better, he believed, for Burnside to follow the overland route, thus keeping his army between Lee and Washington. Besides, Burnside's idea resembled yet another drive on Richmond, when the best way to take Lee out was to take him on in central Virginia. Paying a visit to Burnside's head-quarters, Halleck tried to talk his subordinate out of his idea, but also failed to order him to follow orders. Instead, he simply forwarded the plan to Lincoln, once more abdicating his responsibility as general-in-chief to make decisions and direct military operations. In turn, the president gave his cautious, qualified approval. As Halleck told Burnside, "He thinks it will succeed, if you move very rapidly; otherwise not."[4]

Whatever chance Burnside had of moving rapidly—and his men covered the distance to Falmouth, opposite Fredericksburg, in two days—was thwarted when the pontoons necessary to cross the Rappahannock at Fredericksburg failed to materialize on time. Halleck had not really understood Burnside's plan. He assumed that Burnside would simply use the fords along the Rappahannock west of the town to cross the river, and that the pontoons would be used to forward supplies, not soldiers, across the river. In turn Burnside refused to force a crossing prior to the arrival of the pontoons, lest the crossing force find itself isolated by a rain-swollen river.

It was a lost opportunity, more so because Lee was not sure what Burnside intended to do. Given Burnside's experience with water-borne operations, he speculated that the Union commander might again try the James River approach. In anticipation, he prepared to shift his line of operations southeast to the North and South Anna rivers. Not until November 20 did he conclude that Burnside would gather his entire force opposite Fredericksburg. In light of what would happen, his observation that if Burnside attempted a crossing at Fredericksburg, he would "resist" it, "though the ground is favorable for him," suggests that he had yet to appreciate his army's position. The Army of Northern Virginia concentrated around Fredericksburg and awaited Burnside's next move.[5]

Lincoln traveled to Aquia Creek to meet Burnside and decide what to do next. The general wanted to cross the Rappahannock at Fredericksburg and take the city. The president offered his own idea, which was to continue to outflank Lee by landing additional forces at Port Royal, downstream on the Rappahannock, and along the north bank of the Pamunkey River to the south. Lee would have to retreat southward or risk being cut off from Richmond. This would take time to organize, but Lincoln was willing to allow for that. Only when Halleck objected to the president's idea did Burnside forge ahead with the idea of crossing the Rappahannock and driving Lee away. If nothing else, the discussion revealed the confusion and division in Washington, for neither Lincoln nor Halleck seemed willing to take charge. Each simply vetoed the other's plans. That Lincoln, for all of his insistence on an overland route, had offered a plan that resembled some of McClellan's own thinking was left for others to discuss.[6]

George G. Meade expressed his frustration with the progress of events. Bad weather had hampered army movements, and the roads were in no condition to support the amount of wagon traffic needed to supply the army. "In view of these obstacles," he remarked, "it is most trying to read the balderdash in the public journals about being in Richmond in ten days." He attributed the stalled course of the campaign to "taking the wrong line of operations, the James River being the true and only practicable line of approach to Richmond." One need not even attack the Confederate capital itself: "the proper mode to reduce it is to take possession of the great lines of railroad leading to it from the South and Southwest, cut these and stop any supplies going there, and their army will be compelled to evacuate it and meet us on the ground we can select ourselves." What seemed wise militarily was impracticable politically: "The blind infatuation of the authorities in Washington, sustained, I regret to say, by Halleck, who as a soldier ought to know better, will not permit the proper course to be adopted, and we shall have to take the consequences." The next day Meade went so far as to question whether the Confederates would make their stand at Fredericksburg, "as it is decidedly against their interest. Their policy is to draw us as far as possible from the Potomac and then to attack our rear, [and] cut off if possible our lines of communication and supply." To prevent that, Union commanders would have to detach forces to protect those supply and communication links, weakening the main army to the extent that the Confederates might attack to advantage.[7]

Meade's analysis of the options open to both sides suggested the degree to which he perceived the clash of military and political priorities. Ironically, in saying that it was better to fight near Washington rather than go all the way to Richmond, his views reflected those of Lincoln, even as he disagreed with the president on Lincoln's preference for an overland drive. However, while Meade grasped the Confederate style of counterattacking, his sense that Lee would do best to draw the Yankees into the Confederate interior did not accord with Lee's own desire to take the offensive, which would result in battles being fought closer to Washington than Richmond—exactly as Lincoln seemed to prefer. Meade's assessment demonstrated an awareness of the importance of logistics for both sides. His preferred approach remained to be tested, although McClellan had thoughts along the same line before Halleck directed him to abandon his position along the James. For the moment, however, it would be Burnside who would be calling the shots at Fredericksburg, and Lee did not have to move much at all.

On December 11, Burnside's engineers went to work on constructing five pontoon bridges to span the Rappahannock opposite Fredericksburg. Confederate infantry stationed in the city hampered their efforts. In response Union artillery posted east of the river began blasting away at the town. After the first two bridges were complete, Union infantry hurried across and cleared the Confederates from the town. That afternoon and into the next day the Union forces deployed across the river. Opposite them James Longstreet perfected his defenses on Lee's left, dominated by Marye's Heights just west of Fredericksburg, while Jackson had to make do with far more level terrain on the right.[8]

In years to come Burnside would insist that his subordinates, notably William B. Franklin, botched his attack order calling for an assault on the Confederates' extreme right. Union forces forced Jackson back, before Jackson checked them and threw them back, due in part to Franklin's unwillingness to commit more men to the assault (he cited Burnside's vaguely worded orders as justification for his decision). Meanwhile, in Fredericksburg, Union forces would advance to serve a diversionary purpose. Unfortunately, as they moved forward, they ran head-first into one of the strongest natural defensive positions of the entire war. High on the heights, Longstreet had deployed his artillery, ready to sweep the open plain west of the town. While much of his infantry lined up in front of his guns, of special importance was a sunken road, a natural fortification in which about 2,500 men waited, ready to deliver devastating volleys. As Lee watched, he remarked, "It is well that war is so terrible, or we should grow too fond of it." But Fredericksburg was terrible. Wave after wave of Federal attackers surged forward, emerging from the town, only to be cut down as survivors hugged the earth. Nightfall mercifully cut the slaughter short.[9]

Just over ten percent of Burnside's command became casualties at Fredericksburg. The loss in absolute terms was no larger than that suffered at Antietam or the Seven Days. However, the horror of the bloodbath at Marye's Heights could not be denied, and Lee's army, some 73,000 strong, suffered just over 5,000 casualties. The next day Burnside remained in place, having been dissuaded from personally leading an attack. Lee, awaiting another assault, did not counterattack. As evening came, the

Union forces recrossed the river. "They went as they came, in the night," Lee told his wife. "They suffered heavily as far as the battle went, but it did not go far enough to satisfy me."[10]

Lee did not think that Burnside would go into winter quarters after withdrawing across the Rappahannock. He anticipated that the Union commander would soon strike at Port Royal. If that happened before Lee could counter it, he planned to retire to the North and South Anna rivers and make a stand there. He believed it better to draw the enemy away from its supply head. He regretted that Burnside ceased attacking after December 13. He had prepared for a renewal of the contest, and, "had I divined that was to have been his only effort, he would have had more of it."[11]

FRUSTRATION

At first glance it would have seemed that Fredericksburg was an ideal Confederate victory. The Federals had suffered greatly, while Lee's army could quickly make good its losses. Outside of the reaction to the one-sided nature of the bloody affair, however, Lee realized that the victory itself did not shift the balance of power at all, and that the situation after the battle was much as it had been before Burnside had forced a crossing of the Rappahannock. In short, as horrible as it was, Fredericksburg resolved nothing.

It appeared in January that Burnside was preparing to advance again. No sooner had Lee detected enemy movement than he renewed his plea for more men. "It has occurred to me that the people are not fully aware of their danger, not of the importance of making every exertion to put fresh troops into the field at once." It was critical to "arouse the people to a sense of the vital importance of the subject." Ironically enough, seemingly easy victories such as Fredericksburg simply complicated matters. Lee feared that recent triumphs might "betray our people into the dangerous delusion that the armies now in the field are sufficient to bring this war to a successful and speedy termination." Nor did Lee mince words when he said that given the increasing size of the Union armies, future Confederate victories "can only be achieved by a terrible expenditure of the most precious blood of the country. This blood will be on the hands of the thousands of able bodied men who remain at home in safety and ease, while their fellow citizens are bravely confronting the enemy in the field, or enduring with noble fortitude the hardships and privations of the march and camp." Those at home had "yet to learn how often advantages, secured at the expense of many valuable lives, have failed to produce their legitimate results by reason of our inability to prosecute them against the reinforcements which the superior numbers of the enemy enabled him to interpose between the defeat of an army and its ruin."[12]

In those words Lee perhaps unwittingly revealed the challenges he faced in trying to bring the Yankees to decisive battle. Outnumbered, sometimes by a significant margin, he had to be audacious and resourceful in securing the upper hand, but even when he was able to deliver a telling blow, he was unable to exploit it, in part because of the blood spilled in delivering the blow itself. Thus it did not matter whether he could parry and counterthrust, because he would never be strong enough to take more than temporary advantage of the opportunities created by his skill. "The lives of our soldiers are too precious to be sacrificed in the attainment of successes that inflict no loss upon the enemy beyond the actual loss in battle," he explained to Secretary of War James A. Seddon. "Every victory should bring us nearer to the great end which it is the object of this war to reach."[13]

Lincoln did not quite know what to make of the defeat at Fredericksburg. Aware of the political fallout that was sure to follow—especially on the eve of the issuance of the Emancipation Proclamation—he remarked, "If there is a worse place than hell, I am in it." However, he did his best to bolster the morale of the men by issuing a proclamation, praising their courage and declaring, "Although you were not successful, the attempt was not an error." More chilling was his cold-blooded calculus that if there were a Fredericksburg fought every week, the result would eventually annihilate the Army of Northern Virginia at a far lower human cost than would result from a prolonged conflict characterized by deaths from disease as well as combat. It might be what one of the president's secretaries called "awful arithmetic," and, as he observed, "No general yet found can face the arithmetic, but the end of the war will be at hand when he shall be discovered."[14]

It was a troubled Ambrose Burnside who directed that the Army of the Potomac resume offensive operations some four weeks after Fredericksburg. After his December defeat he began to hear that several of his subordinates were openly critical of how he had handled the army. He fretted over signs of "a want of confidence or cordial cooperation" among his generals. A staffer observed that "jealousies and political intrigues are greater enemies than an open foe." Wing commander William B. Franklin and one of his corps commanders, William F. "Baldy" Smith, contacted Lincoln directly by letter to propose renewing the James River approach; near year's end, two more generals decided to protest personally to the president.[15] In short, the back door to the White House remained open to grousing generals, by order of the president, who did not appear to realize how the resulting disruption would impair Burnside's ability to command. Burnside visited Washington on New Year's Eve, prepared to talk about his plans to renew the offensive, only to be greeted with news of his subordinates' treachery. Enraged, Burnside suggested that if he did not have the confidence of his officers and the public, perhaps it was time for someone else to take over.[16]

Lincoln turned to Halleck for advice. He was becoming frustrated with the general-in-chief's unwillingness to take charge, overlooking that perhaps one reason why Halleck failed to assert himself was that Lincoln reserved the right to intervene, and was not reluctant to act upon that right. Yet the president grew exasperated when a meeting he had with Stanton and Halleck led to no decision. On the very day he signed the Emancipation Proclamation, he composed a rather stern letter to Halleck. With Burnside's generals opposing their commander's plan, what was to be done? "If in such a difficulty as this you do not help, you fail me at precisely in the point for which I sought your assistance." Halleck should go down to the Army of the Potomac, review the situation, talk to the generals, and make a decision: "Your military skill is useless to me, if you will not do this."[17]

Stanton handed Halleck the president's letter at a reception (hardly the place, one would think, to transact official business). The general-in-chief bristled, then wrote out his own resignation. That was not what Lincoln desired, and, to patch things up, he withdrew his letter, whereupon Halleck withdrew his resignation. That, however, left things up in the air with Burnside. For the moment, Lincoln refused to take Burnside up on his offer of resignation, but he failed to support his general's plan to swing west, cross the Rappahannock, and hit Lee. Rather, he endorsed the views of Halleck, who once more pointed out his belief that "our first object was, not Richmond, but the defeat or scattering of Lee's army," Although Halleck favored an advance, he left it to Burnside "to decide upon the time, place, and character of the crossing which you may attempt." In other words, there would be no orders from Washington. Lincoln added his own advice. "Be cautious," the president wrote, "and do not understand that the government, or country, is driving you"—a comment which stood in marked contrast to Lincoln's badgering of McClellan.[18]

In the end, however, it was not Lincoln, or Halleck, or Lee who stopped Burnside in his tracks. It was the weather. No sooner had the movement gotten underway than heavy rains turned the roads into mud, with wagon wheels slowly churning in the muck. Generals cackled and grumbled. Burnside, having taken enough, demanded that either Lincoln remove nine men from command (four of whom would be dismissed from the service) or replace him. The president chose the latter course, although some of the dissenters found themselves transferred elsewhere. There was no use in trying anything else.

To replace Burnside, Lincoln named one of the men who had been most actively intriguing against him, Joseph Hooker. At first glance it seemed a good choice, although one that came with challenges. Hooker had gained a reputation as an able division commander, so much so that his nickname, derived from a newspaper misprint, was "Fighting Joe." However, the truth was that it might have been better had Hooker been known as "Bragging Joe" or "Backstabbing Joe," for those names were equally warranted. Hooker had risen to corps command during the Maryland campaign, and his men had spearheaded the initial Union assault at Antietam. While feeding reinforcements into the fight and attempting to get a better view of the action, Hooker had received a painful wound in the foot, which forced him to retire from the field. Recuperating in Washington, Hooker lost little time in explaining to anyone who would listen that had he and not McClellan been in command that September day, Lee would have been smashed to pieces, and under no conditions would the Army of Northern Virginia been allowed to recross the Potomac River. Unfortunately, "anyone" included Abraham Lincoln. Already pained by McClellan's lack of aggressiveness, Lincoln found in Hooker a general who talked as Lincoln believed generals should fight. The president passed over Hooker when it came to removing McClellan, although Burnside understood that if he did not accept the command in November, it would pass to Hooker. After Fredericksburg Hooker again made clear his feelings about his superior officer's incompetence, waging another aggressive campaign in lobbies, hearing rooms, and offices.

Lincoln knew full well about Hooker's willingness to talk. He had even heard that Hooker declared that the country might be better off under a dictator, and that Hooker had someone in mind for that job, too. Nevertheless, Hooker seemed to be the sort of fighter Lincoln claimed he needed, and so the president set his reservations aside and named Hooker to command the Army of the Potomac. The appointment came with some housekeeping, for Baldy Smith and William Franklin found themselves banished from Virginia in the wake of their attempt to circumvent Burnside by contacting the president directly. Burnside was reassigned to Ohio, where he added to his laurels when he ordered the arrest of Democratic gubernatorial candidate Clement Vallandigham on charges that the Copperhead was preaching treason, an act that caused Lincoln a few more headaches. Hooker also extracted a promise from Lincoln that he would have direct access to the president, bypassing general-in-chief Henry W. Halleck. Hooker and Halleck were old foes from the prewar days in California, and matters had not improved in the interim. The arrangement did not augur well for unity of command in Virginia. Having complained that Halleck was not doing his job, Lincoln now ensured that he would not be able to do it. Having seen (and even facilitated) the backstabbing and intrigue among the generals of the Army of the Potomac, Lincoln punished a few generals while rewarding one with the command of that army. However, he did leave Hooker with one observation: "I much fear that the spirit which you have aided to infuse into the Army, of criticizing their Commander, and withholding confidence from him, will now turn upon you."[19]

News that there was a new commander of the Army of the Potomac did not deter Robert E. Lee from contemplating his next move. The Confederate chieftain was torn between preference and necessity. In January he had thought about splitting his army in two, sending one portion down to North Carolina while the remainder worked its way through the Shenandoah Valley.[20] However, his army needed to replenish its supplies, and Union activity elsewhere was cause for concern. He found himself compelled to earmark two divisions under the command of James Longstreet to respond to evidence of renewed Union activity along the North Carolina coast and southeast Virginia. A secondary objective would be to forage through the area, serving to relieve Lee of some of the supply pressures that plagued him. As February began Lee also discussed with Davis and Seddon the possibility of a Federal attack upon Charleston, South Carolina, or Savannah, Georgia.[21]

Throughout February Lee tried to discern what Hooker might do. Even more frustrating was the news that the United States Congress had decided to strengthen Lincoln's ability to wage war. "Nothing can now arrest during the present administration the most desolating war that was ever practiced, except a revolution among their people," he told his son. "Nothing can produce a revolution except systematic success on our part."[22] Offensive operations, however, would have to await Longstreet's return. During March Lee and Longstreet discussed exactly how long Longstreet should remain in southeast Virginia and northeast North Carolina. Worried about the depleted state of his army, Lee opined that any additional detachments would force him to withdraw to the North Anna River. He preferred "to keep the enemy at a distance & trust to striking him on his line of advance."[23] When Lee learned that the Union high command had decided to send the IX Corps, stationed at Fort Monroe during the winter, westward to Kentucky (and not south toward North Carolina), he wanted Longstreet to be returned to him. Attempting to head off any suggestion that it might be a good idea to transfer Longstreet west, Lee suggested that perhaps he would seek to disrupt any offensive by Hooker by swinging northward through the Shenandoah and pushing back the Union forces that had reoccupied the area around Winchester. Should Hooker stay on the defensive, "the readiest way of relieving pressure" on other armies "would be for this army to cross into Maryland."[24]

For weeks Davis sought Lee's approval to a westward transfer. Lee stood firm in rejecting the idea. It would be better to reinforce the western armies from forces deployed elsewhere in the Confederacy, including the South Atlantic coast. It would be even better, he suggested, if Joseph Johnston would simply concentrate the forces at his command in the West and strike back at the Federals. He welcomed a Union setback at Charleston and reports of Ulysses S. Grant's abandoning operations against Vicksburg, Mississippi, as evidence that threats elsewhere were receding, while reminding Davis that Hooker's strength would erode due to the expiring enlistments of those volunteers who had signed up for two years of service back in the spring of 1861. "If we could be placed in a condition to make a vigorous advance at that time I think the Valley could be swept . . . and the army opposite me may be thrown north of the Potomac. I believe greater relief would be in this way be afforded to the armies in middle Tennessee and on the Carolina coast than by any other method." Before long he declared that he planned to advance at the beginning of May. At the same time he ordered the preparation of a map of the area northward from the Shenandoah Valley to southeastern Pennsylvania, including Harrisburg and Philadelphia as well as a small town named Gettysburg.[25]

CHANCELLORSVILLE

As Lee planned to undertake offensive operations, so did Joseph Hooker. First, however, he had to restore the morale of the Army of the Potomac. The adoption of a system of corps badges bolstered spirits (even as it made it easier to identify units and deserters), and so did a system of furloughs, policed camps, and reviews. Nor did it hurt that spring was coming, a welcome respite from a cold, damp winter. In April Hooker invited President Lincoln to review the result. "The army never looked better and but for the small regiments in some corps would certainly impress one with its invincibility," noted one division commander. "If properly handled I feel that it must carry everything before it."[26]

Hooker did not intend to test Lee's defenses at Fredericksburg again with the bulk of his forces, especially as Lee had refined his fortifications. Nor would he heed Lincoln's advice, which was grounded upon what by now had become a mantra with the chief executive: "our prime object is the enemies' army in front of us, and is not with, or about, Richmond." For the moment, the president advised, it was best not to attack the Confederates in their fortified positions, "but we should continually harrass and menace him, so that he shall have no leisure, nor safety in sending away detachments. If he weakens himself," Lincoln concluded, "then pitch into him."[27] That seemed to suggest that the president was willing to abandon the idea of seeking victory in the East for the notion of pinning Lee in place. It overlooked the contraction in Union manpower that would happen when the two-year troops that had enlisted in the spring of 1861 left the ranks. Nor would it benefit a man who fantasized about dictatorships to rest content with simply holding the line.

Rather, Hooker decided that he would leave two corps to keep an eye on the Confederates while he swung to the west, had three (and potentially five) corps cross the Rapidan and Rappahannock line at several places, and have those columns converge on Chancellorsville, located ten miles west of the rear of Lee's Fredericksburg line. George Stoneman would lead the way with a deep cavalry raid that would circle round before threatening the Confederate communications. With some 134,000 men under his command, Hooker outnumbered Lee by more than two to one. At the least Lee would be forced to abandon his defensive lines and retreat southward; with any luck, if Lee stayed and fought, Hooker might well crush him.[28]

Lee decided not only to stay and fight, but also to meet Hooker's challenge aggressively. Leaving 10,000 men at Fredericksburg, he marched westward to confront Hooker's swing across the Rapidan and Rappahannock. It did not hurt that Hooker decided to halt his advance at Chancellorsville, a house located at a five-road junction. Learning that Hooker's right flank was not anchored anywhere, Lee decided once more to attack. Splitting his command yet again, he dispatched Stonewall Jackson with some 26,000 men through the heavily-wooded area west of Chancellorsville (known as "the Wilderness") with orders to hit the Union right. Throughout the day of May 2, Jackson's column threaded its way through the woods along roads and paths. The route of the march lengthened further when Jackson found a jump-off point for the assault that would place him squarely on the Union right while remaining undetected. At one point, Union corps commander Daniel Sickles, spotting the Confederates as they began their march, probed southward, but pulled back after a short firefight.

Late that afternoon, Jackson's men slammed into the XI Corps, which was holding the Union right, and drove it back over a mile. Jackson urged his men to keep on pressing, only to be hit by a volley from a North Carolina regiment that mistook the general and his staff for Union horsemen. Sad as that news was, Lee continued to press forward. Early on May 3, Jackson's replacement, Jeb Stuart, seized control of a hill from where he could position artillery to shell the Union line at Chancellorsville. One of the shells struck Hooker's headquarters at the Chancellor house, dazing Hooker himself. His temporary replacement, Darius Couch, began to pull back and contract his line still more. That was good news for Lee, who learned that at Fredericksburg John Sedgwick had managed to break through the thinly-manned Rebel line and was marching westward toward the rear of the main Confederate force. Lee quickly moved to check Sedgwick, and did so at Salem Church, midway between Fredericksburg and Chancellorsville. Sedgwick chose to withdraw north of the Rappahannock on the night of May 4, allowing Lee to turn his attention back to Hooker's main force. Believing that he had cornered his foe against the river, Lee planned to launch an all-out assault on May 6. However, the Army of the Potomac managed to scramble across the river on the evening of May 5. When he learned of this turn of events, Lee exploded. "You allow those people to get away. I tell you what to do, but you don't do it!" he complained to an officer. "Go after them, and damage them all you can!"[29] In fact, given that Hooker's men had fortified the position, it might well have been Malvern Hill all over again, with Lee's men suffering the damage. Lee's luck had held. After entertaining hope for Hooker's success based upon early reports, Abraham Lincoln learned of the final outcome. "My God! My God! What will the country say! What will the country say!"[30]

In years to come many observers would term Chancellorsville Lee's greatest military masterpiece. It offered sufficient evidence of his audacity. To divide one's army not one but twice to attack a foe over twice his strength. . . . that was nothing if not daring, regardless of what one thought of the skill of the enemy generals. Yet victory did not come cheap. Jackson died on May 10, the most famous of approximately 13,000 Confederate casualties. In short, the battle was as costly as Antietam, and if Lee had inflicted about 17,000 Union casualties, the fact remained that he had enjoyed a far better ratio of losses at Fredericksburg with a similar result. Chancellorsville offered more evidence of the indecisiveness of battle. Jackson's flank attack was nearly a complete surprise, and yet it stalled as night came, just as Longstreet's August 30 assault at Second Manassas ran out of momentum. Lee told one officer that he was "depressed" after Chancellorsville, even more dissatisfied than he had been after Fredericksburg, at his inability to convert victory on the battlefield into something more than the wearing away of both armies. If such blows as these fell short, what was needed to claim decisive victory? Could one always count on the friction among the Union generals and the inability of their commanders?[31]

Lincoln hurried down to Hooker's headquarters to find out exactly what had happened at Chancellorsville. As he visited the Army of the Potomac and spoke with the corps commanders, the president expressed the opinion that while "the disaster was one that could not be helped. . . . its effect, both at home and abroad, would be more serious and injurious than any previous act of the war." He urged Hooker to contemplate taking the offensive again, because it would "help to supersede the bad moral effect of the recent one, which is sure to be considerably injurious;" however, he did not "wish anything done in desperation or rashness."[32]

Given this sort of advice—do something, because we need to spark support, but minimize risk as much as possible—it was almost inevitable that Hooker would do nothing. As before, Hooker promised action. This time, no action followed, which to Lincoln's mind smacked too much of McClellan. Summoning the general to Washington, Lincoln listened as Hooker explained that an offensive would have to await the reorganization of the army in the aftermath of those expiring two-year enlistments. . . . something Hooker had known all along. To the president it was the same old story again. He dropped his previous plea for action. For now, Hooker could attend to housekeeping matters. "Still, if in your own clear judgment, you can renew your attack successfully, I do not mean to restrain you."[33]

At the same time, Lincoln felt compelled to confide to Hooker some rather disturbing news. "I have some painful intimations that some of your corps and Division Commanders are not giving you their entire confidence," he wrote, adding that this "would be ruinous, if true." In short, Hooker was now the victim of the very behavior he had once practiced on McClellan and which had doomed Burnside—just as Lincoln had feared when he had placed Hooker in command. The president did not reflect that his own behavior in interviewing subordinates and in hearing out their complaints about superiors had also promoted divisiveness among the office corps. Nor was this pattern limited to the Army of the Potomac. Lincoln's willingness to consider the constant carping of John A. McClernand had contributed to strained command relations in Ulysses S. Grant's Army of the Tennessee.[34]

In short, little had changed north of the Rappahannock. Although Hooker's losses at Chancellorsville far exceeded those of Burnside at Fredericksburg, no one spoke darkly of what had happened. Nor was his performance on that field superior to that of his predecessors at Fredericksburg and Antietam. For the moment, however, his position was safe. There were rumors that Lincoln was casting about for a replacement, with corps commander John F. Reynolds's name being bandied about, but Reynolds, aware of the political pressures that came with the top spot, wanted no part of it. The president decided to put the best face on things, remarking that "he was not disposed to throw away a gun because it missed fire once; that he would pick the lock and try it again."[35]

Lee reorganized his army in the wake of Jackson's death. No one was quite ready to take Jackson's place, so Lee decided to transform his two infantry corps into three corps, offering commands to two able division commanders, Richard S. Ewell and Ambrose P. Hill. Ewell was just returning to field service after recovering from a serious wound suffered at Second Manassas, which had cost him a leg. Hill had long enjoyed a reputation as a blunt fighter, with his fiery red shirt heralding his arrival. These two generals would join James Longstreet, who had returned to the Army of Northern Virginia.

Although Hooker also had to wrestle with matters of reorganization, most of that had to do with a significant reduction in strength following the expiration of the enlistments of those men who signed up for two years. The impact was perhaps most visible in the disappearance of the fabled 5th New York, which ceased to exist, although soldiers still owing time were transferred to the 146th New York. When it came to corps commanders, however, Hooker was in fairly good shape. Winfield Scott Hancock, who had earned the sobriquet "the Superb" as a division commander, took over the II Corps, and Alfred Pleasanton replaced Stoneman at the head of the cavalry corps. Other than that, however, the command structure was much as it was before Chancellorsville, meaning that generals had already enjoyed some experience with their responsibilities.

Even as the armies reorganized and refitted, however, the war in the East had taken an interesting turn, at least from the point of view of Union military planners. Lincoln and Halleck now preached the gospel that the main target of Union military operations in the East should be the destruction of the Army of Northern Virginia. They also preferred that this destruction would come about while the Army of the Potomac shielded Washington and committed itself to an overland campaign, with Halleck's approach of choice remaining an advance supported by the Orange and Alexandria Railroad. Advice from Washington discouraged thinking about Richmond as an objective, and said little about logistics, whether in regard to destroying the support for Lee's army or in the difficulties that accompanied protecting a line of supply in support of an overland operation (which was why both Burnside and Hooker looked to the Potomac and Chesapeake as parts of their logistical lifeline). That Richmond's value was as much logistical as political (both as a source of supply and a nexus for railroads), and that one could bring Lee's army out into the open if one threatened Richmond, seemed lost on Lincoln and Halleck. Moreover, if the target of Union military operations in the Eastern Theater was the destruction of Lee's army, by now it should have become evident that one decisive blow would not be enough to accomplish that task. Only in a series of battles would the "awful arithmetic" of attrition take full effect. It might be too much to ask that an public anxious hear about one big final battle. One Fredericksburg was enough. Yet the terrible logic of attrition seemed to favor Union fortunes in the long run, and that was the case even in a defeat such as Chancellorsville.

At the same time, Halleck also appeared to favor a view of the overall military situation that emphasized Union opportunities to make the West the theater of decision. He reminded Ulysses S. Grant, who was struggling in the effort to take Vicksburg, that "the opening of the Mississippi River will be to us of more advantage than the capture of forty Richmonds." Had Halleck followed his argument to its logical conclusion, he might have argued for a shifting of resources and energy westward, leaving Union forces in the East to assume a defensive posture. What rendered such a daring recasting of priorities improbable was the fact that the public kept looking to the East as the place where the war would be won or lost.[36]

Such ideas had implications for Confederate planning. While Confederate forces might shift westward to block Union advances, it was unlikely that the Confederacy could achieve much more than that, absent a major blunder on the part of Union commanders. If the Confederacy was to win the war, it would be in the East. Moreover, it could not win simply by fending off Union blows, for over time the impact of grinding attrition would become apparent. If Lee benefited from the preference of the Union high command to pursue an overland approach (and to reject any notion of reviving in concept McClellan's Peninsula campaign), he knew he could not afford to respond passively. Instead, he sought to "baffle" Union designs and launch counterpunches of his own to tip the balance in his favor. Even victories such as Fredericksburg and Chancellorsville fell short of that objective. Lee believed that if the Confederacy were to win the war, it would have to do so in the East and that his army under his leadership could achieve that goal over the Army of the Potomac. He also believed that he could use the resources at his command and Lincoln's concern about defending Washington to advantage.

Twice the Army of the Potomac had attempted to cross the Rappahannock; twice Lee had defeated it. Yet that was all. Although reduced in strength by expiring enlistments as well as battle losses, the Army of the Potomac remained a formidable foe, and Lee's victories, one of which had been costly in its own way, had done nothing to shift the balance of power in Virginia. At a time when Union forces were on the move elsewhere, especially in Mississippi, Lee would have to do more than simply maintain his position, lest the rest of the Confederacy crumble around the Old Dominion.

Abraham Lincoln (Library of Congress)

George B. McClellan (Library of Congress)

Henry W. Halleck (Library of Congress)

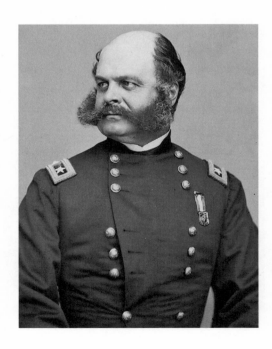

Ambrose E. Burnside (Library of Congress)

Joseph Hooker (Library of Congress)

George G. Meade (Library of
Congress)

Ulysses S. Grant (Library of Congress)

Philip H. Sheridan (Library of Congress)

Jefferson Davis (Library of Congress)

Robert E. Lee (Library of Congress)

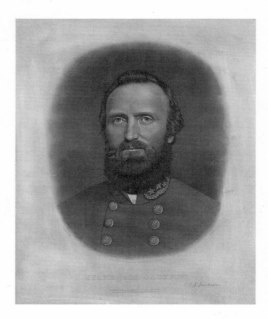

Thomas J. "Stonewall" Jackson
(Library of Congress)

Joseph E. Johnston (Library of Congress)

James Longstreet (Library of Congress)

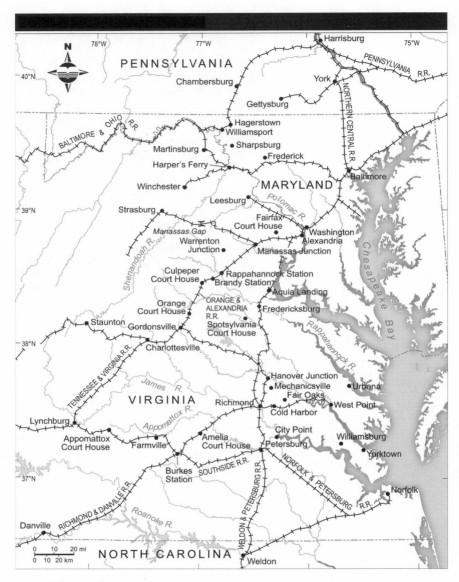

Eastern Theater of Operations

FIVE

GETTYSBURG: THE STALEMATE CONTINUES

Mid-May 1863 found both the Army of the Potomac and the Army of Northern Virginia occupying basically the same positions they had the previous month. The Confederate high command at Richmond contemplated its options. At the same time that Lee was checking Hooker at Chancellorsville, Ulysses S. Grant was preparing to move against Vicksburg, having crossed the Mississippi at the same time Hooker had crossed the Rapidan and Rappahannock. Union troops were but a short distance from Jefferson Davis's own plantation. Was it time to respond by transferring units from the Army of Northern Virginia west, either to confront Grant directly or to create a diversion by advancing against William S. Rosecrans's Army of the Cumberland in central Tennessee? No, Lee argued. If anything he should be reinforced as a prelude to launching a Confederate offensive across the Potomac. The onset of summer, he believed, bringing with it diseases foreign to Yankee immune systems, would be far more effective in diminishing Grant's command than pitched battle; besides, it would be time-consuming and awkward to effect such a transfer. In addition, unless Lee was reinforced, he was certain he would have to withdraw to the Richmond defenses, thus wasting what he had just achieved at Chancellorsville.[1]

Lee pressed his argument during a visit to Richmond in mid-May. He prevailed once more with his plan to take the initiative in Virginia, but must have been chagrined to learn that the president could spare but three brigades of George Pickett's division. That was not enough. Lee believed that "the plan of the enemy is to concentrate as large a force as possible to operate in Virginia"—an interesting statement in light of his earlier argument that Hooker's strength would decline due to expiring enlistments. Not that Lee was altogether hesitant—as he wrote John Bell Hood upon his return to army head-quarters, "I agree with you in believing that our army would be invincible if it could be properly organized and officered. There never were such men in an army before. They will go anywhere and do anything if properly led. But there is the difficulty—proper commanders. Where can they be obtained?"[2]

Given that Lee had been the beneficiary of the abilities of several trusted lieutenants, his query strikes one as being somewhat ungracious. However, in the aftermath of Chancellorsville, he would have to see whether Hill, Ewell, and others would rise to their new responsibilities. At the same time, the note exuded confidence about the fighting prowess of his men. He believed that he would have "demolished" Hooker if Longstreet had been present. For the next several weeks he pressed for reinforcements as he laid out additional justifications for his campaign, almost as if he was not sure whether he had already been persuasive enough to Davis. As the month came to a close he worried that Hooker would beat him to the punch, and that "the contest of the summer would take place in Virginia. "I fear the time has passed," he lamented, "when I could have taken the offensive with advantage."[3]

This sentiment soon passed. By early June, Lee pressed once more to take the offensive. "I think if I can create an apprehension for the safety of their right flank & the Potomac, more troops will be brought from their line of operations in the South," he told Davis. "But to gain any material advantage, I should if possible have a large force, as their army by all accounts is represented as very large." The tug of war con-tinued, with Secretary of War Seddon forwarding warnings about a possible Union attack in North Carolina. Lee responded by asserting that without reinforcements, he would have to remain on the defensive. Unless the Army of the Potomac "can be drawn out in a position to be assailed," it was only a matter of time before it would "renew its advance upon Richmond, and force this army back within the intrenchments of that city."[4]

INVADING PENNSYLVANIA

On June 9, 1863, a review of the Army of Northern Virginia's cavalry near Brandy Station was disrupted by news that Union horsemen had crossed the Rappahannock. What followed was the largest cavalry battle of the war. Jeb Stuart eventually drove the intruders away, but not without some difficulty, and the eventual Union withdrawal did not conceal the fact that for once the Yankee cavalry had held their own and embarrassed Stuart in the process. Now, more than ever, Lee wanted to justify his decision to take the offensive. On the day after the battle, as lead elements of Richard Ewell's Second Corps made their way toward the Shenandoah Valley, Lee suggested to Davis that given the dwindling resources of the Confederate it would be good to encourage calls for peace from the North as a way to weaken enemy resolve, regardless of whether those who called for peace would accept disunion or simply favored a peaceful negotiated reunion.[5]

The same day Lee's drive northward began in earnest. What he was seeking to achieve remains a matter of discussion. Once more there was talk of taking the war to the enemy in order to remove the scourge of war from Virginia, allowing the farmers to plant and harvest. Invading Confederates could strip the Yankee countryside of much-needed food, provisions, and livestock, and the presence of a Rebel army north of the Potomac might increase the calls for peace at any price. Move northward enough and several cities might be alarmed. Perhaps one could strike at rail lines and coal fields in Pennsylvania. But whether Lee envisioned his movement as simply one grand raid or whether he wanted something more remains a matter of debate. He confided to Confederate general Isaac Trimble that he hoped to pick off the Army of the Potomac piecemeal. His confidence in his men's fighting ability suggests that he had no reservations about committing them to battle or doubts about the outcome. If the war was going to be won on the battlefield, he believed that the Army of Northern Virginia would lead the way.[6]

Whether the Army of the Potomac would cooperate was another question. Receiving reports that Confederate units were withdrawing from their positions west of Fredericksburg as June began, Joseph Hooker decided to cross the Rappahannock at the city to see what Lee was up to. Informing Lincoln of that decision, he learned that the president was not enthusiastic about the idea. Perhaps Lincoln was haunted by the ghosts of Marye's Heights; perhaps he was concerned that Hooker was being blinded by an "on to Richmond" obsession. In truth, Hooker wanted to threaten Richmond to fix Lee in place and counter any Confederate ideas of a shift westward preparatory to another invasion of the North. The president disagreed: "I would not take any chance of being entangled upon the river, like an ox jumped half over a fence, and liable to be torn by dogs, front and rear, without a fair chance to gore one way or kick the other." Lincoln also revealed that he had rethought the wisdom of allowing Hooker to bypass Halleck in the command structure. He notified Hooker that he had passed along the general's plan to Halleck for his professional opinion. It should have come as no surprise to Hooker when Halleck concurred with Lincoln's assessment.[7]

The clash at Brandy Station was a sign that Lee was on the move. Reporting news of the battle, Hooker, bypassing Halleck once more, reiterated his preference to move against Richmond in order to pull Lee back and give the rebellion "a mortal blow." Again Lincoln objected. "I think *Lee's* Army, and not *Richmond*, is your true objective point," he reiterated. If Lee pushed northward through the Shenandoah, "follow on his flank, and on the inside track, shortening your lines, while he lengthens his. Fight him when opportunity offers. If he stays where he is, fret him, and fret him." Halleck agreed. Another presidential visit to the front seemed in the offing, but news that Ewell was approaching Winchester gave Lincoln another idea. "If the head of Lee's army is at Martinsburg and the tail of it on the Plank Road between Fredericksburg and Chancellorsville, the animal must be very slim somewhere. Could you not break him?" Such a question appeared almost rhetorical, yet the president privately groused that his generals "appeared to know but little how things are, and showed no evidence that they ever availed themselves of any advantage."[8]

Lee was not going to wait to see what Hooker would do. Already Ewell's corps was marching northward through the Shenandoah Valley, and on June 13 it made contact with Union forces outside of Winchester. During the next two days Ewell drove the Yankee defenders away, although he failed to gobble them up altogether. On June 15 Confederate forces splashed across the Potomac once more. This time Lee did not dally in Maryland or bother himself with capturing Harpers Ferry; he headed north to Pennsylvania. It seemed his objective was the state capital at Harrisburg. Hooker and Halleck debated what to do, with Hooker looking to bring Lee to battle and Halleck preferring that the Army of the Potomac simply follow Lee and protect Harpers Ferry. Making matters worse, Lincoln decided to reinstate the chain of command completely and have Hooker report to Halleck.[9]

On June 22 Lee sent Stuart off on a raid with the mission of gathering supplies and shielding Ewell's right flank as it entered Pennsylvania. The next day he added to this initial directive by telling him he could sweep all the way around the Army of the Potomac and rejoin Ewell. Such a move would brush by Washington, and that city was never far from Lee's mind. Perhaps, suggested Lee, Davis could unite the unopposed Confederate forces in North Carolina and southern Virginia under Beauregard and move the newly-fashioned field army to Culpeper, from where it could menace Washington, thus diverting forces from the Army of the Potomac just as Lee was in Pennsylvania. "The well known anxiety of the Northern Government for the safety of its capital would induce it to retain a large force for its defence," Lee reasoned, recalling what had happened in the spring of 1862, "and thus sensibly relieve the opposition to our advance." Meanwhile Hill and Longstreet made ready to cross the Potomac to join Ewell.[10]

Back in Washington, Lincoln fretted that the Army of the Potomac might let slip what he regarded as a golden opportunity. Believing that Lee was at his most vulnerable in the North, the president looked for Hooker to strike a decisive blow. And yet that was just the issue on which all else depended; could Hooker deliver? "We cannot help beating them, if we have the man," he told Welles on June 26. "How much depends in military matters upon one mastermind! Hooker may commit the same fault as McClellan and lose his chance. We shall soon see, but it appears to me he can't help but win."[11]

Within a day Lincoln had cause to reconsider. Halleck refused to accede to Hooker's request to issue orders to the Harpers Ferry garrison to attack Lee's supply line. This stalemate approached the ridiculous, for Hooker wanted to do what Lincoln had thought he ought to do (strike at Lee's lengthening logistical tail), and here was Halleck, ostensibly in accord with Lincoln's view, depriving Hooker of an opportunity to realize those wishes. In response, Hooker asked to be relieved as commander of the Army of the Potomac. If he had designed the move to force Lincoln's hand in his favor, his tactic backfired. A general who was willing to forfeit his command on the eve of battle was not a general to be trusted in battle. It looked as if Hooker was looking to evade responsibility. Lincoln did not hesitate. Hooker was out; in his place Lincoln settled upon George G. Meade, a solid general.

Lincoln made his disappointment with Hooker evident the next day at a cabinet meeting. Recently he had "observed in Hooker the same failings that were witnessed in McClellan after the battle of Antietam—a want of alacrity to obey and a greedy call for more troops which could not and ought not to be taken from other points." Once more Little Mac served as a point of reference. Lincoln abhorred inaction, insubordination, and an incessant call for reinforcements. Indeed, he rejected suggestions to call on McClellan to take charge of units being formed in Pennsylvania, and reminded New Jersey governor Joel Parker of his belief that Lee's invasion "presents us the best opportunity we have had since the war began."[12]

GETTYSBURG

No sooner had Meade taken over the Army of the Potomac than he began to make plans for a defensive line in northern Maryland along Pipe Creek, just south of the Maryland and Pennsylvania state line. He would first shield Washington and Baltimore, then advance his forces to make contact with Lee, and hope that he could draw the Confederates away from the Susquehanna. Coincidentally, Lee, upon learning that the Army of the Potomac had crossed its namesake river and was under a new commander, directed Ewell to abandon the effort to take Harrisburg and instead move southwest toward the road junctions at Cashtown and Gettysburg in the southern part of the state. Given that his men were foraging along their line of march, an order to concentrate meant he was looking toward giving battle, although Lee remained unsure where and when he would fight, due in part to his uncertainty about the location of Union forces. Stuart was out of touch with his commander, finding his way back to Lee blocked by the movements of the Army of the Potomac. Cavalry clashes with the stubborn Federals further complicated his task. Although Lee had some cavalry available, he did not use it to advantage in discerning Meade's location, and so it would be left to the infantry to find out where the enemy might be. In turn Meade had his cavalry out in front, with two brigades of John Buford's division entering Gettysburg, a crossroads town that was the seat of Adams County, on June 29 before fanning out north and west of town. Behind them was John Reynolds with the I Corps, just over a day's march away.

On the morning of July 1 lead elements of a Confederate division under Henry Heth made contact with one of Buford's brigades of Union cavalry west of Gettysburg. At about the same time Ewell's lead elements made contact with Union cavalry north of town. Dismounted Union troopers forced the Confederate infantry to deploy in line of battle. Then, as the Confederates advanced, Buford's cavalrymen gave way to Reynolds's arriving infantry. Within hours Heth was in hot combat against the Union I Corps. As noon approached, so did several more Confederate divisions belonging to Ewell's Second Corps, this time from the north of town. As they converged on Gettysburg, they encountered a second Union infantry corps, the ill-fated XI Corps, which had given way just two months before under the weight of Jackson's attack at Chancellorsville. One of Ewell's divisions, under Robert Rodes, was roughly handled by a brigade from I Corps, but that proved a momentary setback. To the west William Pender's division of A. P. Hill's Third Corps joined Heth in battling the I Corps. The Confederates were able to bring more men to bear on the Union defenders, who were awkwardly deployed, and by mid-afternoon the Union line began to give way. Retreating Yankees made their way through town streets and alleys, taking up position just south of the town on a hill where the local citizenry buried its dead. Lee himself arrived in time to decide what to do next. He sent orders to Ewell to assault that hill—Cemetery Hill—"if practicable," and cautioned him against bringing on a general engagement. When Ewell replied that he would welcome the use of Richard Anderson's newly-arrived division to drive the Yankees away, Lee denied the request, saying that he needed to retain Anderson in reserve in case of a disaster.[13]

Ewell thus found himself in a tough spot. His two divisions on the field had fought and marched in the hot July sun; his reserve division had not yet arrived. To form his men for an attack required him to swing around the town, lest the attackers present easy targets for the Union cannoneers, who were swinging their guns into place on Cemetery Hill. How was he to mount such an attack without bringing on a general engagement? Was not Lee betraying his own hesitation in refusing Ewell the use of another division? And what was he to make of reports that Union forces were approaching from the east to threaten his left flank? As Ewell contemplated what to do, he saw another wooded hill just east of Cemetery Hill, and decided that perhaps that hill, known as Culp's Hill, presented a more promising target. By the time Ewell's trailing division arrived, however, he learned that Union forces had also made their way to Culp's Hill. In the face of evidence of an enemy force positioned on good ground being reinforced, Ewell decided that it was not "practicable" to launch a final assault.[14]

In years to come much would be made of Ewell's decision not to attack. Lee himself suggested that Ewell needed direct and explicit orders to attack, which raised the question of why Lee did not issue such orders. Other critics would pine for the return of the departed Jackson, as if Stonewall would have swept all before him. The fact is, however, that the Union forces had found themselves a good piece of terrain upon which to mount a defense, with a road network that would feed reinforcements into battle. During the night several more Union corps arrived, and those who were not already stationed on Cemetery and Culp's Hill stretched southward from Cemetery Hill along a ridge (now called, logically enough, Cemetery Ridge) toward two hills south of town, now known as Little and Big Round Top. More Confederate divisions arrived as well.

At the close of battle on July 1, Lee had several choices. The first was whether to stay and fight or break contact with Meade. Having planned for the concentration of his army, Lee must have been anticipating that battle would be imminent. If he did not act on that belief, he would have to disperse his forces again to enable them to forage successfully. If he chose to fight, he had to set forth a plan of battle. Should he hit the Union right, wrapped around the eastern face of Cemetery Hill and Culp's Hill, where he might sever the turnpike system leading back to Baltimore? What about targeting the Union left, presently ill-defined, stretching southward from Cemetery Ridge? Or should he punch ahead at the Union center at Cemetery Hill and the northern edge of Cemetery Ridge? Perhaps he should sweep around one flank, more likely the Union left flank, and seek ground from where he could stand or attack as circumstances dictated.

Longstreet preferred the last plan. Images of Fredericksburg danced in his imagination. Why attack the Federals by charging across fields against hills and heights when by maneuver the Confederates could sweep around the Union left and place themselves between the Yankees and Washington, forcing the bluecoats to attack? Such a plan would depend on Ewell pulling back from his position, which would involve a good deal of marching. Ewell, seconded by division commander Jubal Early, preferred to stay where he was, although he did not want to spearhead an attack on the Union right. Lee then decided to replicate Jackson's flank march at Chancellorsville, with Longstreet leading the strike force. An early morning reconnaissance brought back news that the Union left was indeed vulnerable; however, in retrospect it is clear that the reconnaissance had been poorly conducted, and its information was badly flawed. Finding that Lee was set upon attacking, Longstreet reluctantly set his superior's plan in motion, after gaining Lee's approval to allow a late brigade to arrive so that it could be thrown into the assault.

In the past Robert E. Lee had often enjoyed the cooperation of a Union general as he planned his devastating attacks. Such was the case at Second Manassas and Chancellorsville. But things didn't go quite as planned at Gettysburg, although the unintended consequences were not altogether adverse to Confederate fortunes. Longstreet's flanking movement became something of a fiasco, as he failed to secure an initial route of march that would remain concealed from Union observation. A time-consuming countermarch meant that the earliest he could mount an attack was mid-afternoon. Moreover, when his lead division approached where it was to deploy in line of battle, it came under fire from Yankees of Daniel Sickles's III Corps, located on a ridge along the Emmitsburg Road and anchored at a peach orchard.

That Sickles was where Longstreet found him was due to the Union corps commander's fear that the Confederates would repeat their Chancellorsville gambit, a fear reinforced when forward elements got into a sharp firefight with elements of A. P. Hill's Third Corps behind Seminary Ridge. In moving forward from his position due south of Cemetery Ridge, however, Sickles thinned out his two divisions to the point that they could not occupy a pair of hills, Big Round Top and to its north, Little Round Top, as they would come to be known. Heavily wooded, Big Round Top was hard to utilize; however, a Union signal station on Little Round Top looked westward over the hillside's cleared face, and at one point caught sight of Longstreet's countermarch. Meade was unaware of Sickles's redeployment for hours, due in large part because he believed the more significant threat was to the Union right. Yet as the hours passed his army gained strength. The V and VI Corps arrived during the day and were kept in reserve behind the front line, ready to be sent forward as circumstances dictated.

Undeterred by Sickles's redeployment, Longstreet launched what would be one of the most powerful assaults ever unleashed during the war. He wrecked Sickles's corps, mangled several more Union divisions, and came close to taking Little Round Top and piercing the Yankee line north of that height. Only the timely action of Gouverneur K. Warren in dispatching two brigades to Little Round Top preserved Union control of that position, and reinforcements rushing forward from other parts of the field barely plugged gaps along the southern section of Cemetery Ridge before the Confederates could punch their way through. Moreover, in shifting brigades to fend off Longstreet, Meade thinned his right flank on Culp's Hill, and as it grew dark Ewell ordered his men forward. After desperate fighting the Union lines held at Cemetery Hill. At Culp's Hill only the foresight of brigadier George S. Greene in erecting fortifications allowed the outnumbered defenders to hold on as Confederate attackers occupied positions vacated by Yankee regiments sent over to stop Longstreet. Just a short distance away the Baltimore Pike beckoned. If the Confederates took that road they would sever Meade's line of communications. They failed to do so on July 2.

Much has been written about the performance of the Confederate high command at Gettysburg on July 2, with emphasis placed on the actions of Lee's corps commanders, especially Longstreet. In years to come there would be much heated debate about whether Longstreet's unhappiness verged on insubordination, whether he moved with alacrity once he got the order to march, and whether the delays that ensued insured failure. In the absence of clear written orders from Lee, one must piece together the commander's intent from recollections and other documentation. However, Lee can be faulted on several points. First, whatever his sentiments about Longstreet's reluctance, he permitted Longstreet to await the arrival of his last brigade before moving, so he was well aware that the flank march would not begin until midday. If anything, Lee deferred too much to his subordinates on July 2, as the exchange with Ewell and Early suggests. Although much has been made of the quality of the information brought back by the early morning reconnaissance of the Union left, what stands out is that Lee took no steps to update his information about the Union deployment over the course of the day, and that he appears to have believed that there would be no change in either the size of Union forces or their deployment during the morning and early afternoon of July 2. In short, he assumed that it would be Chancellorsville all over again, and that Meade would prove to be no better an army commander than his predecessor. Moreover, if Longstreet did not perform well in marching and deploying his men, when the attack finally came it was devastating. The same could not be said for the lack of support offered by A. P. Hill, who did not stir to put his men into action at the appointed moment, or Ewell, whose attack could have come earlier and who failed to coordinate the actions of his three divisions.

Meeting with his commanders during the night, Meade decided to stay and fight. Lee was disposed to oblige him, but his plan to resume pressuring both flanks in coordinated fashion collapsed when fighting, precipitated by the Federals, broke out along Culp's Hill before dawn. Eventually Union forces repelled the Confederates in the area. Lee also discovered that Longstreet was not prepared to advance that morning. Given that Longstreet was less than enthusiastic about renewing the July 2 assault (and had compromised the possibility of renewing that attack by not bringing up in timely fashion a fresh division under George Pickett to join that assault), Lee decided upon attacking the Union center on Cemetery Ridge. At the same time, Jeb Stuart, who had arrived at Gettysburg on July 2, would threaten Union forces east of Culp's Hill, although it remains a matter of discussion as to whether his attack was part of Lee's larger plan.

Longstreet, his mind still fresh with images of the slaughter at Marye's Heights the previous December, thought success unlikely, but it was up to him to coordinate the assault forces. Three divisions of infantry would spearhead the charge, with reserves ready to support it. A massive artillery barrage would weaken the enemy position;

then some 12,000 men would advance in the first wave. A series of swales would offer them partial concealment as they made their way to the Emmitsburg Road. Indeed, from Lee's position Cemetery Ridge did not look imposing at all. But the plan started to implode from the outset. The artillery bombardment expended so much ammunition that little was available to support the infantry assault, while decisions by Union commanders to swap batteries and withhold fire gave the appearance that many of the Yankee cannon were out of commission. Although the three divisions moved forward, Isaac Trimble's men on the left soon came under fire, and quickly became disorganized. The other two divisions fared somewhat better, but as they approached the Emmitsburg Road they discovered that they would have to take down the fences on both sides of the lane, exposing them to artillery and rifle fire. There would be much of that, for the Confederate bombardment had largely overshot the Union position, and there was enough Union artillery in line to make things extremely uncomfortable. Still the Confederates came on, until a small group reached the Union line and actually penetrated it in one place. Had any Rebels looked back, however, they would have seen that there was no second wave, no reserve force ready to exploit this single opening, while to the front and the sides the Yankees counterattacked. Elsewhere, as muskets blazed away, Union soldiers yelled, "Fredericksburg! Fredericksburg!"

It was just as Longstreet had feared. The massive assault was a costly, bloody failure. Rebel survivors straggled back across the fields; Lee met them, admitting that it was all his fault. Elsewhere, Union cavalry fended off Stuart east of Gettysburg, while Union horsemen mounted an ill-conceived attack near the Round Tops. After some thought, Meade decided against a counterattack, fearing that he might get as good as his men just gave. Besides, both armies were badly damaged; both had lost important generals. After waiting most of a rainy July 4 for a Union counterattack that never came, Lee commenced making his way back to Virginia.

What had happened? The Lee magic of previous battles was not evident at Gettysburg. The Confederate commander made some fundamental mistakes. He held back forces that might have been used to deal one more blow to the already bruised Union forces on the afternoon of July 1. He did not keep a watchful eye on the arrival of Union reinforcements and Sickles's redeployment on July 2. At best the assault of July 3 was a high-risk proposition, given the previous failure of such assaults on other fields. He found it hard to coordinate operations when his army was strung out for miles on external lines. Nor were his subordinates at the top of their game, although too much has been made of Ewell's hesitation of July 1 and Longstreet's supposed procrastination on July 2. Stuart's absence had left Lee blind, in part because Lee did not use the cavalry still at his disposal for reconnaissance. Perhaps Chancellorsville had left Lee overly optimistic about what he might achieve. Despite later reports that he had said that Meade would commit no blunder on his front, he certainly acted as if the new Union commander was no improvement over his predecessors.

Under the circumstances, Meade performed well at Gettysburg. He was new to his job, and at times he seemed uncertain what to do next, but he did nothing rash and did not fold under pressure. Some of his subordinates performed brilliantly, and when they did not, others rose up and limited the damage. In retrospect, perhaps the astonishing thing about Gettysburg is not that the Union won, but that at long last Lee did not benefit from the mistakes of his opposite number. To pull off a Second Manassas, a Fredericksburg, or a Chancellorsville is much easier if the other side is ill-led: Lee was not so fortunate at Gettysburg.

Gettysburg in itself was not decisive. Although both armies had been severely damaged, neither had been destroyed. At best the bloodshed had worn away more Confederate manpower in the continual attrition of combat. Had the Confederates gained control of either the Taneytown Road or the Baltimore Pike behind Union lines, they might have been able to deliver a devastating blow. But Lee enjoyed no such luck. Now he had to fend off Meade's pursuit as he scrambled southward toward the Potomac with the spoils of weeks of foraging still in hand. The next ten days proved critical to determining the battle's true import.[15]

Meade let July 4 pass without undertaking any significant action with his army, aside from directing his cavalry commander, Alfred Pleasanton, to harass the retreating Confederates. It was time to rest, regroup, and reassess. He congratulated his command for the fighting of the last three days, declaring: "Our task is not yet accomplished, and the commanding general looks to the army for greater efforts to drive from our soil every vestige of the presence of the invader."[16] Much depended on which clause one emphasized. Was the task simply to drive Lee back across the Potomac? Or was it to follow up on Gettysburg with a pursuit designed to cripple the enemy army?

To help reach a decision, Meade that evening gathered his generals for another council of war. By that time, he already had evidence that Lee was preparing to withdraw. Lee had asked to exchange prisoners taken during the battle, which Meade interpreted as an effort to shed the responsibility of feeding prisoners as well as his own men. By late afternoon he received reports that the Confederates were on the move away from the battlefield. Meade had also issued orders to several generals heading nearby commands. He wanted William French, commanding what had been the Harpers Ferry garrison, to move on the mountain passes along South Mountain. Indeed, French had already sent forward a cavalry detachment to destroy Lee's lone bridge over the Potomac at Falling Waters. Meade was less successful with Darius Couch and Couch's subordinate, William F. Smith, who had charge of 9,000 militia at Carlisle, an ideal position from which to come down upon Lee from the north, had it not been for Smith's well-founded opinion that his soldiers were nearly useless.

With all this in front of him, however, Meade listened as his generals advised caution: better to see first what Lee would do; under no conditions attack Lee at Gettysburg; pursue Lee while keeping the Army of the Potomac between the Army of Northern Virginia and Washington, which meant swinging south to Emmitsburg before advancing westward toward Williamsport; and forego a serious direct pursuit against Lee's retreating rear. This was the safe and sure approach, but it meant that Meade hesitated before attempting a gambit that might have reaped great benefits: an immediate strike westward toward Fairfield in the hopes of blocking the Confederates' most direct line of retreat.[17]

Meade's hesitation was understandable, in light of all the pressure he had been under, but it left him open to criticism from his civilian superiors and other generals. Engineer wunderkind and Lincoln favorite Herman Haupt had arrived at Gettysburg on July 4 predisposed to believe that once more a Union army would let a decisive victory elude its grasp by resting in place after a major battle north of the Potomac. Nothing in his conversation with Meade disabused him of this notion, and Haupt took it upon himself to convey his disappointment with Meade's lack of aggressiveness with the authorities in Washington, including Lincoln.[18]

Lincoln was not in a good mood about Meade. Everything he heard in the days after the battle reminded him of McClellan after Antietam. Reading Meade's congratulatory order, with its remark about driving the Confederates "from our soil," the president exploded: "The whole country is our soil!" On July 5 he visited Daniel Sickles, who was already developing his own self-serving version of the battle in order to shield himself from criticism, an account that fingered Meade as a general who would have retreated from Gettysburg had not Sickles advanced his corps. Such an account reinforced the president's concerns about Meade, as did Haupt's report. Lincoln urged Halleck to keep an eye on Meade. At a cabinet meeting on July 7, he told Gideon Welles that "he feared the old idea of driving the rebels out of Pennsylvania and Maryland, instead of capturing them, was still prevalent among the officers."[19]

Lee did a good job of getting his command down to Williamsport, as Jeb Stuart compensated for his shortcomings during the week prior to Gettysburg by shielding the Confederate withdrawal. However, a Union detachment from Harpers Ferry had destroyed the Confederate pontoon bridge at Falling Waters, and Lee would have to wait for high waters to subside before fording the river at Williamsport. The Confederates quickly prepared a fortified line to protect the army while the crossings were readied. Many of them hoped that Meade might test those defenses so that they could cut down charging Yankees. As artillerist Charles Wainwright observed, "It would nearly end the rebellion if we could actually bag this army, but on the other hand, a severe repulse would give them all the prestige at home and abroad which they had lost at Gettysburg, and injure our morale greatly."[20]

Meade agreed. At first he had hoped to catch Lee before the Confederates retreated back to Virginia, but the exhaustion of his own command and the losses suffered in leadership caused him to have second thoughts. "I expect to find the enemy in a strong position, well covered with artillery," he told Halleck, "and I do not desire to imitate his example at Gettysburg and assault a position when the chances are so greatly against success. I wish in advance to moderate the expectations of those who, in ignorance of the difficulties to be encountered, may expect too much." Clearly Meade had Lincoln in mind, and rightly so, as Halleck wired Meade on July 8 that the president "is urgent and anxious" for Meade to catch Lee.[21]

In the weeks after Gettysburg Henry W. Halleck failed to act as a successful mediator between Lincoln and Meade. If anything, he made matters worse. He was unsuccessful in communicating Meade's real concerns to an impatient Lincoln, and he tended to relay Lincoln's anxiety unfiltered to Meade, who was already feeling the pressure of command. The president watched events "with agonizing impatience, hope struggling with fear," in the words of private secretary John Hay. Nor was he alone. Gideon Welles, who was often dismissive of Union generalship, wondered, "Why cannot our army move as rapidly as the Rebels?. . . It has been the misfortune of our generals to linger, never to avail themselves of success,—to waste, or omit to gather, the fruits of victory."[22]

By July 11, both armies were confronting each other near Williamsport. The next evening, Meade called upon his generals once more to decide what to do next. He claimed to be inclined to attack, or at least launch a reconnaissance in force that might, if the opportunity came, be turned into an assault. However, he wondered whether his generals were up to the challenge. He sorely missed Reynolds and Hancock, although doubtless he was glad to be rid of Sickles. The majority of the corps commanders urged him to wait another day. The delay proved crucial. On the night of July 13 Lee succeeded in getting most of his command across the Potomac. The most Meade could do the next morning was to tangle with the Confederate rear guard at Falling Waters.

Lincoln was furious. Something was fundamentally wrong with the Army of the Potomac. "There is bad faith somewhere," he told Welles. At the War Department, the president continued to express his astonishment and disappointment. "We had them within our grasp. We had only to stretch forth our hands and they were ours. And nothing I could do or say could make the army move." Back at the White House, he broke down before his eldest son, Robert. "If I had gone up there," the president declared, "I could have whipped them myself."[23]

Halleck wasted no time in informing Meade of Lincoln's dissatisfaction. Meade responded by asking to be relieved of command. "This is exactly what I expected," he told his wife; "unless I did impractical things, fault would be found with me."

Lincoln backed down, setting aside a letter he had composed to Meade in which he set forth his unhappiness and told Meade, "I do not believe you appreciate the magnitude of the misfortune involved in Lee's escape. . . . Your golden opportunity is gone, and I am distressed immeasurably because of it."[24]

No sooner had Lee made good his escape than he reflected on the campaign, concluding that perhaps things were not as bad as one might suppose. "The army has returned to Virginia dear Mary," he wrote his wife in mid-July. "Its return is rather sooner than I had originally contemplated, but having accomplished what I purposed on leaving the Rappahannock, viz., relieving the Valley of the presence of the enemy & drawing his army north of the Potomac, I determined to recross the latter river." The claim was a remarkable one, in that it might appear that what happened at Gettysburg had no effect at all on the course of the campaign. Within weeks he shifted the army east of the Blue Ridge Mountains. Of the campaign he remarked: "The army did all it could. I fear I required of it impossibilities. But it responded to the call nobly and cheerfully, and though it did not win a victory it conquered a success."[25]

In years to come the Gettysburg campaign in general and the battle for Gettysburg in particular would be celebrated as the "high watermark" of the Confederacy and, sometimes in conjunction with Vicksburg, termed the "turning point of the war." It was no such thing. The chances for Confederate victory remained much as they were before the campaign; at most the Army of Northern Virginia had suffered losses that would be increasingly hard to replace. Nor had victory made the Army of the Potomac and its generals more confident about their chances of defeating the Confederate's foremost military leader. Had the battle or the campaign turned out differently, what followed might have proved decisive, but as it happened, Gettysburg settled little. August 1863 found the Army of Northern Virginia and the Army of the Potomac facing each other in central Virginia once more.

OVERSHADOWED OPPORTUNITIES

In focusing on Lee's invasion of Pennsylvania, his defeat at Gettysburg, and his escape to Virginia, accounts of military operations in the East in mid-1863 tend to overlook other actions, which, had they turned out differently, might have had an important impact on the progress of Union arms. Foremost in terms of its possible impact on public opinion was a series of efforts to take Charleston, South Carolina. In the fall of 1862 there had been talk of taking Wilmington, North Carolina, thus shutting down a major Confederate port. At the same time Assistant Secretary of the Navy Gustavus Fox was quite taken with the notion of a naval expedition against Charleston in which ironclads would run past Fort Sumter and the other coastal forts and pull up outside Charleston itself, forcing the enemy to surrender the city. Rear Admiral Samuel Du Pont did not share Fox's enthusiasm, and for months not much was done to implement the idea. However, when an attempt to take Wilmington went awry at the end of 1862—including the sinking of the USS *Monitor* off Cape Hatteras in bad weather—pressure mounted for the Charleston operation. Feuding among army commanders on the scene guaranteed that it would be a navy-only operation, despite evidence gathered during a series of small operations that the Charleston defenses would prove too much an obstacle.[26]

On April 7, 1863, Du Pont attacked Fort Sumter with nine ironclads. The Confederates in Sumter and nearby Fort Moultrie returned fire, damaging five ironclads severely (one eventually sank). The battle was over within two hours. Clearly naval vessels by themselves could not achieve much, and so planning turned again to an army-navy operation. If Union infantry could establish control of Morris Island, just south of Fort Sumter and east of James Island, a target of operations in 1862, siege artillery could reduce Sumter's brick walls to rubble and open the way for the Union navy to steam into Charleston harbor. However, to gain a position for the artillery, Union forces would have to capture Battery Wagner, just over a mile south of Fort Sumter on the eastern shore of Morris Island. Perhaps a joint army-navy attack on Wagner would prove successful.

General Quincy A. Gillmore pulled together a force to conduct the ground operations. Included in that force were several black regiments, including the 54th Massachusetts Infantry, which had just arrived in South Carolina. An initial effort to take Wagner on July 11 proved premature. A week later, a second assault took place, with ironclads and artillery blasting away for some 36 hours before the infantry, spearheaded by the 54th, sprang forward. Once more the Confederate defenders held their ground and repulsed the attackers with great loss. Among the dead was the commander of the 54th, Colonel Robert Gould Shaw; his regiment suffered severe losses. Much would be said of how the performance of the 54th proved the battle-worthiness of black soldiers, especially at a time when draft riots in New York City had turned into an anti-black race riot, but from a military point of view the assault was another disappointing failure. Gillmore decided to lay siege to the battery, while Du Pont's replacement, Admiral John A. Dahlgren, resumed bombarding Fort Sumter, assisted by Gillmore's land-based artillery. This time Sumter's walls began to crumble; in the days to come Wagner came under heavy fire as well. Realizing that the outer ring of Charleston's defenses was being breached, the Confederates pulled back to James Island, Fort Moultrie, and Charleston itself. By the time Wagner fell on September 7 and Sumter was reduced to rubble, the Union gains proved empty: Charleston remained in Confederate hands.[27]

Although one might concede that the Union occupation of Charleston in 1863 would have been a valuable symbolic victory, the truth remains that it would not have amounted to much else. Charleston was virtually useless in terms of its function as a port. Union military commanders did not think beyond the capture of the city itself, and had given little serious thought to what might come next. So long as the Confederates maintained the defensive lines they had set up in the aftermath of the initial Union incursions along the coast in 1861, the south Atlantic coast would not become a new front, and there would be no threat to the rear of Confederate forces operating in Virginia and points north.

Nor did either side take advantage of what appeared to be an opportunity offered by Lee's invasion of Pennsylvania to threaten their opponent's capital. As Lee prepared to advance north in June, he advised Jefferson Davis to put Pierre G. T. Beauregard in charge of a force that might be formed from units that were not already keeping an eye on Union movements. That force might go to Mississippi, but Lee also entertained the idea of it reinforcing the Army of Northern Virginia. Nothing came of this idea, nor did anything come of Lee's suggestions for a drive into western Virginia. As the Army of Northern Virginia forded the Potomac, Lee once more urged Davis to place Beauregard in charge of a force gathered from the south Atlantic coast, arguing that all signs pointed to the Union pulling its forces out of the area (an incorrect impression). Beauregard could operate in central Virginia, threatening Washington and forcing the enemy to abandon any thought of attacking Richmond. Lee even thought it might force the reallocation of Union forces from the west to the east, which upon reflection appears to be overly sanguine.[28]

Lee continued to press for the formation of a strike force under Beauregard, finding time on June 25 to write two more letters on the subject. "It should never be forgotten that our concentration at any point compels that of the enemy, and his numbers being limited, tends to relieve all other threatened localities," he argued, although the main thrust of his argument was that a force in Virginia would assist his operations north of the Potomac by threatening Washington.[29]

Nothing came of this suggestion. By the time Beauregard could have gathered a force of any significance, it would have been too late to influence the course of events in Pennsylvania. At the same time, however, Union forces in southeast Virginia declined to take advantage of Lee's absence to threaten Richmond. They had occupied West Point, at the confluence of the Pamunkey and Mattapony rivers, in May, but had evacuated at month's end. The following month, John A. Dix took charge of the forces around Fort Monroe. Halleck decided that he would threaten Richmond to draw to the defense of the Confederate capital units that might otherwise be sent to strengthen Lee's Army of Northern Virginia. However, this amounted to little more than a demonstration, although at one point Dix's cavalry reached Hanover Junction, not far from Richmond. Dix contemplated more, but decided that his command (some 32,000 strong) would not be able to take Richmond, especially as Halleck's orders were too vague on that point. At best Dix succeeded in pinning Confederate forces that otherwise might have been dispatched to reinforce Lee, although there remains a sense of missed opportunity in this often-forgotten campaign.[30]

STALEMATE IN VIRGINIA

These abortive moves at Charleston and along the Chesapeake and James rivers receive relatively little attention in accounts of the war, contributing to the impression that the war in the East had boiled down to the actions of the two principal opposing armies. Throughout the remainder of July and August, they perpetuated the strategic stalemate in central Virginia. Events elsewhere stirred matters up. At the end of August Lee visited Jefferson Davis in Richmond. The Confederate general seemed eager to resume the offensive, telling James Longstreet to "prepare the army for offensive operations," for he believed it best "to endeavor to bring General Meade out and use our efforts to crush his army while in its present condition." President Davis had different ideas, however: Longstreet would be taking the offensive, but it would be in Georgia. The massive troop transfer that Lee had prevented in June, he could not block in September. Throughout July and August William S. Rosecrans's Army of the Cumberland had outmaneuvered Braxton Bragg's Army of Tennessee, forcing the Confederates to abandon southeastern Tennessee, including the critical rail junction of Chattanooga, and retreat into northern Georgia. There Bragg proposed to launch a counterattack against Rosecrans's increasingly dispersed forces, and Longstreet with two divisions would take a long winding path of railroads to reinforce Bragg in time to deliver the blow. Davis proposed that Lee consider going west as well, but once more he demurred.[31]

Lee was not pleased with Davis's decision. He continued to believe that it was his army that deserved to be strengthened, so that he could resume offensive operations. He viewed Longstreet's detachment as a short-term expedient. "If I was a little stronger," he informed Davis, "I think I could drive Meade's army under cover of the fortifications of Washington before he gathers more reinforcements. When he gets all his reinforcements I may be forced back to Richmond. The blow at Rosecrans should be made promptly and Longstreet returned." He repeatedly pressed the matter, displaying more than slight impatience. Even after news arrived that Bragg had defeated Rosecrans at Chickamauga on September 19-20, 1863, Lee urged that Longstreet sweep quickly through East Tennessee. "No time ought now to be wasted," he declared. "Everything should be done that can be done at once, so that the troops may be speedily returned to this department." Congratulating Longstreet on his performance, Lee beseeched: "Finish the work before you, my dear general, and return to me. I want you badly and you cannot get back too soon."[32]

When news of what had happened at Chickamauga reached Washington, Lincoln decided that it was time to respond to the shift in Confederate forces. Orders had previously gone out to Grant and other western generals to reinforce Rosecrans, although far too late to have any impact at Chickamauga. Now the president decided to shift two corps from the Army of the Potomac westward. Chosen for the task were the XI and XII corps. With them, in overall command, Lincoln dispatched Joseph Hooker, a decision that pleased Meade far more than did the weakening of his army. Meade had been contemplating taking the offensive himself when news came of the transfer. Once more divided counsels had produced sparse results. "Your bricks and mortars may be of the best," remarked one of Meade's staff officers, "but, if there are three or four chief architects, none of whom can agree where to lay the first brick, the house will rise slowly."[33]

That comment summarized the chaos within the Union high command during the preceding two months. Meade had intended to give battle to Lee at the end of July, but when the Confederates evaded a confrontation, Lincoln shook his head in disappointment. "I have no faith that Meade will attack Lee," he told Gideon Welles. "I believe he can never have another as good opportunity as that which he trifled away. Everything since then has dragged with him. No, I don't believe he is going to fight." Now, having learned of Longstreet's departure, Meade sensed an opportunity. Deploying his army for an advance, he wired Washington to see what his superiors wanted: Lincoln equivocated, preferring to wait and see what would develop in response to an advance. Puzzled, Meade observed: "I can get a battle out of Lee under very disadvantageous circumstances which may render his inferior force my superior and which is not likely to result in any very decided advantage, even in case I should be victorious." Such waffling did not inspire confidence, and when Meade offered that perhaps it would be better to cross the Rappahannock at Fredericksburg or renew operations along the James River, he added, "I take it for granted, either of these contingencies is out of the question." The shadows of 1862 continued to haunt everyone.[34]

Lincoln found Meade's logic confounding. "I am not prepared to order, or even advise an advance in this case, wherein I know so little of particulars, and wherein he, in the field, thinks the risk is so great, and the promise of advantage so small," he told Halleck. If that was the case, however, why not send some of Meade's men elsewhere where they might do some good? Indeed, why not stand on the defensive altogether, freeing up a considerable force for offensive operations? Certainly there was no reason to advance upon Richmond. "If our army can not fall upon the enemy and hurt him where he is," he reasoned, "it is plain to me it can gain nothing by attempting to follow him over a succession of intrenched lines into a fortified city." The president's point was plain: forget capturing Richmond. Once more he declared that the Army of the Potomac should "make Lee's army, and not Richmond, its objective point."[35]

Thus put, Lincoln's conclusion—that the stalemate would continue—offered precious little hope for success in the very theater where northern public opinion looked for great success. Perhaps it would indeed be better to concentrate one's energies elsewhere, but it was dangerous to believe that the northern people would accept the relegation of the Eastern Theater to secondary importance. Nor did Lincoln make any effort to affect public opinion in this regard. He might compose carefully worded missives to justify emancipation, for example, but no such effort was made to shift public perceptions of the war and to educate people as to the military situation.

Circumstances called for what preplanning would not permit: in reaction to Chickamauga, Lincoln finally transferred forces from Virginia westward. Meade hoped for a lessening of expectations commensurate with the lessening of his strength. As he explained, "if people believe that Lee has no army, and that I have an immense one, it is hard to expect them not to inquire why I do not do something; but when they come to know that just as I was about trying to do something, my army was suddenly reduced to a figure a little greater only than Lee's and that he occupies a very strong position, where the natural advantages in his favor more than equalize the difference in our forces, they will understand why I cannot do anything."[36]

No sooner had Meade set forth his reasoning than Lee, learning of his opponent's reduction in strength, decided to take advantage of the opportunity to go on the offensive. His decision not to mention his plans to Davis suggested that communications between generals and presidents were flawed on both sides. Perhaps he saw a chance to reprise his campaign against Pope that had been crowned with triumph at Second Manassas. This time, however, Lee was not to enjoy a repeat of his earlier successes. An initial assault by A. P. Hill against a Union position at Bristoe Station on October 14 proved a bloody setback. Meade pulled back to the familiar area around Manassas Junction and Centreville and waited in prepared positions for an attack that never came. Lee contented himself with destroying railways before pulling back. "This was a deep game," Meade ruefully observed, "and I am forced to admit that in the playing of it he had got the advantage of me." Perhaps, but Lee had been thwarted in bringing him to battle. There would be no Third Manassas.[37]

Nevertheless, Lincoln and Halleck were disappointed that Meade had not done something more impressive. The president was disheartened, while the general-in-chief, as Meade observed "was very urgent that something should be done, but what that something was he did not define." That was vintage Halleck. Even more bizarre in its way was Lincoln's offer, made as the campaign neared its close. "If Gen. Meade can now attack [Lee] on a field no worse than equal for us," he told Halleck, "and will do so with all the skill and courage, which he, his officers and men possess, the honor will be his if he succeeds, and the blame may be mine if he fails." Skeptical, Halleck preferred to echo Lincoln's complaint that the result was "the same old story we had from all our Potomac generals."[38]

In short, the president, the general-in-chief, and the commander of the Army of the Potomac were never on the same page. Lincoln and Meade never could get in sync. Halleck was worse than useless. As Welles noted during the campaign, the general-in-chief "should, if he has the capacity, attend to these things, and if he has

not should be got out of the way."[39] The president had lost faith in Meade, questioning whether he had very much to do with the victory at Gettysburg (it did not help
that he proved all too willing to listen to Daniel Sickles's self-serving renditions
of the clash, which sparked another investigation by the Joint Committee on the
Conduct of the War into that battle).[40]

In early November Meade commenced his offensive. Within days, after short, sharp
actions at Rappahannock Station and Kelly's Ford in which thousands of prisoners fell
into Union hands, he had forced Lee to abandon his line along the Rappahannock and
retire behind the Rapidan. Buoyed by the cheers from his men, Meade was eager to
fight, but even then he could still hear echoes of the reaction to the previous month's
campaign. He hoped that his latest triumph would "convince the intelligent public
that my retreat to Centreville was not to avoid battle, and that Lee, who was not outflanked, or had his communications threatened, but was attacked in front, and
yet withdrew, is really the one who avoided battle." He was also pleased when Lincoln
telegraphed his approval of the move.[41]

Disappointed that Lee had not accepted his offer of battle but had withdrawn
behind the Rapidan, Meade pressed on, determined to bring matters to a head. Bad
weather and the need to repair the Orange and Alexandra Railroad that served as his
supply line hindered his movement, but he believed that once he got going, "we shall
have a great and decisive battle." But within days his hopes unraveled. Delays in movement allowed Lee to respond to the Union advance and prepare new field fortifications. When corps commander Gouverneur Warren assured Meade he had identified
a weak spot in the Confederate position along the right flank, Meade hurried to mass
nearly 30,000 men to launch a powerful assault, supported by another attack column
15,000 strong with orders to hit the Confederates at the same time. Just as the plan was
about to be put into operation, however, Warren changed his mind. The Confederate
position was now impregnable, he reported, and he had decided on his own accord to
suspend the attack. After finding out that Lee had strengthened his lines elsewhere,
Meade, wisely deciding that the risks were too high and the reward not worth
the chance, withdrew. "There will be a great howl all over the country," he predicted.
"Letter writers and politicians will denounce me." Eventually "the Administration will
be obliged to yield to popular clamor and discard me." So it would be, he thought,
even as he maintained that he had "acted from a high sense of duty, to myself as a soldier, to my men as their general, and to my country and its cause, as the agent having
its vital interests solemnly entrusted to me, which I have no right wantonly to play
with and to jeopardize, either for my own personal benefit, or to satisfy the demands
of popular clamor, or interested politicians."[42]

To date there has been only one study of the war in the East from the end of the
Gettysburg campaign through Mine Run—a concise volume by Meade's chief of staff,
Andrew A. Humphreys. The reason is obvious. "Nothing" happened. There was no

big battle, just what appears to be a series of thrusts and parries across the chessboard of war in Virginia. Major events happened elsewhere, notably at Chickamauga and Chattanooga, but the story of the war in Virginia in the summer and fall of 1863 is largely passed over in the rush to move the narrative from the drama of Gettysburg to Grant's arrival in March 1864.

Yet, if this period is not marked by a big battle, a closer look at it reveals many of the dynamics that shaped other campaigns. It also calls into question key parts of the traditional narrative. Lee's offensive spirit and preference for maneuver was far from broken after Gettysburg. He was eager to resume offensive operations, either by moving northwards himself or by preparing to counterpunch should Meade initiate a campaign. Aware of the importance of public opinion, he repeatedly argued that steadfast popular support was essential to Confederate success: "Nothing is wanted but that their fortitude should equal their bravery in insure the success of our cause." Acutely sensitive to criticism, Lee was even willing to offer his resignation in the face of public disappointment at the outcome of the Gettysburg campaign, despite his insistence that, properly understood, it had been a success. But even Lee was worried about whether his own men shared his expressed faith in the cause. As Longstreet's divisions moved westward, he noted that the corps commander wanted to swap two Georgia brigades for other brigades stationed elsewhere, for he feared that once back home, the Georgia troops might desert. Nor did the Confederate commander agree with his civil superior about the proper strategy to pursue across the board. He resisted the detachment of Longstreet's force, looked for its quick return, and seized upon the first opportunity to launch his own offensive without informing Davis of his intentions (indeed, he waited until Davis had left Richmond to visit the Army of Tennessee to move).[43]

George Gordon Meade struggled with the expectations of his superiors and public opinion. He was well aware that the way to win applause was to advance southward, bring the enemy to battle, and win a decisive victory. However, when he contemplated such a move, events conspired to thwart him, most notably when Lincoln decided to detach two corps and send them westward after Chickamauga. He received absolutely no assistance from Henry Halleck, who continued to render worse the relationship between Meade and Lincoln. Lincoln himself offered uncertain guidance while grousing about Meade's ability. Navy secretary Gideon Welles noticed as much. When Lincoln told Meade that if he took the offensive in October, Lincoln would take all the responsibility for defeat while according Meade with all the credit for a success, Welles confided to his diary: "This is tasking Meade beyond his ability. If the President could tell him how and when to fight, his orders would be faithfully carried out, but the President is overtasking Meade's capability and powers."[44]

Meade had decided that he would not advance unless he saw a good chance to win. He believed that the failure of previous advances limited his options. There would be no revival of the Peninsula campaign, and no recrossing the Rappahannock at Fredericksburg. That left the area south of the Rappahannock and the Rapidan, just west and south of the Chancellorsville battlefield, as the most likely area for future operations. It was not until November, however, that he finally advanced, and the abortive assault at Mine Run may have sealed his fate.

In short, Gettysburg was not the decisive battle it is often portrayed to have been. Lee retained his aggressive edge, even after dispatching Longstreet westward. The Army of the Potomac remained wary of its foe, and events soon suggested that not all of its generals were over their fear of Bobby Lee. If Meade had proved that he would not be the general who would lose the war, he also proved that it was unlikely that he would be the general who would win it. And so the two armies went into winter quarters, not all that far from where they had settled down after Burnside's abortive Mud March fiasco in January 1863. The strategic stalemate continued.

SIX

GRANT TAKES COMMAND

As 1863 gave way to 1864, everyone was aware of the important role that the progress of Union arms would play in the coming year's presidential contest. The Union had enjoyed signal success in the West in 1863, highlighted by the capture of Vicksburg and the triumph at Chattanooga, both credited in large part to Ulysses S. Grant. However, military affairs in the East seemed to be much as before, with the opposing armies confronting each other in central Virginia. Given the public attention paid to the Eastern Theater, it looked as if the war was far from over. After a year in which Robert E. Lee had steadfastly resisted efforts to go west to help Confederate fortunes there, the year opened with increasing discussion about bringing Grant east, not as commander of the Army of the Potomac, but as the new general-in-chief. Indeed, Congressman Elihu B. Washburne had already introduced a bill reviving the rank of lieutenant general, and everyone knew that he intended Grant to be promoted to the new rank. Did the new man have new ideas?

As he spent the winter of 1863–1864 in Tennessee, Grant, with Halleck's encouragement, contemplated how he might approach conducting operations in the Eastern Theater. Two officers, William F. Smith and Cyrus Comstock, drew up one possible strategy, and Grant forwarded the proposal to Washington. The plan reflected Smith's belief that McClellan's approach to the problem of Virginia had been correct: after all. "Baldy" Smith, as some called him, had been a brigade and division commander with the Army of the Potomac until he found himself transferred out of that army in the fallout over Burnside's removal. One of the reasons he had been reassigned was that, along with William B. Franklin, he had contacted Lincoln directly after Fredericksburg to advocate a return to operating along the James. The president had dismissed the idea. Now, having impressed Grant by his performance during the Chattanooga campaign, Smith took another crack at proposing a different line of approach. Perhaps, after a year of stalemate, a plan bearing Grant's name might gain attention.

Suggesting that Union leaders abandon "all previously attempted lines to Richmond," Grant argued that in 1864 Union operations should target Raleigh, North Carolina, with a force of 60,000 men moving southward from Suffolk, Virginia. That done, Union forces should secure beachheads at New Bern and Wilmington to supply the incursion into the interior. Such an offensive would threaten the Confederate logistical network south of Richmond, forcing Lee to abandon his defenses in central Virginia and leave the Old Dominion altogether. Union forces would "partially live upon the country and would reduce the stores of the enemy," he observed. A thrust through North Carolina might encourage that state's Confederate soldiers to desert and liberate slaves in its wake. In short, this proposed plan "would draw the enemy from campaigns of their own choosing, and for which they are prepared, to new lines of operations never expected to become necessary."[1]

Halleck rather bluntly dismissed Grant's proposal, although, given that it took him nearly a month to forward his objections, one might assume that he had shared Grant's proposal with other interested parties, including, perhaps, the president (although he implied that he had yet to do so). The general-in-chief reiterated (without attribution) Lincoln's assumption that Lee's army, and not Richmond, was the proper objective point for Union operations in the East, and, as was his wont, he cited Napoleon in support of that principle. Given the tone of his wording, he might as well have cited Lincoln, too, as he repeated the president's notion that it should be easier to defeat Lee nearer to Washington than further away somewhere else. Grant's proposal, Halleck argued, would strip Washington of the forces needed to protect it. There simply were not enough men in uniform to undertake an invasion of North Carolina. Should the Army of the Potomac (some 70,000 strong at the moment) be weakened by 30,000 men earmarked for the North Carolina operation, it would be an open invitation for Lee to strike northward once more. Indeed, Halleck wanted to strip the south Atlantic coast of ground forces to use elsewhere: "I always have been, and still am opposed to all these isolated expeditions on the sea and Gulf coasts."

To Halleck, the problem was simple: the goal of Union operations in the East should be the destruction of the Army of Northern Virginia. "Lee's army is by far the best in rebel service," he observed, "and I regard him as their ablest general. But little progress can be made here till that army is broken or defeated." The story of the war in the East had been one of missed opportunities to do just that. "The overthrow of Lee's army being the object of operations here, the question then arises how can we best attain it?" It seemed best to him to unite the forces in the East and strike southward directly at Lee's army through an overland approach: "And the nearer to Washington we can fight it the better for us. . . . If we cannot defeat him here with our combined force, we cannot hope to do so elsewhere with a divided army." Lincoln could not have said it better himself, although the president had said it before (indeed, he had said as much to Franklin and Smith back in December 1862).[2]

The situation in the East at the time Grant offered his plan remained the same during the winter of 1863–64. In the aftermath of the Mine Run offensive, the Army of the Potomac and the Army of Northern Virginia settled into winter quarters. Neither army was entirely inactive. Lee shuffled off Pickett's division to North Carolina, used Jubal Early to take a poke at the Shenandoah Valley, and shifted forces to intercept Judson Kilpatrick's raid upon Richmond in February and March 1864. Although Lee did not succeed in the last-named venture, Kilpatrick's raid, which featured Ulric Dahlgren's ill-fated expedition to free prisoners, failed in spectacular fashion. Whether Dahlgren also planned to kidnap or kill Jefferson Davis has been disputed then and since, but the operation's failure left things much as they had been months before.

It was a time of reenlistment and reorganization for the Army of the Potomac. The three year terms Union volunteers had accepted in 1861 would expire the following spring, and, despite financial incentives, furloughs, and honorary designations, slightly less than half of the Army of the Potomac's battle-hardened veterans reenlisted. At the same time, conscripts began showing up in large numbers for the first time, and their quality did not match their quantity. Meade chose to reorganize the army's five infantry corps, consolidating them into three corps. Both the I and III Corps had suffered badly at Gettysburg, but survivors did not welcome the dissolution of their corps and their reassignment to the remaining II, V, and VI Corps. The reorganization created new command relationships, some of which would fare better than others.[3]

Robert E. Lee did not intend to sit in place and await the opening of the annual spring Union offensive. "If we could take the initiative & fall upon them unexpectedly we might derange their plans & embarrass them the whole summer," he advised Davis in February. Without a thrust by Longstreet's still-absent corps into Kentucky, Lee advised the return of Longstreet's men to the Army of Northern Virginia, followed by a drive northward against Meade. "We are not in a condition, & never have been, in my opinion, to invade the enemy's country with a prospect of permanent benefit," he reminded the Confederate president. "But we can alarm & embarrass him to some extent & thus prevent his undertaking anything of magnitude against us." If he received sufficient supplies and fresh horses, he reflected weeks later, "I think I could disturb the quiet of the enemy & drive him to the Potomac." As during the previous fall, there was nothing in Lee's correspondence to suggest that Gettysburg had crippled his army or dampened his ardor for taking the offensive, even if one also senses in these letters a shrewd request to be reinforced and resupplied by promising great benefits.[4]

It soon became evident that Lee would be facing a new general when the spring campaign opened. At first Abraham Lincoln had watched quietly as Washburne's bill reviving the rank of lieutenant general made its way through Congress. It was not until he learned from multiple sources that Grant had no interest in the presidency that he believed he could promote a general without elevating a rival. Grant came east to accept his commission on March 1864, and with his third star he assumed the role of general-in-chief, with Halleck functioning as a chief of staff in Washington.[5]

No sooner had Grant accepted his commission than he headed down to Meade's headquarters in Virginia. Accompanying him was William F. Smith, who entertained hopes that he might replace Meade. Meade certainly thought that he would be replaced, perhaps by Sherman. With that in mind he met Grant and indicated his willingness to step aside; that, in turn, impressed Grant so much that he decided to leave Meade where he was. He'd find a place for Smith later. When Grant returned to Washington, Meade accompanied him, because the victor of Gettysburg had to testify before the Joint Committee on the Conduct of the War about Gettysburg. Here was an introduction for Grant to the political meddling and second-guessing that generals in the East had to learn to withstand. That Hooker was among Meade's critics may have endeared him even more to Grant, for Grant had dealt with Hooker during the Chattanooga campaign and found him to be a braggart.

Grant's experiences during his trip east helped him reach a critical decision. Initially he had assumed he would return to Tennessee to direct operations there. Once he had seen Washington for himself, however, he decided that he would come east, in large part to deal with the political interference that plagued operations there, although he had no intention of making the capital his headquarters. Nor would he put up with officers making their way to Washington to air their grievances: all passes for leave would have to go through headquarters.[6]

Grant began drawing up instructions for his generals in line with his overall strategic vision of conducting several campaigns simultaneously that targeted the two main Confederate field armies (the Army of Northern Virginia and the Army of Tennessee) as well as the logistical network of the Confederacy. During the next two months he conferred with generals, pushed forces to the front, and prepared to move during the first week of May. The only significant change Grant made was to bring east Philip H. Sheridan to command the Army of the Potomac's cavalry. Sheridan had seen action under Grant in the West before learning the trade of an infantry division commander. His reputation as a fighter led Grant to believe he could be of best service at the head of his cavalry.

Grant's ascension to general-in-chief caused Lee to reconsider his options for spring. At first he remained unsure whether the Union would concentrate its energies in the West (against Georgia or Longstreet's corps) or in Virginia. Apparently he did not contemplate simultaneous offensives in both theaters. Perhaps the Confederates might launch their own offensive in the West at the first sign that forces might be shifted away from Sherman. A victory "might entirely frustrate the enemy's plans by defeating him," Lee declared. Such a blow "will embarrass, if not entirely thwart the enemy in concentrating his different armies, and compel him to conform his movements to our own;" Success in the West would prevent Grant from concentrating against Richmond. Within days, however, he concluded that Grant would remain in the East, and that before long there would be another offensive against Richmond. Lee's instincts still inclined toward taking the offensive himself. If Davis approved, he proposed to move against Meade's army, provided Longstreet's divisions returned to Virginia and there was sufficient provisions and forage to supply the move. "If I am obliged to retire from this line," he added ominously, "either by a flank movement of the enemy or the want of supplies, great injury will befall us."[7]

That was precisely what Grant aimed to do. Over the next several weeks he modified his North Carolina proposal so that its essential concepts could be employed within the boundaries of Virginia while meeting the concerns of Lincoln and Halleck. He planned to take advantage of Union possession of Fort Monroe to form a new army, the Army of the James, with orders to move up the James River, debark between Richmond and Petersburg at Bermuda Hundred, and then penetrate inland, snapping the rail link between the two cities and threatening each of them. A second column would operate southward in the Shenandoah Valley, denying Lee the valley's resources and its use as a strategic highway. A third offensive, in southwest Virginia, would target the salt mines, lead works, and rail links. Finally, the Army of the Potomac would march south across the Rappahannock and Rapidan rivers, turn west, and hope to force Lee outside his prepared position along Mine Run, where Meade would try at best to beat him and at worse to pin him in place. Trapped, his logistical net eroding, and with Richmond threatened, Lee would be forced to do something, and whatever he did would be at great disadvantage.[8]

In years to come observers would speak of Grant's "strategy of attrition" in 1864, yet one look at this plan reveals that Grant did not look to grind away Lee's army in a series of bloody poundings. Rather, he hoped to slice at Lee's supply lines, and use an advance against Richmond to force the Confederate leader's hand. Perhaps Lee would rush to the capital's defense, with Meade in hot pursuit, hoping to catch the Rebels off balance; perhaps Lee would decide that he had to risk everything upon defeating Meade in open battle. In any case, Grant anticipated a war of maneuver, not head-on collisions.

The plan looked fine on paper, but executing it might be a challenge, in large part because Grant found himself bound by political considerations when it came to who would head the supporting columns—especially as 1864 was an election year. Nowhere was this more evident than along the James River and in the Shenandoah Valley.

After Grant, Benjamin F. Butler was the ranking Union general in Virginia, and the Democrat-turned-Republican politico headed the Army of the James. Renowned for his reputation as an administrator of occupied territory, he had displayed no skill as a field commander, and had enjoyed little opportunity in that regard. Grant tried to mitigate this by providing Butler with two corps commanders who reputedly knew their business. One of these was William F. Smith, who had helped Grant frame his initial thinking about how to approach operations in the East. In the Shenanadoah Valley Grant found himself saddled with Franz Sigel, an undistinguished general whose main value appeared to be the electoral clout he wielded through his German heritage.

In retrospect the appointment of these two generals to important positions due to their political importance in an election year proved disastrous, although their mere presence suggests that Grant did not possess the free hand often attributed to him: Lincoln's political needs merited heeding. Yet one can go too far with this explanation, for if these generals failed to perform their missions and Grant's offensive suffered as a consequence, many people in the North might wonder whether victory was as far off as ever and consider voting for someone other than Lincoln. Nor did keeping Butler in command ensure his political loyalty, for by summertime Butler would be knee-deep in intrigue against the administration. If what happened at the ballot box was influenced by what happened on the battlefield, Lincoln was taking a risk by entrusting military results to Butler and Sigel, whatever Grant's wishes might be.

In pondering what the Army of the Potomac might do, Grant considered moving by Lee's left, into central Virginia, or by his right, entering the Wilderness at the beginning of his march. Logistics played an important part in his decision. To strike towards Lee's left was to extend the Union supply lines along several railroads that would be vulnerable to Confederate raiders, most notably the detachment of partisan rangers led by John Singleton Mosby. By moving eastward across Lee's right, how-ever, Grant could establish railheads and supply depots along the Virginia coastline, using the Chesapeake to advantage. In the end, Grant chose the latter, although it was not due solely to logistical considerations, he later reflected. For he was new to the war in Virginia; he did not know the capabilities of the officers and men under his command. It would take him some time to appreciate their good qualities and understand their shortcomings. After all, the Army of the Potomac was not Grant's army either literally (it remained under Meade's command) or figuratively. It would take trial and error to learn about his generals. Some of the latter proved costly.[9]

THE OVERLAND CAMPAIGN

On May 4, 1864, the Army of the Potomac commenced yet another offensive. Two corps crossed the Rapidan-Rappahannock river network and entered the vicinity of the

Wilderness, west of the Chancellorsville battlefield. Grant hoped that he would be able to move at least two corps quickly through the thickets and undergrowth in this heavily-wooded area, which was haunted by the ghosts and human remains of the preceding spring. He preferred to meet Lee out in the open south and west of the Wilderness. The massive supply train slowed down the pace of march, while James H. Wilson fumbled his task of reconnaissance in his first experience as a commander of a cavalry division. Grant and Meade decided to slow down while everyone caught up. Observing the movement, Lee made ready to respond, dispatching two corps eastward along the road network while calling for Longstreet's corps to make haste to join them.[10]

The next morning lead elements of Richard Ewell's Second Corps encountered Gouverneur K. Warren's V Corps along the Orange Turnpike, running east and west through the Wilderness. Grant and Meade decided to break with their plan and fight Lee where he was. Within hours Ambrose P. Hill's Third Corps collided with first a division from John Sedgwick's VI Corps and then Winfield Scott Hancock's II Corps along the Orange Plank Road, which ran roughly parallel to the Orange Turnpike. Arriving from the north was the remainder of Sedgwick's corps and Ambrose Burnside's IX Corps, while Longstreet's First Corps approached from the west. Early on May 6 Hancock struck hard at Hill, forcing the Confederates back to a point where Lee himself attempted to rally his men. Fortunately for the Confederates, Longstreet arrived in time to stabilize the line; he then launched a counterattack that drove Hancock back. As dusk came the Confederates struck again, this time at the extreme Union right, bending it back and causing much chaos before running out of steam.[11]

Undeterred, Grant decided to move by Lee's right flank once more. This time the crossroads at Spotsylvania Court House was his target. If he beat Lee there and held onto his prize, he would have the inside road to Richmond, and that would force Lee to attack or to retreat. Lee responded rapidly. A combination of Confederate good fortune and a Union traffic jam resulted in the Confederates winning the race to the Spotsylvania crossroads. For the next ten days Grant shifted forces back and forth in an effort to find a weak point in Lee's line. He experimented with various offensive tactics designed to punch a hole through the Confederate defenses. Twice he came close to succeeding. Both times the blows were struck at the Confederate center, which took the form of a protruding salient that could be attacked from multiple angles. On the afternoon of May 10, a Union assault hit a weak point near the base of the salient. Emory Upton, the officer in charge of the attack column, had instructed his twelve regiments to rush forward without pausing to fire until they had broken through. The attack failed due to lack of support. Two days later, as dawn approached on May 12, Grant launched a massive assault against the Confederate center, with soldiers pouring forward through the fog and mist. This time good fortune smiled on the Federals. Lee, having previously directed his artillery away from the center, changed his mind and ordered them back just in time to be captured before they were unlimbered and in place. If the assault two days previous failed because too few men were involved, however, the assault of May 12 failed because too many men were crowded in a small piece of terrain. Initially the Yankees captured great numbers of Rebels as they bashed through the Confederate line. Once more Lee used his personal presence to rally his men, and the Confederates did what they could to hold off the attackers until a new defensive line was completed at the base of the salient. What followed was hour after hour of hellish combat, until the Confederates withdrew to the protection of their new position.[12]

Grant believed he had Lee right where he wanted him. On May 11 he informed Washington that he intended "to fight it out on this line if it takes all summer." Lee seemed pinned in place, helpless to lend assistance anywhere else. But Grant was frustrated by the slow responsiveness of some of his subordinates and the pervasive feeling still evident among some of his officers that Lee would prevail somehow. In the Wilderness he had whittled and smoked incessantly, not because Lee worried him, but out of impatience and concern about his own army's failure to respond quickly and energetically to his touch. By the end of the second day of combat, when an officer expressed concern that another Confederate attack bore all the signs of a Lee offensive, Grant had had enough. "Oh, I am heartily tired of hearing about what Lee is going to do," Grant snapped. "Some of you always seem to think he is suddenly going to turn a double somersault, and land in our rear and on both of our flanks at the same time. Go back to your command, and try to think what we are going to do ourselves, instead of what Lee is going to do." During the next two weeks he would have more cause for frustration as he saw more missed opportunities.[13]

Phil Sheridan gave Grant cause for some satisfaction. His troopers and Meade's infantry had become entangled on the march to Spotsylvania. The resulting chaos had cost just enough time to allow the Confederates to secure that town and its crossroads. The confusion caused much consternation at Union headquarters, climaxing with a confrontation between Meade and Sheridan. When Grant heard that Sheridan had declared that it would be best to let him loose to take on the Confederate cavalry and track down Jeb Stuart, he decided to give Sheridan a chance to prove himself. With some 10,000 troopers Sheridan swept around Spotsylvania and headed south toward Richmond on May 9. The following day Stuart led 4,500 horsemen to intercept the Yankees. On May 11 the two forces collided at Yellow Tavern, some six miles north of Richmond, and in the resulting clash Stuart fell mortally wounded. Although tempted to head toward Richmond, Sheridan swung east and south once more, linking up with Butler's Army of the James. Although the loss of Stuart damaged the Confederates, Sheridan's failure to return to Grant for some two weeks meant that Grant and Meade were short of cavalry to reconnoiter Confederate positions.

In the North people welcomed the news that at last Union forces had advanced after a battle in Virginia. After all, many onlookers had predicted that in this clash of titans Grant would prevail with one mighty blow. However, within a few days the reports of battle after battle frayed some nerves. As New York's George Templeton Strong put it, it was wise to be skeptical about whatever one heard at first, for "we are so schooled in adversity that we presume all good news apocryphal." Even so, reports remained optimistic, indeed "splendid beyond our hopes. But will it last?" Sure enough, several days later he observed that the prevailing mood was "despondent and bad. There is no news from the front to justify it, but people have taken up with an exaggerated view of Grant's hard-won success in opening the campaign," so any evidence that Lee was still in the field left them "disappointed, disgusted, and ready to believe any rumor of disaster and mischief that wicked ingenuity of speculators can devise and inculcate." Indeed just such an attempt was made the day after Strong wrote about it when speculators released to several papers a forged proclamation purporting to come from the president, calling for more troops in the wake of a disaster.[14]

As the two main armies faced each other at Spotsylvania, Grant's three other offensives in Virginia failed to achieve their objectives. Then the Union advance into southwest Virginia fizzled out, although it destroyed a bridge and nearly two dozen miles of railroad. The withdrawal of those forces, however, meant that the Confederates did not have to commit manpower to protect the area. Far more spectacular was Franz Sigel's abortive offensive. After marching slowly southward while fending off guerrillas and partisans, Sigel confronted John C. Breckinridge's tiny command, numbering a mere 5,335 men in all (against Sigel's 8,940) at New Market. Normally, Sigel would have been expected to attack, but when he did not, Breckenridge decided that the terrain favored launching his own assault. Aided by Sigel's mishandling of his men, Breckenridge carried the day. Sigel withdrew northward, and Breckenridge headed eastward to join Lee.

If matters in western Virginia were not going well for the Union, neither was there good news from the James River. On May 5, Butler commenced landing his command of some 26,000 men at Bermuda Hundred, located where the James and Appomattox rivers met. The Richmond and Petersburg Railroad was some seven miles away from the landing point. Petersburg was perhaps a ten-mile march, less if Butler seized City Point, on the south bank of the James a mile from Bermuda Hundred. Richmond itself was about fifteen miles away. It was the first time since July 1862 that such a large body of Union infantry was so close to the Confederate capital, which was lightly defended. Butler proved deliberate, even cautious, fortifying his position while launching tentative probes against the rail line and Petersburg. He also fell to arguing with his corps commanders, William F. Smith and Quincy A. Gillmore, and decided to await Grant's approach, giving the Confederates enough time to reinforce the Richmond defenses, with P. G. T. Beauregard taking command.

On May 13 Butler pushed against Confederate defenses at Drewry's Bluff south of Richmond. Beauregard wanted Lee to hurry down, detaching 15,000 men so Beauregard could dispatch Butler before turning on Grant. Jefferson Davis, heeding the recommendation of his newly-appointed adviser, Braxton Bragg, declined, urging Beauregard to go ahead with what he had at hand. On May 16 Beauregard did just that, driving Butler away from Drewry's Bluff. Butler regrouped his command at Bermuda Hundred, and Beauregard promptly erected fortifications that effectively sealed the Army of the James in a pocket. More Confederates marched north to reinforce Lee.[15]

Thus, within two weeks of crossing the Rapidan, Grant learned that all his other offensive moves had gone for naught. Confederate successes across the board meant that Lee would be reinforced instead of having to consider weakening his force or moving quickly to fend off a Yankee thrust. Newspaper correspondent Noah Brooks remarked: "The great public, like a spoiled child, refuses to be comforted, because Richmond is not taken forthwith, and because we do not meet with unbroken success at every point." As Benjamin B. French, commissioner of public buildings in Washington, DC, noted, "I begin to imagine that Grant is not going to beat Lee as easily as everyone seemed to suppose."[16] It was time to improvise.

Although most traditional accounts treat the opening battles of the Overland campaign separately, it is instructive to treat the Wilderness and Spotsylvania as one nearly-continuous engagement. Neither side achieved all each had desired. Grant's early wish to force Lee out into the open west of the Wilderness near the Mine Run battlefield had failed, and, despite repeated efforts, he had failed to deliver a deathblow to the Army of Northern Virginia. That should not minimize the significant damage he did inflict, however. By the end of the fighting at Spotsylvania Lee's losses were sizable, in the neighborhood of his losses at Gettysburg. That Grant had done this while learning the capabilities of a new army and its generals (and learning that they would not be as responsive to his orders as he might have wished) was notable. That the education was a costly one cannot be denied, for Grant lost some 36,000 men in two weeks.

The results were equally mixed for Lee. In contrast to Fredericksburg and Chancellorsville, he had not driven his opponent back across the Rappahannock-Rapidan boundary. Nor was his offensive skill what it had once been, and indeed he had been fortunate in several instances not to have suffered more. His losses had been substantial—at least 24,000 men killed, wounded, or missing. All three of his infantry corps commanders—the wounded Longstreet, the ailing Hill, and a fatigued and less than alert Ewell—had given way to replacements, while Stuart was dead. He would have to make do with new generals. Finally, Lee had not been able to get inside Grant's head and intimidate him as he had his predecessors. Grant's relentless determination was something new in a Union commander, and it was Lee who now had to adjust.

Only by setting these battles in the context of Grant's larger plan can one assess what happened during the first two weeks of campaigning. Grant had indeed retained the initiative, and Lee was pinned in place. However, the other three offensive thrusts planned by Grant had failed to achieve their objectives. Most importantly, they had failed to keep reinforcements away from Lee, and they had failed to force Lee to move quickly to protect his logistical network or Richmond. It made no sense to "fight it out on this line if it takes all summer" if nothing would be achieved by that. Grant would have to find another way to put pressure on Lee's rear. The Army of the Potomac would advance toward Richmond, forcing Lee to follow, whereupon Grant hoped to catch the Confederates out in the open.[17]

Thus opened the second phase of the Overland Campaign, with Grant moving ever closer to Richmond, trying to draw Lee out of his trenches. On May 19 Grant started moving again by Lee's right, shifting his supply depot southward. He sent one corps ahead as bait, hoping to lure Lee out into the open, but Lee chose instead to head toward the North Anna River, where he would set up a defensive line. When Grant pressed forward, securing several footholds on the south bank of the North Anna, Lee sensed an opportunity to spring a trap of his own. The Union flanks might be south of the river, but the center remained north of it; the river separated both flanks from the center. Having impressively fortified his position, Lee might now strike at either flank, secure in the knowledge that Grant would find it difficult to shift forces back and forth across the North Anna. But no attack came, and little evidence survives that one was planned, contrary to postwar accounts that only poor health prevented Lee from striking a telling blow.[18]

Grant contemplated what to do next. He had already sent orders to General David Hunter, who had replaced Sigel, to strike southward through the Shenandoah Valley toward Charlottesville and Lynchburg, where he could destroy the James River Canal and the nearby railroad. As for the Army of the Potomac, Grant at first favored breaking his pattern of moving across Lee's right, considering instead a move against Lee's left, where he could bear down on Richmond for the north, taking supplies via rail. Eventually, however, he gave in to Meade's preference to continue moving by the left, a decision made in the aftermath of a Meade temper tantrum in which he expressed frustration about being overshadowed by Grant and his army's performance being demeaned by others.[19]

Grant had expected a Confederate attack at North Anna. When none was forthcoming, he concluded that perhaps nearly three weeks of fighting had sapped the fighting spirit of the Army of Northern Virginia. Thus he pressed southward once more believing that one more blow might break the Rebel resolve. In order to increase the likelihood of success, he called for William F. Smith's XVIII Corps to leave Bermuda Hundred and come north via the Pamunkey River to reinforce the Army of the Potomac. By month's end the Yankees were six miles northeast of Richmond.

On June 1 Union and Confederate forces clashed at Cold Harbor, five miles northeast of Richmond. The Yankees gained control of this critical road junction. Encouraged, Grant decided to launch a major assault the next afternoon, only to have his will thwarted in a tangle of confusing orders and mistakes in direction. Grant postponed the attack until the early hours of the following morning, June 3. He left the planning of the assault itself to Meade.

Whether an assault on June 2 would have achieved a breakthrough is an open question; that the delay proved deadly is not. Lee's men used the extra time to refine and improve their fortification, establishing crossfires and protected areas that meant that the Union attackers would cross a killing field. At the same time, Union corps and division commanders failed to take advantage of the additional time afforded them to make adequate reconnaissance and other preparations, let alone provide for cooperation and coordination. Thus, when three Union corps advanced early on the morning of June 3, they were unable to exploit what precious little opportunity presented itself. Instead, Confederate fire proved so withering that Union soldiers hit the dirt, one way or another. By mid-morning it was clear that nothing could be done. Meade, exasperated by messages from subordinates who expressed a willingness to try again provided other commands supported them, snapped that each corps commander should proceed on his own. Once Grant realized what was happening, he directed Meade to call off the offensive.[20]

Grant had misread the situation. The Confederates were not on the point of breaking. Their failure to attack could be explained in other ways. Moreover, the inability of his subordinates to work together meant disaster. Unfortunately for his reputation and for understandings of the campaign, Cold Harbor became the prime count in the indictment of Grant as a mindless, heartless butcher who from the beginning had sought to wage a war of bloody attrition against Lee. Before long, exaggerated accounts of the battle had upwards of 7,000 Union soldiers killed or wounded in thirty minutes, a wild distortion in terms of time and casualties. Even then, Cold Harbor was not as bloody as Fredericksburg or the final Confederate assault at Gettysburg; it was not even as costly as the May 12 assault at Spotsylvania. Rather, it was the futility of the effort that stuck in people's minds.

CROSSING THE JAMES

Grant had taken a chance at Cold Harbor, and he had failed, and failed badly. The second phase of the campaign, forced on him to some degree by the failure of supporting offensives, was over. But the defeat did not deter him. Rather, Grant commenced in earnest to consider an idea that had been in his mind before the Overland Campaign had commenced, when he had requested that pontoons be ready to support a possible crossing of the James River. Now Grant decided that he would shift his army around Lee's right once more, but this time he would break contact, head south for the James, cross it, and strike at Petersburg. In short, now he would undertake what he had proposed the previous winter: cutting Richmond off from the south. Grant looked to Hunter to threaten Lee's lines of supply to the west, and dispatched Sheridan once more on June 7 to assist Hunter by attacking the Virginia Central Railroad and supply depots at Gordonsville and Charlottesville.

At the same time Robert E. Lee pondered his next move. Although his men had beat back the Yankee attackers at Cold Harbor, they still confronted an enemy just miles from the Confederate capital. "We must destroy this army of Grant's before he gets to the James River," he told Jubal Early. "If he gets there, it will become a siege, and then it will be a mere question of time." Yet he was also aware that to the west Hunter was making his way southward along the Shenandoah Valley, and if he reached Lynchburg, Richmond's logistical net would be compromised. At first he directed Wade Hampton, Stuart's successor as cavalry commander, to turn back Sheridan. Hampton succeeded in doing just that at Trevilian Station, southeast of Gordonsville, on June 11 and 12. Sheridan abandoned any notion of taking Gordonsville or Charlottesville or of linking up with Hunter. He had done next to nothing to the Virginia Central Railroad. Rather, he made his way back to Grant's army, although by the time he arrived he could not influence the outcome of operations at Petersburg.[21]

Lee did not rest content with this triumph. Even as he heard reports that a Union offensive had tested the Petersburg defenses on June 9, he decided that he would have to counter Hunter's drive through the Shenandoah. He ordered Early to take his corps (augmented by Breckinridge's Valley veterans) to take on Hunter. Should Early drive Hunter away, he should consider the feasibility of continuing northward though the valley, crossing the Potomac, and threatening Washington. That move had been successful in easing pressure on Richmond in 1862; perhaps it would work yet again. In ordering Early away, Lee acknowledged that he was placing Richmond at risk, but he saw no alternative, even as he reported that Grant's army was breaking contact and that he was not quite sure where it was going, although he named the James River as a probable destination.[22]

Thus in the immediate aftermath of Cold Harbor both Grant and Lee thought in daring ways. Grant would be open to a devastating attack from Lee if he did not skillfully manage his shift southward across the James, and so he hoped that Sheridan's raid would serve as a diversion as well as a way to bolster Hunter's efforts. Ironically, Lee's decision to counter Hunter and Sheridan with Early and Hampton stripped him of forces that he might have used to attack Grant, precisely because he was convinced that such an attack would be futile. The only question remaining was whether Grant could take advantage of Confederate weakness and confusion to strike a telling blow that would make the crossing of the James not only daring but also decisive.

An early mishap presaged what was to come. On June 9 Butler actually directed an assault on the Petersburg defenses, and the attackers were driven off after a brief but sharp clash. The blow was too light to promise victory yet heavy enough to telegraph a contemplated punch. Beauregard realized that the city's defenses were but weakly held and secured some reinforcements, but Lee remained where he was, still trying to divine Grant's next move. Meanwhile, Grant's men prepared new fortifications behind the Cold Harbor lines to serve as a defensive shield. On June 12—the same day Early received his orders from Lee—Grant's men began to move. Before long Lee responded by pressing forward, only to discover that the Yankees were gone and no one was quite sure where they were going.

On June 14, Smith's XVIII Corps, which had moved by water from White House down the Pamunkey and York, around Old Point Comfort, and up the James to Bermuda Hundred, started once more across the Appomattox. Meanwhile Winfield S. Hancock's bloodied II Corps crossed the James and moved west toward Petersburg. Although Grant had intended Hancock to link up with Smith and attack Petersburg, Hancock did not know this until the afternoon of June 15, by which time Smith had already started to make preparations—rather deliberate ones—for an assault. As dusk came Smith launched his attack, which enjoyed early success. However, Smith declined to follow up. Perhaps memories of Cold Harbor were fresh in his head; perhaps he believed that he was about to hit the lead elements of Lee's army; perhaps his poor health proved too much of an obstacle to overcome. Whatever was going to happen would have to happen the following day. Unfortunately, that proved to be too little, as neither Smith nor Hancock pressed forward vigorously. Meade came to the front, as did reinforcements, and another late afternoon attack enjoyed some early success. But by June 17 Beauregard had prepared new defenses, and those defenses were being filled by Lee's veterans, as Lee was now fully aware of Grant's thrust south across the James. The Union attackers were tired and their generals sick (Hancock seriously so, due to the aftereffects of his Gettysburg wound) or exhausted, and by June 18 it was evident that Petersburg would remain in Confederate hands for the time being.[23]

By the end of the third week of June, siege operations around Richmond were well under way. Critics of Grant's strategy would declare that he had spilled the blood of tens of thousands of young men to reach a position that McClellan had reached with far less cost of life two years before. That superficial similarity obscured real differences in the situation. In 1862, McClellan did not have as firm a hold on Richmond as Grant had at this time; while in 1862 Lee was in position to drive McClellan away, such an ambitious offensive was no longer an option. The Army of Northern Virginia had not been so much worn down through attrition as it was damaged from top to bottom. No longer could one argue that its generals were clearly superior to its counterparts; no longer could Lee launch devastating blows against the main Union field army. Unless Grant chose to abandon his efforts, they would result, sooner or later, in the fall of Richmond, so long as the Lincoln administration remained in power.

Yet Grant had reason to be less than satisfied with that result. He had failed to meet the high expectations in the North that spring. He had punished Lee, but at a high cost, and without decisive results. If he currently had Lee pinned against his own capital, it was not clear whether he could force the issue. To the undiscerning eye the stalemate simply continued. Lincoln understood as much. In mid-June he advised newspaper reporter Noah Brooks to "do all you can to correct the impression that the war in Virginia will end right off victoriously. To me the most trying thing in all of this war is that the people are too sanguine, they expect too much at once." For his part, the president would "be satisfied if we are over with the fight in Virginia within a year."[24]

EARLY'S RAID

Until election day, the best way Lee could break Grant's grip would be by forcing him to abandon his offensive in Virginia. It was unlikely that Grant would leave of his own volition. In turn that meant that the Confederates would have to create their opportunity elsewhere and create a crisis that might force Grant to respond. The most likely way to do this was to turn to that old favorite, the Shenandoah Valley. Stonewall Jackson's operations in the Valley in 1862 had compelled Lincoln to retain reinforcements earmarked for McClellan, which in turn fed McClellan's belief that he was fighting at a disadvantage and that his plan of campaign was being sabotaged by his own superiors. Threatening Washington had worked before; perhaps it would work again.

The opportunity was there. The very day that Grant's last assaults before Petersburg ground to a halt, General David Hunter tested the defenses of Lynchburg, Virginia, and found them too strongly held. Without too much thought, he decided to abandon his campaign. However, he chose to withdraw toward West Virginia, leaving open the route to the Shenandoah Valley and places north. Jubal Early wasted no time; by month's end he was halfway to the Potomac. On July 5 his men forded the river. Washington was not far away, and at the moment not many Union soldiers were in the area—Grant having drained the capital defenses for reinforcements in May.

It was just the move Lee had wanted Early to make. "I think I can maintain our lines here against General Grant," he had written Jefferson Davis in June. "He does not seem disposed to attack, and has thrown himself strictly on the defensive." Only the lack of supplies might force Lee to attack, something he claimed "I should not hesitate to do but for the loss it will inevitably entail" and the dire consequences that would attend defeat. Days later he added that he believed the best strategy was "to draw the attention of the enemy to his own territory. It may force Grant to attack me, or weaken his force." He was heartened to learn that a New York paper was puzzled as to the goal of Early's invasion: "It seems. . . . to have put them in bad temper as well as bad humour." The price of gold, often a barometer of public confidence, soared, indicating a heightened sense of war-weariness and lack of confidence in military prospects.[25]

Indeed, it was a close-run thing. Grant was not aware of Early's absence or location until July 4. Two days later he decided to send a division of the VI Corps up to Washington via Baltimore. That day Early was at Hagerstown, just north of Sharpsburg. Three days later, along the Monocacy River, a Union force of some 6,000 men cobbled together from various units tried to check Early's advance, but the best they could do was to delay it. That same day two more divisions of the VI Corps embarked on transports and headed toward Washington. They arrived on July 11, just as Early's men approached the Union capital from the north. So did the XIX Corps, fresh from New Orleans, which Grant had diverted from a planned landing at City Point. The sight of so many Yankees convinced Early that whatever opportunity he might have had to march down Pennsylvania Avenue had passed, and he withdrew the following day, recrossing the Potomac on July 14.[26]

Early's offensive was perhaps Lee's best chance to lift the siege of Richmond and Petersburg, but from the beginning it had been a long shot. Only the failure of Union intelligence to keep track of Early's location made victory possible. Even then, Grant's ability to use waterborne movement meant that he could shift forces more quickly over significant distances. Moreover, Early's move drew Grant's attention to securing the defense of Washington. Ever looking for the advantage in a situation, he welcomed the chance to catch part of Lee's army in the open. "We now want to crush out and destroy any force the enemy have sent north," he wired Halleck. "Force enough can be spared from here to do it."[27]

Early's withdrawal, therefore, came as unwelcome news to Grant. So did the failure of Union forces to track him down or work together to protect the capital. As Benjamin B. French saw it, the result was more of an embarrassment and a scare than anything else. According to French, "My friend Abraham has got to do something to retrieve this awful blunder or he is 'a goner!' " To make things worse, a few weeks later Early crossed the Potomac once more, entered Pennsylvania, and a Confederate detachment set fire to Chambersburg. The Confederate dash proved more embarrassing than threatening, but in an election year, embarrassing was bad enough.[28]

Early's thrust across the Potomac also distracted the northern public from Union successes in Georgia. "Our people—who are, as usual, more intent upon what passes around them than that at a more remote point—do not appear to realize the great importance of the successes which Sherman has achieved in the Southwest," correspondent Brooks observed. Atlanta was more important economically than Richmond, Brooks noted, although he conceded that "the moral effect of the political Capital of the Confederacy would be greater than would be the surrender of the economic Capital, at Atlanta doubtless is."[29] Nevertheless, in an election year, military appearances and public perceptions became political reality. If people believed the East was more important than the West, then, in some sense, it was, at least so far as Lincoln's reelection fortunes went.

IN THE TRENCHES AT PETERSBURG

As Early danced back and forth across the Potomac, it looked as if the stalemate at Petersburg would continue for the foreseeable future. Several early efforts by Union forces to improve their position and threaten Lee's supply lines led to insignificant results aside from extending the lines held by the opposing sides. Meanwhile, Grant struggled to resolve several problems in his command structure. It was evident that there was friction among his army and corps commanders in both the Army of the Potomac and the Army of the James, and William F. Smith was managing to stir up trouble in both armies with his criticism of Butler and Meade. Nor was Grant happy with the performance of Henry W. Halleck. The chief of staff remained openly skeptical of Grant's plan, taunting one aide by asking when Grant intended to take Richmond. However, he panicked as Early approached Washington and proved ineffective in managing the Union forces in the area. Grant contemplated trying to solve multiple problems by sending Meade to take charge at Washington. He also thought about putting William B. Franklin in command, and Lincoln may have suggested none other than George B. McClellan for the job. None of these proposals survived, and neither did Grant's effort to relegate Butler to a desk job at Fort Monroe, with a new general to be placed in charge of the Army of the James. There the political costs of offending Butler proved too onerous, especially at a time when Lincoln had just accepted the resignation of political rival Salmon P. Chase as secretary of the treasury and had pocket-vetoed a congressional Republican proposal for reconstructing southern civil governments. The only general who found himself without a job was the carping Smith, who had become too disruptive.[30]

As if these squabbles were not bad enough, Grant lost a chance to deliver a telling blow against Lee near Petersburg. A Pennsylvania regiment populated by miners proposed digging a tunnel below the Confederate fortifications, filling it with explosives, and blowing a hole in the Rebel line. Burnside, in whose corps the regiment served, approved the idea, and improved on it, directing Edward Ferrero to drill his division of black soldiers to exploit the opening created by the mine's detonation. Meade, by now skeptical of Burnside's abilities, was less than enthusiastic about the plot, Grant, willing to try anything, supported it, and laid the groundwork for success by making the mine part of a larger plan that would at least thin out the Confederate lines at the point of contact. Toward that end Grant directed Hancock and Sheridan to swing northward toward the Richmond defenses; although the advance made little progress, it did divert some Confederate forces away from Petersburg, just as Grant wished.

On the eve of the mine operation, however, Meade declined to authorize the use of the black division to lead the assault, arguing that the army risked coming under public criticism for using the blacks as cannon fodder should the assault fail. Grant agreed; Burnside decided to select the new spearhead division by letting his subordinates draw straws. As fate would have it, the choice fell upon Burnside's worst division commander, and when the mine was exploded early on the morning of July 30, the ensuing assault was botched and then repulsed. "It was the saddest affair I have witnessed in this war," Grant sadly remarked. "Such opportunity for carrying fortifications I have never seen and do not expect again to have." He had not exercised sufficient oversight of the operation, a mistake given that he knew how poorly Meade and Burnside worked together as well as Burnside's own shortcomings. Burnside soon joined Smith on the shelf.[31]

The next day, Grant met with Lincoln at Fort Monroe. The president was not interested in placing either Franklin or Meade in charge of the forces around Washington; the idea of naming McClellan to the spot went nowhere. Finally Grant proposed putting Phil Sheridan in charge, and Lincoln agreed. At first even this idea stalled, for Halleck proved obstinate, and Grant wavered. Intervening, Lincoln told Grant that nothing would "be done nor attempted unless you watch it every day, and hour, and force it." Thereupon Grant did just that. Grateful that Hunter, who was Sheridan's senior, willingly relinquished his department command, Grant placed Sheridan in charge, directing him go after Early and strip the Shenandoah Valley of provisions, forage, and livestock.[32]

It proved to be a long August for Grant. Gone were the chances of a spring victory; gone too were the opportunities briefly glimpsed during the first six weeks of besieging Richmond and Petersburg. It looked as if stalemate had prevailed again, at a time when the Lincoln administration desperately needed to convince voters that the president was on the right path. "Our slow progress, wretched finances, and difficult recruiting can be endured or remedied," observed George Templeton Strong; "but if the national backbone become diseased and degenerates into cartilage or gelatin, we are a lost people." But that was exactly what seemed to be happening. On the eve of the Democratic presidential convention, which convened at month's end, Strong concluded that "Lincoln manifestly loses ground every day. The most zealous Republican partisan talk doubtfully of his chances."[33]

While Sheridan prepared his army for offensive action, Grant tried once more to threaten Lee's supply line. Lincoln encouraged him, telling him, "Hold on with a bulldog grip, and chew and choke, as much as possible." However, Grant's next attempt to take a bite out of Lee's supply line by cutting the Weldon Railroad south of Petersburg proved costly, with one Union division nearly dissolving under the pressure of a Confederate counterattack. Days later another Confederate effort to drive the Yankees off the railroad dealt a serious blow to Hancock's II Corps, which had been worn down by months of combat. Although the Yankees held on to the railroad, the impact was simply to lengthen Lee's line of supply, not sever it completely. Thus, as the Democrats convened in Chicago to select their nominee for the fall presidential contest, they took stock of the military situation and framed a platform that declared the war a failure and called for an end to hostilities followed by a conference of the states which would restore the Union through peaceful means. With that done, they nominated George B. McClellan for president and looked forward with optimism to the coming campaign.[34]

Their joy was short-lived. On the day McClellan was nominated, Confederates failed to drive away Sherman's army at Jonesborough, Georgia. The following day, realizing that he could no longer hold onto Atlanta, John Bell Hood, commander of the Army of Tennessee, ordered an evacuation. Lead elements of Sherman's army occupied the city on September 2, and Sherman announced his victory to Washington. Although Hood had escaped to fight another day, most observers overlooked that in celebrating the capture of an important enemy city, an accomplishment long equated with victory. In this case, the fact that the victory was largely symbolic did not make it any less real. Sherman had basically already removed Atlanta from the board as a railroad hub, but its occupation signaled the end of strategic stalemate.

In the aftermath of Atlanta's fall, Lee found himself nearly helpless. This had not been the case in campaigns past, where Confederate successes in the East did much to conceal setbacks in the West. But Lee needed men. He recommended to Davis that all whites with the armies be pressed into combat service, leaving blacks to assume roles as "teamsters, cooks, mechanics, and laborers. . . . It seems to me that we must choose between employing negroes ourselves, and having them employed against us." For the moment that would be as close as he would come to recommending enlisting blacks as combat soldiers. He also pressed Davis to order that the exemption status of men be reexamined, for he was sure that people were shirking duty: "The time has come when no man capable of bearing arms should be excused, unless it be for some controlling reason of public necessity."[35]

The problem facing Lee and his fellow Confederate generals was one of time as well as resources. The capture of Atlanta had cast a pall over Confederate hopes that a war-weary northern public would turn away from Lincoln and elect McClellan president. Unless something happened in the next two months to reverse the sway of public opinion, Lincoln would be reelected. At first Grant did not realize that in fact it was up to the Confederates to reverse the momentum building in favor of

Lincoln's reelection in the aftermath of Atlanta's fall. Anxious to do something, he told Sherman, "We want to keep the enemy continually pressed to the end of the war. If we give him no peace whilst the war lasts the end cannot be distant."[36]

Sherman understood Grant's impatience, but he also doubted his ability to do much. He soon saw that Atlanta was something of an albatross around his neck, because Hood's army remained at large, a threat to cut his communications from Atlanta northward to Chattanooga. He began prodding Grant to allow him to march through Georgia to a point on the coast, leaving George H. Thomas behind to keep Hood in check. Although Grant eventually approved Sherman's plan, he made sure that Sherman would not commence his march until after the presidential election, lest some unforeseen disaster negate the political benefits of the fall of Atlanta.

As Grant and Sherman discussed Sherman's next move, Hood did his best to slice Sherman's rail connections northward from Atlanta to Chattanooga. Sherman had prepared for this by fortifying points along the railroad, which meant that what success Hood enjoyed in interrupting Sherman's communications was temporary and easily repaired. It soon became evident that while Hood could harass and annoy Sherman; he could not do more. Retreating into northern Alabama, Hood soon rethought his earlier efforts. Deciding to advance northward into Tennessee, he made preparations for such a strike—but he would not be able to move in force until after the November election. While Hood's offensive would eventually cause Grant some anxious moments, it would have been far better had Hood moved while the outcome of the election remained in doubt.

VICTORIES IN THE VALLEY

Thus, in the aftermath of Atlanta, there remained only two places where military events might reverse Union momentum: the Richmond-Petersburg front and the Shenandoah Valley. Lee knew he was not going to be able to dislodge Grant on his own: the Union commander would have to make a misstep or suffer a setback. His last chance resided with Jubal Early's men in the Shenandoah Valley. It would be Phil Sheridan's job to see that Early could not do in September and October what he had done during the summer.

Grant was growing impatient for Sheridan to act. He reminded Sheridan of the need to strip the valley bare so that the Confederates could no longer draw subsistence from it. He kept a careful eye on reports and rumors of the movements of Confederate forces between Lee and Early, seeking to ascertain when and where to strike next. Finally he could wait no longer. On September 15 he traveled to Sheridan's headquarters at Harpers Ferry. In his pocket he carried a plan of campaign. It remained there, for Sheridan assured his superior that he was now ready to move against Early's forces at Winchester. Grant thus left Sheridan to set his own plan in motion; by

September 19, he was back at City Point. That very day Sheridan struck at Early's line, and after some initial difficulty drove the Confederates through the town. The news cheered Grant, who celebrated as he had when he had heard of Atlanta's fall—by ordering an artillery salute.[37]

Sheridan pressed forward in pursuit of Early. On September 22 he struck again at Fisher's Hill. Once more Early folded under pressure; once more the Confederates abandoned the field; once more Confederates in the trenches around Richmond and Petersburg cowered as Grant's artillery celebrated the news of yet another victory. Grant himself then sought to add to the string of victories by thrusting to the north of the James, with Forts Harrison and Gilmer as the target, then attacking south against Lee's communications. The thrust above the James, while it made some progress, fell short of realizing Grant's hopes that perhaps Richmond itself might fall, whereupon Grant, believing that Lee must have shifted his forces north to meet the blow, hoped for more progress south of the James. He was to be disappointed again, but in the process Lee's lines grew thinner yet again. If it was not a resounding Union victory, one worth another cannonade, it was at least not a setback. Indeed, Grant believed that the fall of Richmond was not far away: "I believe the enemy look upon the city as doomed."[38]

As Grant was testing Lee's lines, Sheridan was laying waste to the Shenandoah Valley, while Early could do little more than fret at him. By early October Grant believed that before long Sheridan would be able to return two infantry corps to the Richmond-Petersburg front, men who were sorely needed if there was to be another offensive against Lee's army. He even contemplated an amphibious strike against Savannah to help Sherman out.[39]

Fortunately for Grant, the political signs favored Lincoln's reelection, freeing the general from having to take any risks or order an immediate offensive. On October 11 voters in Indiana, Ohio, and Pennsylvania cast their ballots in a series of state contests, with the Republicans emerging victorious. As these contests were fairly good predictors of what would happen in November, the administration could rest somewhat easier, and so could Grant, who was preoccupied with negotiating with Sherman as to the latter's planned march and pondering how to deal with Hood's army. Affairs in Virginia offered far less cause for concern. Although Sheridan did not act on Grant's request to cut the Virginia Central Railroad near Charlottesville and passed on his superior's request to do damage to the James River Canal, he did a fairly thorough job when it came to stripping the Shenandoah of its resources. That done, the feisty cavalryman visited Washington to confer with Stanton and Halleck about what to do next.

Sheridan returned to Winchester on the night of October 18. The next morning he headed southward to rejoin his army, which was encamped along the banks of Cedar Creek some twenty miles to the south. Soon he could hear the sounds of battle raging in the distance, but didn't know their source. Exploiting weaknesses in the deployment of Sheridan's army, Jubal Early had launched a surprise attack at dawn, driving the Yankees some distance away. Sheridan galloped southward, and by the time he encountered his army at 10:30 a.m., his men had already rallied and were holding off the Confederate attackers. Early's attack had lost momentum as many of his men stopped to loot the camps they had captured and partake of the still-warm breakfasts that had been prepared. The pause proved fatal; having achieved surprise and initial success, Early and his generals were unable to exploit their advantage. By mid-afternoon Sheridan and his subordinates were ready for revenge, and before long the Confederates had been driven away. Although Sheridan did not destroy Early's army, his victory at Cedar Creek eliminated it as a serious threat. The Shenandoah Valley was no longer a major Confederate strategic asset.[40]

The great value of Sheridan's victory was in its dramatic nature. Stories soon spread describing how he had single-handedly rallied a shattered and demoralized force before striking a decisive blow. Once more Grant greeted the news by ordering several more hundred-gun salutes; once more the Confederates ducked and covered their ears. Cedar Creek capped Sheridan's efforts in the Shenandoah, and removed it once and for all from Lee's bag of tricks. Yet Grant failed to exploit the victory as he might have. Although he mounted yet another operation against Lee's flanks as October drew to a close, it did not amount to much. Once more Union infantry was stopped short of its objective—in this case the South Side Railroad, running west from Petersburg south of the Appomattox River—while Grant's feint north of the James never amounted to any more than a diversion. This was in part because Grant had taken care to ensure that there would be no unnecessary or costly attacks by instructing Benjamin Butler not to assault fortified positions. By now a pattern was evident: Grant would strike at one of the Confederate flanks, and then hold on against a Confederate counterattack. Sometimes he would feint toward one flank to divert Confederate forces from his true target at the other end of the line. Each time some progress was made, but it fell far short of the sort of dramatic victory Grant dearly desired. In reporting the setback Grant underplayed his frustration with the result; nor did he chastise Sheridan when that general once more refused to comply with his request to strike at the James River Canal and the Virginia Central Railroad.[41]

If Grant seemed frustrated, at least he knew that as election day approached that the recent success of Union arms had gone a long way towards assuring Abraham Lincoln's reelection. For Robert E. Lee, the past two months had been a vast disappointment, with Lee unable to do much to change the outcome. He could not have strengthened Early very much without weakening his own lines to the breaking point, and he was far too weak to mount a substantial offensive himself. "The inequality is too great. . . . I always find something to correct on the lines," he told

Jefferson Davis, "but the great necessity . . . was the want of men."[42] If he had fended off Grant's efforts to attack his flanks, he realized that he had still failed to relax Grant's grip on Petersburg. Moreover, he had at last lost the Shenandoah Valley, which had been essential to him in so many ways.

And then, on November 8, came the final blow. It was delivered not by Grant's army in combat but by voters in the North and in the ranks of the Union armies. Abraham Lincoln had won reelection by a decent popular majority and an overwhelming victory in the electoral college. The war would continue. Lee's hope that he could demoralize northern will through frustrating Grant proved futile; although he had thwarted Grant's efforts to win a decisive battlefield victory in 1864, he had failed to reverse the tide of events elsewhere. What could he do now?

SEVEN

TO APPOMATTOX

With the reelection of Abraham Lincoln in November 1864 the Civil War entered a new phase. Confederate strategy throughout 1864 had been predicated upon wearing down support for the war in the North, leading to Lincoln's defeat. With the president's triumph at the polls, it was hard to see exactly how the Confederacy could win the war outright. One might more persuasively reason that continued conflict could lead to better terms of capitulation. Still, if the Confederacy continued to hold out, something might happen which would cause the Union to give up the fight short of complete victory, although what that event might be remained elusive.

Moreover, with the November election now a thing of the past, it was no longer morale in the North but within the Confederacy that was critical. Would Confederates continue to think that this was a war worth waging? Victory seemed further off than ever. Union armies were now in the Confederate heartland, turning more of what was once homefront into battlefront. It was harder to move troops and supplies from place to place, and Confederate numbers were dwindling. Did the Confederacy possess both sufficient means and ample will to persist?

William T. Sherman meant to find the answer. For two months after the capture of Atlanta he pondered exactly what to do. He quickly discovered that he could not bring John Bell Hood's Army of Tennessee to bay, and that so long as he held onto Atlanta, his logistical link to the North through Chattanooga remained slender and vulnerable. Atlanta itself, once the goal of his operations, was now an albatross around his neck. He hit upon the notion of cutting through the Confederacy yet again, this time by marching through Georgia's interior to the Atlantic coast. The simple sight of a Union army marching unopposed through the Confederacy might strike a devastating blow against Confederate morale, and would deprive foraging soldiers of needed food and livestock.

At first Grant wanted Sherman to take care of Hood prior to embarking upon a new campaign, but before long he was convinced that so long as Sherman left behind enough men to keep an eye on Hood, he could do as he pleased. In agreeing to Sherman's plan Grant made explicit the link between Sherman's operations and his own, eradicating the boundary that once separated the Eastern and Western theaters. In targeting Savannah, Sherman would capture from land a city Union forces had long observed from sea. The next stop would be a movement north to join forces with Grant himself.[1]

As for Grant's own operations in Virginia, with the presidential election having come and gone, it was at last simply a matter of time before he would occupy Richmond and Petersburg. Gone was the need to produce dramatic results in a timely fashion with an eye on public opinion in the North. There was no need to take any risks or suffer any severe losses. Grant decided that it was best not to renew offensive operations against Lee for the winter. Better to keep the Army of Northern Virginia pinned in place while offensive operations unfolded elsewhere. Key among these operations were Sherman's march through Georgia and an effort to take Wilmington, North Carolina, that would close the last major Confederate port on the Atlantic coast. At the same time Grant kept a watchful and increasingly worried eye on Hood's army as it invaded Tennessee. Anxious to see Hood stopped, he urged George H. Thomas to take action, but delays in gathering and supplying a sufficient force along with bad weather postponed Thomas's offensive until mid-December, just as an increasingly impatient Grant started to go west to relieve Thomas personally. However, when news came of Thomas's smashing victory, Grant returned to Virginia.

Whereas Thomas's triumph at Nashville came as Sherman reached the outskirts of Savannah, the effort to take Wilmington suffered a serious setback, thanks in large part to the presence of Benjamin F. Butler. Much to Grant's displeasure, the Massachusetts general accompanied the expedition to take Fort Fisher, some twenty miles downriver of Wilmington at the mouth of Cape Fear River. He hoped to reduce the fort by packing an old frigate with explosives, towing it near the fort, and then setting it off. As impressive as the explosion was when it came on the day before Christmas, it left no impact, and when Admiral David D. Porter's flotilla failed to reduce the sand-and-dirt fortification, Butler decided to withdraw his men from their beachhead. Furious, Grant, now freed from political considerations, secured Butler's removal, and then charged General Alfred Terry with taking the fort. This time the naval bombardment did its work, enabling Terry's men to storm the fort on January 15 and overrun its defenders. The Union victory shut off the final remaining Confederate port, although it would not be occupied for another five weeks.[2]

Thus, as January drew to a close, the eastern Confederacy was sealed off from Europe. Savannah was in Union hands, and it was only a matter of time before Charleston and Wilmington suffered the same fate. After first considering shipping Sherman's forces north from Savannah, Grant decided to let them make their way by foot. Sherman was putting the finishing touches on preparations for his next march, this one through the Carolinas. Ahead of him were scattered Confederate forces; meanwhile, Grant maintained his bulldog grip on Lee. Together these Union armies were poised to crush what remained of the Confederacy in the Eastern Theater.

Robert E. Lee was not quite ready to concede defeat. Less than two weeks after Lincoln's reelection he was busy contemplating "striking Grant a blow." Whether he had enough men to do just that was another question entirely. Replying to requests for forces to help defend South Carolina, he observed that if he weakened his force to any significant extent, he would have to yield Richmond to Grant: "It will be impossible for me to send sufficient troops from this army to oppose Sherman and at the same time resist Grant." As one way to remedy his manpower shortage, he called for the more systematic collection of supplies, and he wanted to do what he could to shore up his forces from desertions; otherwise, "I apprehend dire results."[3] At the same time, he resisted efforts to increase his military authority, only to find himself confirmed as general-in-chief as February opened. It did not matter. Lee still lacked enough men to act, although he was rather vague as to what he wanted to do in any case.

With Lincoln's reelection, the premise of Lee's strategic planning—that of the need to erode northern morale in order to secure a negotiated peace that would recognize Confederate independence—was rendered problematic. He had failed to turn the tide in Virginia. Early's efforts to threaten Washington had fallen short, and now he was on the verge of conceding control of the Shenandoah Valley to Phil Sheridan's forces. Nor was there any easy way to wriggle free from Richmond and Petersburg. With the advent of winter supplies were running short and roads were in bad condition. Even if Lee evacuated the Confederate capital, what could he do to reverse the momentum of events? Better to remain in place, weather the siege for a few more months, and gather supplies so that when he finally moved, his army (or what was left of it) could eat as it marched along dry, clear roads.

Besides, there were people who wanted to explore a different ending to hostilities through negotiation. In January 1865 Francis P. Blair, a wizened Democratic politico whose political career dated back to the days of Andrew Jackson, journeyed to Richmond to propose to Jefferson Davis that both sides reach an armistice, followed by a joint military expedition to oust the French from Mexico. Apparently fighting side-by-side in a common cause would rekindle feelings of reconciliation and reunion.

Davis rejected the scheme, but he could not so easily set aside the wishes of those in his own government, led by Vice President Alexander H. Stephens, who wanted to see for themselves what sort of settlement they might negotiate. Stephens led a three-man delegation to Hampton Roads, Virginia, where Lincoln agreed to meet them. Fresh from securing congressional passage of a proposed Thirteenth Amendment to abolish slavery—the "king's cure" the president had long sought—Lincoln proved most flexible on how reunion and emancipation were to be realized, so long as they were the basis of any settlement. However, the Confederate representatives were not quite willing to give up the fight yet, and Davis certainly was not.[4]

The generals got into the act at the end of February. By that time prisoner exchanges had resumed, and Edward O. C. Ord, who had replaced Butler as commander of the Army of the James, was meeting with James Longstreet, who had returned to active duty after recovering from his Wilderness wound. The two prewar friends soon wondered whether there was some way for them to bring this all to an end. Perhaps the process could be initiated by Louise Longstreet and Julia Dent Grant, who were cousins, exchanging social visits (which would have meant that Mrs. Grant would have entered Richmond and Petersburg before her husband). Grant had little use for the notion of spousal diplomacy, although the idea gained enough traction among the Confederate high command that Mrs. Longstreet was ready to go. Days later Lee wrote Grant, suggesting that it might be a good idea if the two commanders met to consider "the possibility of arriving at a satisfactory adjustment of the present unhappy difficulties by means of a military convention" so as to leave "nothing untried which may put an end to the calamities of war," Grant forwarded the message to Washington and requested instructions. Back came word from Lincoln through Stanton that he should not enter into any negotiations except for Lee's surrender, and that it would be up to others to determine the resolution of political questions.[5]

One reason both sides had so much time to talk was that neither really wanted to break winter quarters yet. The roads were not in any condition for Lee to stage an evacuation of the Confederate capital, and it was not clear where the Army of Northern Virginia would go in any case. It was extremely unlikely that the Confederates would break Grant's grip: the best they could hope for was to slip through his fingers. Aware that when spring came and the roads dried Lee would move as quickly as he could, Grant contemplated how to cut him off. In February he moved to sever yet another Confederate supply link, the Boydton Plank Road. Once more the two armies clashed near Hatcher's Run. This time Union forces prevailed, even though they did not reach the road. Grant's grip had tightened again. Meanwhile he looked to Sheridan to complete clearing the Valley of Confederates, pursuing what remained of Early's army, and coming down to join Grant's armies. If he could also destroy the James River Canal and the Virginia Central Railroad, so much the better. Grant had been after Sheridan to cut those Confederate supply links for some time, but it was not until March that Sheridan complied with the request, and when he did so, he ignored Grant's preference that he continue southward and sever more rail links before joining with Sherman in North Carolina. The fiery cavalryman wanted to rejoin Grant and be in at the kill.[6]

Thus both sides were waiting for the weather to improve, with Grant concerned that Lee might make a break for it, and Lee growing ever more anxious to do just that. For weeks the Confederate commander read with dismay reports of Sherman's marching northward towards Richmond. No sooner had Lee been named general-in-chief in February 1865, than he reinstalled Joseph E. Johnston as commander of the Army of the Tennessee. He argued that the best chance the Confederacy had for victory was to unite the two remaining field armies and seek to beat back the Yankee forces one at a time, "as separately they do not seem able to make head [way] against the enemy." But nothing happened. No one heeded his recommendations to pursue a scorched earth policy to deprive Sherman's soldiers and Schofield of supplies as they made their way through the Carolinas; nor did there seem to be much haste to comply with his recommendations to shift supplies to Lynchburg in anticipation of Richmond's evacuation.[7]

It was left to Sherman's men to do the burning and destroying, although exactly who was responsible for Columbia, South Carolina, going up in flames remained a matter of dispute. With the South Carolina state capital in Union hands, Charleston fell to Union forces. The cradle of secession was feeling the impact of Union anger. Confederate desertions mounted, especially from North Carolina units. Lee concluded that letters from home from people "very despondent as to our success" induced men to leave. Lee's efforts to remedy his manpower shortage by turning to enlisting blacks had not borne much fruit, either. Only in the appointment of Johnston did he get his way.[8]

As long as Lee's strength dwindled through desertion, Grant saw no need to mount an ambitious offensive operation until the weather improved. He hoped Lee would stay just where he was. He explained to Meade at the beginning of March that to attack the Confederate intrenchments around Richmond and Petersburg "is not worth the risk to be run." Better to allow Sherman and Sheridan to complete their campaigns without worrying about encountering Lee.[9] But once the temperature rose and the roads dried, Grant had to be ready to move, lest Lee get the jump on him.

The Confederate chief offered a realistic assessment of the Confederacy's military situation, declaring that "it is full of peril and requires prompt action." However, he was not surprised by what confronted him. "While the military situation is not favorable, it is not worse that the superior numbers and resources of the enemy justified us in expecting from the beginning," he told Secretary of War John C. Breckinridge. "Indeed, the legitimate military consequences of that superiority have been postponed longer than we had reason to anticipate. Everything in my opinion has depended and still depends upon the disposition and feelings of the people." That said, he did not believe that holding on to cities staved off defeat. "The greatest calamity that can befall us is the destruction of our armies," he wrote Davis. "If they can be maintained, we may recover from our reverses, but if lost we have no resource."[10]

Whatever had to happen had to happen quickly. Lee could not wait for Sherman to reach Grant's army: he would have to evacuate his position and move to join Johnston. He targeted Burkeville Junction, west of Richmond and Petersburg, as a point upon which his forces would unite. Meanwhile he kept a watchful eye on Grant's efforts to extend his left westward around Petersburg. Should the Union lines continue to stretch westward, Lee would have to thin out his defenses or counterattack before Union forces blocked his route to Burkeville.[11]

One way to thwart Grant's movements was to strike Union lines near City Point. Any success might force the Union commander to shift forces back to protect his supply depot, thus contracting his lines and opening the way for Lee to move west and south to join Johnston. On March 25 the Confederates launched an assault against Fort Stedman, just south of the Appomattox River, at the right end of Union fortifications opposite Petersburg. The idea was to punch a hole in the Union line, then broaden the gap by turning right and left. If all went well, Confederate cavalry might head toward City Point itself. Not only was that the location of Grant's massive supply base, it was also where one could find Abraham Lincoln, the president having just come down to confer with his commanding general and get away from Washington for a while.

The timing of the assault seemed perfect, for Grant had just issued orders for an offensive thrust against Lee's extreme right south of Petersburg. If successful, the Confederate attack would disrupt these plans. However, the Confederate thrust, despite enjoying some initial success, soon sputtered, and a Union counterattack quickly regained what had been lost. Lincoln himself rode out to see what had happened. He reported to Stanton that his son Robert, now a captain on Grant's staff (the better to keep him out of harm's way) "just now tells me there was a little rumpus up the line this morning, ending about where it began."[12]

A disheartened Lee informed Davis of the failure at Fort Stedman. "I fear now it will be impossible to prevent a junction between Grant and Sherman, nor do I deem it prudent that this army should maintain its position until the latter shall approach too near," he told his civil superior. Meanwhile he estimated Johnston's army as some 13,500 strong, with that number dwindling due to desertion. Together Grant and Sherman would outnumber Lee and Johnston by close to 100,000 men. The import of these numbers was obvious, but Lee rested content with concluding that he had laid this information before Davis, "knowing that you will do whatever may be in your power to give relief."[13]

Grant intended to give Lee no rest. For months he had hoped that Lee would stay just where he was. He explained to Meade at the beginning of March that to attack the Confederate intrenchments around Richmond and Petersburg "is not worth the risk to be run." Better to allow Sherman and Sheridan to complete their campaigns without worrying about encountering Lee. By mid-March, however, plans were taking shape for another swing around the Confederate right, with Sheridan spearheading an effort to break the South Side and Danville railroads. "I am anxious to have Lee hold on where he is a short time longer so that I can get him in position where he must lose a great portion of his army," Grant explained to his father.[14]

Sheridan's sweep westward toward Burkeville and the railroads would place Lee in a difficult position. However, whether the scope of the operation would expand beyond that depended on events. Grant told Sherman that while at the start he had "no distinct view further than holding Lee's forces from following Sheridan," he would ride to the front and "take advantage of anything that turns up." If Lee sent a force to pursue Sheridan or vacated his lines, Grant would attack the Confederates out in the open. Finally, on March 24, he issued orders outlining the operation, which would commence March 29. Two infantry corps would support Sheridan's cavalry. Grant would thin his lines and redeploy his men to hold his fortifications. The action at Fort Stedman had no effect on his planning, although it alerted him that the Confederates were finally ready to act.[15]

In directing his generals, Grant made it clear that he did not intend to attack Lee in his intrenchments. Rather, he hoped to force the Confederates out of their fortifications and engage them in open combat. Before long, however, he detected that perhaps Sheridan needed to swing out all the way to Burkeville. "I now feel like ending the matter if possible to do so before going back," he told Sheridan. Better for the cavalryman to take on the Confederate right flank and see how much of Lee's line they could gobble up. Bad weather on March 30 threatened to delay the movement, but Sheridan insisted that he could forge ahead, and Grant consented, relieved that at last one of his generals was not eager for an excuse to hold back one more day. That was fortunate, for Grant had contemplated a frontal assault against the Petersburg lines in the belief that Lee must have weakened them to counter Sheridan.[16]

By March 31 the Confederates had moved out in force to counter Grant's movement. George E. Pickett established a defensive position at a road junction called Five Forks, several miles west of the end of Confederate fortifications. To the east of that junction the Confederates mounted a series of attacks in an effort to drive back threats to their right flank, with Gouverneur Warren's V Corps taking as much as it could handle. Eventually Warren placed his men astride White Oak Road, thus isolating Pickett from the main Confederate line. Unaware of this, Pickett's men and Confederate cavalry roughly handled Sheridan's horsemen, driving them back, but failed to capture Dinwiddie Court House, possession of which remained essential for Union success in moving men to the left. That evening Warren dispatched infantry to help Sheridan, and Pickett prudently withdrew to Five Forks. Lee, after all, had told him to hold the junction at all hazards to prevent Grant from curling around the Confederate right, severing the remaining rail lines, and threatening his line of retreat.

April 1 dawned with Lee contemplating an attack against Grant's fortifications to force the Union general to pull back to his lines. Nothing happened. Meanwhile, Sheridan's cavalry and Warren's infantry converged on Five Forks. In a reversal of classic tactics, Sheridan's horsemen would deal with the Confederate center and right at Five Forks, while Warren was given the job of working around Pickett's left and in the process isolating Pickett from Lee.

It was George Pickett's bad fortune to choose this day to conduct a shad bake with several of his generals, including cavalry commander Fitzhugh Lee, nephew of the commanding general. Thus they were not at the front when Sheridan and Warren struck. It was Warren's misfortune that he moved his corps into position to attack what Sheridan had told him would be the Confederate position, only to discover that the Confederates were no longer there. As a result, Warren's three divisions lost formation, and their corps commander scrambled to rectify that problem. With Warren off to find one division, Sheridan wheeled the other divisions into an assault on Pickett's line, breaking it. Pickett pulled back what remained of his command, leaving Five Forks to Sheridan. The Confederate line was now compromised, and before long it would collapse. Even so, Sheridan, furious with Warren's performance, relieved him of command, an act that seemed astonishing at the time and remained controversial for decades to come. In truth, Sheridan overreacted and acted harshly, for whatever Warren's previous shortcomings as a corps commander, he did not deserve removal for his actions that day. Nevertheless, the message was loud and clear: this time even perceived mistakes would not be tolerated.[17]

The news of Five Forks was disastrous to Confederate prospects. Grant's taking of Dinwiddie Court House, Lee told Davis, "seriously threatens our position": Richmond and Petersburg were in danger. If Grant proceeded to cut the South Side and Danville railroads, it would be necessary to evacuate. With Five Forks in Union hands, the South Side Railroad was vulnerable. Lee believed he could not hold his lines past the evening of April 2. Even so, he hoped that afternoon that in advancing "the enemy might expose himself in some way that we might take advantage of, and cripple him." Given what Lee had already said about the relative strength of the two armies, it is difficult to see how he could cling to that notion, and in any case he did not do so for long. At last he told Davis directly what he had tried to argue all along: "I think it is absolutely necessary that we should abandon our position tonight."[18]

Grant launched an assault against the Petersburg lines that day. He might have been better advised to continue swinging left to block Lee's routes to the southwest, but he surmised that the Confederates were already stretched to the breaking point. Throughout the day, the Confederates struggled to resist the advancing Union forces, but it was not long before Union infantry stood astride the South Side Railroad and was pushing forward toward Petersburg. Here and there the defenders managed to check the Union advance, but at best it was a delaying action until nightfall. At that time Lee planned to evacuate both Richmond and Petersburg and head west to Amelia Court House to pick up supplies, and then turn southward to link up with Johnston.

For the Confederates, the next three days were a series of disappointments and delays that presaged disaster. Not all of the bridges spanning the Appomattox River that Lee had counted on for his withdrawal were in useable condition, creating traffic jams and delays. Upon arriving at Amelia Court House, along the Danville Railroad, on April 4, Lee discovered that the supplies he had hoped would be waiting for him there had not yet arrived. The time spent in gathering together and resupplying the Army of Northern Virginia proved crucial, for by the time Lee was ready to move toward Burkeville he learned that Union forces were poised to block his advance at Jetersville, midway between Amelia Court House and Burkeville, with the latter about to fall into Union hands. The route to North Carolina was no more.[19]

That Union forces were already at Jetersville was due to Grant's determination to pursue Lee and cut off his line of retreat. To conduct a successful pursuit, one needed not to follow a retreating foe, but to get ahead of his retreat. Thus Grant entered Petersburg on April 3 only long enough to meet with Lincoln and to issue orders for a pursuit. It would be left to other Union forces, led by black soldiers, to enter Richmond itself, which by that time was in flames due to fires set by the retreating Confederates. Reporting the result to Sherman, Grant remarked: "This Army has now won a most decisive victory and followed the enemy. That is all it ever wanted to make it as good an Army as ever fought a battle."[20]

Yet even that would no longer suffice: it was time to bring Lee to bay one final time. By April 5, just as Lee was pulling his command together, lead elements of Edward O. C. Ord's Army of the James reached Burkeville. Grant himself was at Jetersville. Lee thus had no choice but to continue to move west to Farmville, where once more he would try to avoid Grant's advance and head for Danville, from where he might try again to head to North Carolina.

Once more Grant had to make sure to keep the pursuit going. Meade advocated advancing upon Amelia Court House; Sheridan, realizing that such a move would end up following Lee rather than heading him off, wanted to move due west once more. Grant directed Sheridan to move as he pleased, but, aware that an ailing Meade might be a bit touchy about giving in to Sheridan, allowed Meade to send his infantry on to Amelia Court House. Fortunately, Meade soon learned of Lee's withdrawal, and he decided to move westward in an effort to cut him off as well.

On April 6 Lee's army nearly unraveled altogether. As it moved westward, various commands lost contact with each other, opening gaps that could be readily exploited by pursuing Federals, as they did at Sailor's Creek, less than ten miles east of Farmville. That afternoon, John B. Gordon, in charge of what was left of the Confederate II Corps, barely fended off Andrew A. Humphreys's II Corps to protect the Confederate wagon train, while to the southeast Horatio Wright's VI Corps and Sheridan's cavalry closed in on Richard Ewell's command, nearly swallowing it up whole. Coming upon what was left of Ewell's forces, Lee gasped, "My God! Has the army dissolved?" To a large extent, it had.[21]

Elsewhere that day Lee's army had fended off Federal threats rather easily, and before long Lee looked to concentrate his army at Farmville, where, resupplied, he could prepare his next move. Danville seemed an impossible goal, but moving westward toward Lynchburg via Appomattox Court House did not. More supplies would be waiting for Lee at Appomattox Station, and from there he could continue his retreat and look for a place where he would be safe.

Grant continued to move on, having informed Sherman that "Rebel Armies now are the only strategic points to strike at." Even as Humphreys and Wright jabbed at Lee's rear, Grant moved with John Gibbon's XXIV Corps (part of Ord's army) and the V Corps (now commanded by Charles Griffin, who replaced Warren), as Sheridan's horsemen fanned out ahead. The cavalryman had informed Grant in the aftermath of Sailor's Creek that "if the thing is pressed I think Lee will surrender." By April 7 he had entered Farmville on Lee's heels. At that time Grant opened negotiations with Lee for the surrender of Lee's army, informing his opposite number that the events of the last week "must convince you of the hopelessness of further resistance."[22]

Victory seemed so close. Lincoln could sense it: upon reading Sheridan's dispatch describing the triumph at Sailor's Creek, the president wired Grant, "Let the *thing* be pressed." Grant needed no such urging, and in any case Lee's response to his letter gave little room for hope, for the Virginian did not share his own sense of the hopelessness of further resistance. Perhaps Lee was simply buying time; perhaps he was slow to come to terms with what was happening. For the moment, he was willing to inquire what terms Grant might offer.[23]

The pursuit continued on April 8. Grant replied to Lee's query by outlining rather simple terms. Lee snapped that he did not intend to propose the surrender of his army (rendering curious his interest in what terms Grant might offer) and declared that he did not think "the emergency has arisen to call for the Surrender of this army." Nevertheless, while he would not meet Grant to surrender his army, he would meet to discuss "as far as your proposal may affect the C. S. forces under my command & tend toward the restoration of peace." This formulation suggested that Lee was avoiding the issue even as he was slowly coming to accept the result, provided it came under some name other than surrender.[24]

Unknown to Lee, the emergency had indeed arisen. On April 8 Sheridan's cavalry reached Appomattox Station and captured Lee's supplies. Griffin and Gibbon were close on his heels, and they were now approaching Appomattox Court House, where Lee arrived that afternoon. Meanwhile, Humphreys and Wright kept nipping at Lee's heels. Since the commencement of the campaign, Lee had lost over half of his army to battle and desertion, and of the 25,000 or so who remained, only a third were armed. Most people would define that situation as critical, even an emergency, regardless of what Lee said.

Evidently the Confederate commander needed vivid evidence of his situation. It appeared on April 9. Early in the morning, Confederate infantry approached Union cavalry, and prepared to disperse it, when suddenly the Yankee horsemen gave way, revealing the presence of Griffin and Gibbon blocking the Confederate advance. Humphreys and Wright were moving up behind the Rebel rear. The end had come: as Lee put it, "there is nothing left for me to do but to go and see General Grant, and I would rather die a thousand deaths."[25]

The war in the East was over.

AFTERWORD

Many people believe that the Civil War was won in the West. Much could be said about that argument, but, in the end, it's a matter of opinion, nothing more. What seems less open to debate is that the Confederacy's best chance to win the war was in the Eastern Theater, and it was in the East where one most clearly sees the interaction between political leadership, military operations, civil-military relations, and public opinion. The public most often focused its attention on the ebb and flow of events in the East, as did European powers. Had there been the sort of victory in the East that there was at Vicksburg, for example, the result might have been even more devastating to the loser. But no such victory came until the spring of 1865.

The Eastern Theater is more about what could have been and what almost was than about what actually happened. It was the theater of war in which the Confederacy was most likely to claim victory, and where it was most likely by force of arms to prevail. That it failed to do so was not preordained. At the same time, it was not until Ulysses S. Grant came east in 1864 that Union forces were able to break the pattern of Confederate triumphs south of the Potomac and Union successes north of it that had prevailed since Lee's ascension to command of the Army of Northern Virginia. Grant took away Lee's ability to reverse the tide of military fortunes. If he could not secure the sort of decisive Union battlefield triumph that would insure

Lincoln's reelection in 1864, he held Lee in check while Union forces elsewhere under his overall direction achieved the victories that convinced a majority of northern voters that the Union was on the path to winning the war.

Assessing what happened in the Eastern Theater and its import for why the United States prevailed in the American Civil War presents some interesting challenges. Although the story of the four years of conflict offers ample opportunity to compose lively and compelling narratives of dramatic battles and charismatic leaders, it is far harder to determine what it all meant. Take, for example, Gettysburg. Each year sees new books about nearly every aspect of the campaign and the battle, but rarely do the findings appreciably change our understanding of Gettysburg's place in a broader context. The Confederate defeat in Pennsylvania by no means doomed the quest for southern independence, and Union victory did little to ease northern minds about Robert E. Lee's ability or prevent Lee himself from contemplating future aggressive moves.

Thus, if anything, the recurring pattern evident in the war in the East reinforces the argument that most battles during the Civil War were bloody, indecisive affairs, their impact measured by how the commanders used those battles, how the public North, South, and abroad viewed those battles, and by the long term impact of attrition on both sides. If Robert E. Lee fended off his foes during his first twenty-three months in command, he failed to score any decisive game-changing victories himself. Yes, he drove McClellan away from the outskirts of Richmond (at high cost) in 1862, but it was the decision to transfer the Army of the Potomac away from the James that proved more important. Yes, he could declare victory at Second Manassas, Fredericksburg, and Chancellorsville, but even he came to view such battles as hollow triumphs. He saw that true opportunity lay north of the Potomac, and each time he attempted to make use of that opportunity he was stymied, although he proved fortunate enough to stave off disaster and return to Virginia. For all the plaudits he won, he could not do much more than to hope that his successes would raise Confederate morale and depress support for the Union war effort. By 1864 that was all that was possible for him to do, because he had lost the ability to prevail in a decisive manner on the battlefield proper.

Ulysses S. Grant dealt a significant although not fatal blow to the strategic stalemate in the East. Several times during the Overland Campaign decisive victory eluded him; nevertheless, he seized the initiative from Lee and never gave it back, despite Lee's best efforts to regain it. Jubal Early's raid may have created a momentary scare, but it paled in comparison to previous Confederate crossings of the Potomac, and eventually Grant used Phil Sheridan to terminate that option. His bulldog grip at Richmond and Petersburg prevented Lee from countering Union successes in the West in an election year. While the glory went to Sherman and Sheridan, it was Grant who made sure that Lee had no chance to steal it back. Grant's ability to prevent Lee from winning in the East made it possible for Union arms to build upon his own previous accomplishments in the West and drive forward to victory, but even then people saw in Lee's surrender the end of the conflict. Thus, even at war's end, the East retained pride of place in the public consciousness. Never mind that the Confederacy seemed doomed in any case: it was the news from Richmond, then Appomattox that signaled the end of the conflict in most minds. Believing as much made it so.

———

Ulysses S. Grant had a way of reducing matters to their essentials. "The art of war is simple enough," he once explained; "find out where your enemy is, get at him as soon as you can, and strike him as hard as you can, and keep moving on." Yet, as Carl von Clausewitz once observed, "Everything in war is very simple, but the simplest thing is difficult."[1] This is especially true when it comes to reviewing the options each side had in the Eastern Theater.

For the Confederacy matters were relatively simple. The Army of Northern Virginia could fend off offensive thrust after offensive thrust and rest content with waging defensive war. Lee realized that over the long term the attrition of battle and campaign would tell against the Confederacy. So long as the Lincoln administration remained wedded to an overland approach, however, he knew he could trade blow for blow while waiting for an opportunity to strike back. If he was to do something more than that, however, he would have to launch offensives of his own, hoping to keep his opponent off balance, prey on Lincoln's concern about Washington's security, and deliver blows that might damage not only the Army of the Potomac but also northern morale. Given the cost of offensive operations, however, Lee could not sustain such a stance for long, and even a success, if costly, might drain him of the ability to exploit it by following up and delivering another telling blow. If Lee gambled, perhaps he had to. He remained thankful that no Army of the Potomac commander followed McClellan's water-borne approach, although Grant's 1864 campaign incorporated elements of that concept. He also resisted transferring units out of Virginia, because he believed that his army had the best chance of delivering the military triumphs needed to declare victory.

As long as Lee followed a basic operational and tactical pattern, he was in good shape. That pattern consisted of pinning the enemy in place, moving a mobile force to threaten a flank or weak point, and attacking with that mobile force. Such was the idea at the opening of the Seven Days. It characterized the Second Manassas campaign; and it reached its apogee at Chancellorsville. At other times Lee remained largely on the defensive (Antietam and Fredericksburg) or counterpunched as needed. When those tactics failed, most notably at Malvern Hill and Gettysburg, things did not go well for the Confederates. Although Lee was aggressive in the Wilderness and to a lesser extent at Spotsylvania, over time those opportunities grew fewer, and Lee could not always take advantage of them, as at North Anna. Even when Lee's efforts met with success, however, he concluded that his triumph was less than complete, and at times the cost in casualties meant that eventually the attrition would tell on his army.

By the summer of 1862 the Union had simplified its choices by defining the Eastern Theater as Virginia and points north. Thus, the promise inherent in using a foothold along the coast of the Carolinas as a way to sweep into the Confederate interior never gained traction. Before long operations in South Carolina and Georgia focused on enforcing the blockade and taking port cities, while the beachheads in North Carolina were never exploited. In 1864 Grant found himself roundly rebuked when he suggested that a thrust into North Carolina would slice the logistical network of the Confederacy, mobilize slaves, and capitalize on a growing resistance to the Richmond government. It would also take the war out of Virginia, where Union operations had not always fared well. By the time the Carolinas were in play again, the Confederacy was struggling to survive.

Once the theater of operations was defined, the Union high command had to answer three basic questions. First, was the objective of operations territorial (namely Richmond) or the destruction of the opposing army? All too often this was treated as an either/or choice, especially by Lincoln (although Halleck mimicked it). It need not have been, and in fact to treat it as an either/or choice constrained operational creativity. Threatening territorial points of great importance drew one's foe to defend them (as Lee knew full well when it came to Washington).

Second, should Union forces (a) advance through central Virginia, relying on retaining control of a railroad for supply; (b) advance using the tidewater with its rivers and railheads as points of supply; or (c) swing south to the James River-Fort Monroe area and advance westward to Richmond, either to take the Confederate capital itself or to sweep to the south to cut it off from the Confederate heartland? These options were shaped primarily by logistics. Much is made of the fact that the east-west route of most Virginia rivers offered defensive positions for the Confederates to defend, but those rivers also offered Union forces supply routes if they marched by the left flank southward along the tidewater. The Shenandoah Valley offered its own set of problems, but through the end of 1863 Union strategy focused more on holding the northern end of the Valley at Harpers Ferry than considering how to deny it to the Confederates as a source of supply and a route for maneuver.

Finally, should the Union high command treat Virginia as the theater of decision, as public opinion would seem to dictate? Here Lincoln and others wavered. At times in 1863 it became evident that if the Army of the Potomac could simply keep the Army of Northern Virginia in check, surplus troops could be transferred westward (as both sides did in September 1863). It might have been a good idea to experiment with a defensive posture, but Lincoln refused to sell the rationale for it to the northern public. Having portrayed the East as the theater of decision, it proved to be too much to abandon that notion, even as it was in the West that Union arms enjoyed significant success in 1863.

It was left to Ulysses S. Grant to pull all of these threads together and offer new answers, some reflecting second-best choices and not the initial preferences exhibited in his North Carolina plan. One targeted both Richmond and Lee's army by forcing Lee to fight to defend his capital and maintain his line of supply. One advanced both overland via the tidewater route and exploited Union control of the waterways to approach Richmond from the east. One also eliminated the Shenandoah Valley as a source of supply and as a place for Confederate maneuvers to exploit, particularly when it came to threatening targets north of the Potomac. Finally, one pursued operations in both theaters simultaneously, spreading Confederate resources thin, denying the enemy the initiative, and waiting to see where the Rebels would give way. There would have been no capture of Atlanta or marches through Georgia and the Carolinas if Grant had not held Lee in a death grip at Richmond. In 1862 and 1863 Grant achieved success in the West. In 1864 his brand of waging war in the East made it possible for Sherman to claim the victor's laurels in the West.

Thus, to say the war was won in the West is in its way as simplistic as saying that Gettysburg represented the turning point of the conflict: taken to extremes, in fact, these arguments sound nonsensical. Given the importance of public support for the success of the war effort of either side, if the public focused its attention on the East, then the East retained its importance. Appearances contribute to reality, and never more so than in a war where ultimately victory and defeat depended on which side's will to fight would dissolve first.

NOTES

INTRODUCTION

1. By "military strategy" I mean not what is defined as "policy" (war aims) or "national strategy/grand strategy" (the use of military, diplomatic, economic, and other resources to achieve the ends of policy) but the use of military force to achieve victory through military operations (frequently called campaigns), in this case in the Eastern Theater. Thus my understanding of the term "military strategy" and "operations" mirrors that of James McPherson in *Tried by War: Abraham Lincoln as Commander in Chief* (New York: Penguin, 2008), p. 5, and I share with Brian Holden Reid, *America's Civil War: The Operational Battlefield, 1861–1863* (Amherst, NY: Prometheus Books, 2008), an interest in the operational art, which seeks through military campaigns to achieve the goals set forth by military strategy. For a somewhat different set of definitions, see Donald Stoker, *The Grand Design: Strategy and the U.S. Civil War* (New York: Oxford University Press, 2010), pp. 5–11.

2. Lincoln to Agénor–Etienne de Gasparin, August 4, 1862, Roy P. Basler, et al., eds., *The Collected Works of Abraham Lincoln* (New Brunswick, NJ: Rutgers University Press, 1953), 5:355–56 (hereafter *CWAL*).

PROLOGUE

1. For an account of the opening months of the war, see James M. McPherson, *Battle Cry of Freedom: The Civil War Era* (New York: Oxford University Press, 1988), chapters nine and ten; on Butler and contrabands, ibid., pp. 355–56.

2. Ibid., p. 334; Scott to George B. McClellan, May 3, 1861, U.S. War Department, *The War of the Rebellion: Official Records of the Union and Confederate Armies*, 128 vols. (Washington, DC: Government Printing Office, 1881–1901; hereafter *Official Records*), series I, volume 51, part 1, pp. 369–70.

3. Bruce Catton, *The Coming Fury* (Garden City, NY: Doubleday, 1961), pp. 406–10, 436–37.

4. McPherson, *Battle Cry of Freedom*, p. 336.

5. On First Manassas (also known as First Bull Run), see William C. Davis, *Battle at Bull Run* (Garden City, NY: Doubleday, 1977); Ethan S. Rafuse, *A Single Grand Victory: The First Campaign and Battle of Manassas* (Wilmington, DE: Scholarly Resources, 2002); David Detzer, *Donnybrook: The Battle of Bull Run, 1861* (New York: Harcourt, 2004); and John Hennessy, *The First Battle of Manassas: An End to Innocence, July 18–21, 1861* (Lynchburg, VA: H. E. Howard, 1989).

6. Maria Lydig Daly, *Diary of a Union Lady, 1861–1865*, ed. Harold Earl Hammond (New York: Funk and Wagnalls, 1962), p. 39.

7. George Templeton Strong, *Diary of the Civil War, 1860–1865*, ed. Allan Nevins (New York: Macmillan, 1962), pp. 168–69.

8. Ibid., pp. 169–70.

9. Catherine Ann Devereux Edmondston, *"Journal of a Secesh Lady,"* eds. Beth G. Crabtree and James W. Patton (Raleigh, NC: North Carolina Division of Archives and History, 1979), pp. 79–81.

10. Steven E. Woodworth, *Davis and Lee at War* (Lawrence, KS: University Press of Kansas, 1995), pp. 48–50.

CHAPTER ONE

1. In *The Fourth Battle of Winchester: Toward a New Civil War Paradigm* (Kent, OH: Kent State University Press, 2002), Richard M. McMurry uses a counterfactual narrative to advance the argument that the war was won in the West. While there is merit in much of what he argues, one cannot dismiss the power of perception, which privileged the East.

CHAPTER TWO

1. David W. Miller, *Second Only to Grant: Quartermaster General Montgomery C. Meigs* (Shippensburg: White Mane Books, 2000), pp. 92–93; McClellan to Scott, April 27, 1861, Stephen W. Sears, ed., *The Civil War Papers of McClellan: Selected Correspondence, 1860–1865* (New York: Ticknor and Fields, 1989), pp. 12–13 (hereafter *Papers of McClellan*).

Even Ethan S. Rafuse, who places McClellan's plan in a more generous light, admits that it presented "a logistical nightmare." Rafuse, "Impractical? Unforgivable? Another Look at George B. McClellan's First Strategic Plan," *Ohio History* 110 (Summer–Autumn 2001), pp. 153–64 at 160.

2. On Scott see Allan Peskin, *Winfield Scott and the Profession of Arms* (Kent, OH: Kent State University Press, 2003), and Timothy D. Johnson, *Winfield Scott: The Quest for Military Glory* (Lawrence, KS: University Press of Kansas, 1998).

3. Daly, *Diary of a Union Lady*, p. 35.

4. Miller, *Second Only to Grant*, p. 99.

5. Lincoln, Memoranda of July 23 and 27, 1861, *CWAL*, 4: 457–58.

6. McClellan to Lincoln, August 2, 1861, *Papers of McClellan*, pp. 71–75.

7. Mark A. Snell, *From First to Last: The Life of Major General William B. Franklin* (New York: Fordham University Press, 2002), p. 70.

8. McClellan to Scott, August 8, 1861, *Papers of McClellan*, p. 80; McClellan to Mary McClellan, August 8, 1861, ibid., p. 81.

9. McClellan to Edward D. Townsend, May 17, 1861, ibid., pp. 19–20; McClellan to Troops of the Department of the Ohio, May 26, 1861, ibid., p. 25.

10. McClellan to Townsend, July 5, 1861, ibid., pp. 44–45.

11. Clayton R. Newell, *Lee vs. McClellan: The First Campaign* (Washington: Regnery Publishing, 1996) offers the most detailed study of these operations.

12. Steven E. Woodworth, *Davis and Lee at War* (Lawrence: University Press of Kansas, 1995), pp. 58–60.

13. Ibid., p. 53.

14. Ibid., pp. 60–64.

15. Ibid., pp. 65–68.

16. Howard K. Beale, ed., *The Diary of Edward Bates, 1859–1866* (Washington, DC: Government Printing Office, 1933), p. 194 (September 30, 1861); Michael Burlingame and John R. T. Ettlinger, *Inside Lincoln's White House: The Complete Civil War Diary of John Hay* (Carbondale; Southern Illinois University Press, 1999), p. 25 (October 10, 1861).

17. For Ball's Bluff, see James Morgan III, *A Little Short of Boats: The Fights at Ball's Bluff and Edward's Ferry, October 21–22, 1861* (Cincinnati: Ironclad Publishing, 2004).

18. Burlingame and Ettlinger, *Inside Lincoln's White House*, pp. 28–29 (October 26, 1861).

19. Ibid., p. 30 (November 1861).

20. Ibid., p. 11 (April 25, 1861).

21. E. B. Long with Barbara Long, *The Civil War Day By Day: An Almanac, 1861–1865* (Garden City, NY: Doubleday, 1971), p. 88 (June 29, 1861).

22. See William H. Roberts, *Now For the Contest: Coastal & Oceanic Naval Operations in the Civil War* (Lincoln, NE: University of Nebraska Press, 2004), pp. 41–44.

23. Rowena Reed, *Combined Operations in the Civil War* (Annapolis: Naval Institute Press, 1978), 48.

24. Ibid., pp. 8, 19, 50.

25. William Marvel, *Burnside* (Chapel Hill: University of North Carolina Press, 1991), pp. 33–35.

26. Reed, *Combined Operations in the Civil War*, p. 43.

27. McClellan to Thomas, March 13, 1862, *Papers of McClellan*, p. 208.

28. For Secessionville, see Patrick Brennan, *Secessionville: Assault on Charleston* (Campbell, CA: Savas Publishing, 1996).

29. John G. Nicolay and John Hay, *Abraham Lincoln: A History*, 10 vols. (New York: Century, 1890), 4:468.

30. Lincoln to McClellan, December 1, 1861, *CWAL*, 5:34–35; Stephen W. Sears, *George B. McClellan: The Young Napoleon* (New York: Ticknor & Fields, 1988), pp. 130–31.

31. Miller, *Second Only to Grant*, 131; Henry J. Raymond, *Life and Public Services of Abraham Lincoln* (New York: Derby & Miller, 1865), pp. 772–73.

32. Ethan Rafuse, *McClellan's War: The Failure of Moderation in the Struggle for the Union* (Bloomington: Indiana University Press, 2005), pp. 171–72, 177.

33. Ibid., pp. 178–82; Michael Burlingame, ed., *With Lincoln in the White House; Letters, Memoranda, and Other Writings of John G. Nicolay, 1860–1865* (Carbondale: Southern Illinois University Press, 2000), p. 72.

34. Daly, *Diary of a Union Lady*, p. 98; Strong, *Diary*, p. 208 (February 20, 1862).

35. Rafuse, *McClellan's War*, p. 190.

36. Craig L. Symonds, *Joseph E. Johnston: A Civil War Biography* (New York: W. W. Norton, 1992), pp. 142–45.

37. Woodworth, *Davis and Lee at War*, pp. 100–3.

38. Ibid., pp. 103–4.

39. Rafuse, *McClellan's War*, pp. 190–92, 194–95.

40. McClellan to Barlow, March 16, 1862, *Papers of McClellan*, p. 213.

41. McClellan to Nathaniel Banks, March 16, 1862, *Papers of McClellan*, p. 212. On the entire campaign see Stephen W. Sears, *To the Gates of Richmond: The Peninsula Campaign* (New York: Ticknor & Fields, 1992).

42. McClellan to Banks, March 24, 1862, *Papers of McClellan*, p. 217; McClellan to Lincoln, March 31, 1862, ibid., pp. 219–20; McClellan to Mary Ellen McClellan, April 2, 1862, ibid., p. 225.

43. Sears, *To the Gates of Richmond*, pp. 33–34.

44. Woodworth, *Davis and Lee at War*, p. 107.

45. McClellan to Lincoln, April 5, 1862, *Papers of McClellan*, p. 228; Rafuse, *McClellan's War*, p. 207; McClellan to Mary McClellan, April 8, 1862, *Papers of McClellan*, p. 234.

46. McClellan to Lorenzo Thomas, April 1, 1862, *Papers of McClellan*, pp. 222–23; Thomas to McClellan, April 4, 1862, ibid., p. 229 (note); McClellan to Mary McClellan, April 6, 1862, ibid., p. 230.

47. Lincoln to McClellan, April 9, 1862, *CWAL*, 5:184–85.

48. McClellan to Lincoln, April 20, 1862, *Papers of McClellan*, 245.

49. Lee to Jackson, April 21, 1862, Clifford Dowdey and Louis H. Manarin, eds., *The Wartime Papers of Robert E. Lee* (Boston: Little, Brown, 1961), p. 151 (hereafter *WPL*).

50. Sears, *To the Gates of Richmond*, pp. 46–47; see, however, Steven H. Newton, *Joseph E. Johnston and the Defense of Richmond* (Lawrence, KS: University Press of Kansas, 1998), pp. 157–61.

51. Johnston to Lee, April 29, 30, 1862, *Official Records*, volume 11, part 3, pp. 473, 477.

52. David Donald, *Lincoln* (New York: Simon & Schuster, 1995), pp. 350–51; Newton, *Johnston and the Defense of Richmond*, pp. 154–56.

53. McClellan to Stanton, May [8], 1862, *Papers of McClellan*, p. 258; Lincoln to McClellan, May 9, 1862, *CWAL*, 5:208–9; Lincoln to McClellan, May 9, 21, 1862, ibid., 5:208, 227; McClellan to Lincoln, May 22, 1862, *Papers of McClellan*, p. 273.

54. McClellan to Stanton, May 10, 1862, *Papers of McClellan*, p. 261; McClellan to Lincoln, May 14, 1862, ibid., pp. 264–65; Lincoln to McClellan, May 15, 1862, *CWAL*, 5:216; Lincoln to McDowell, [May 17, 1862], ibid., 5:219 and n; Stanton to McClellan, May [17], 1862, ibid., 5:220n.

55. Lincoln to McDowell, [May 17, 1862], *CWAL*, 5:219–20.

56. Lee to Jackson, May 16, 1862, *WPL*, pp. 174–75.

57. On operations in the Valley, see Peter Cozzens, *Shenandoah 1862: Stonewall Jackson's Valley Campaign* (Chapel Hill: University of North Carolina, 2008).

58. Lincoln to McClellan, May 25, 1862, *CWAL*, 5:235–36; McClellan to Lincoln, May 25, [1862], *Papers of McClellan*, p. 276.

59. Gary W. Gallagher, "You Must Either Attack Richmond or Give Up the Job and Come to the Defense of Washington: Abraham Lincoln and the 1862 Shenandoah Valley Campaign," in Gallagher, ed., *The Shenandoah Valley Campaign of 1862* (Chapel Hill: University of North Carolina Press, 2003), pp. 11, 15–16; see, in the same volume, William J. Miller, "Such Men as Shields, Banks, and Frémont: Federal Command in Western Virginia, March–June 1862," pp. 43–85.

60. Woodworth, *Davis and Lee at War*, pp. 127–29.

61. Ibid., pp. 131–32.

62. Ibid., pp. 132–35.

63. McClellan to the Army of the Potomac, June 2, 1862, *Papers of McClellan*, pp. 286–87.

CHAPTER THREE

1. Special Orders No. 22, June 1, 1861, *WPL*, p. 182.

2. Edward P. Alexander, *Fighting for the Confederacy: The Personal Recollections of General Edward Porter Alexander*, edited by Gary W. Gallagher (Chapel Hill, NC; University of North Carolina Press, 1989), p. 91.

3. Lee to Davis, June 5, 1862, WPL, p. 184; Frederick Maurice, ed., *An Aide–de–Camp of Lee* (Boston: Little, Brown, 1927), pp. 69–75.

4. John B. Jones, *A Rebel War Clerk's Diary*, edited by Earl S. Miers (New York: Sagamore Press, 1958), p. 82; C. Vann Woodward, ed., *Mary Chesnut's Civil War* (New Haven, CT: Yale University Press, 1981), p. 287 (June 15, 1862).

5. McClellan to Lincoln, April 20, 1862, *Papers of McClellan*, pp. 244–45.

6. Cozzens, *Shenandoah 1862*, chapters 25–28.

7. Lee to Davis, June 5, 1862, *WPL*, pp. 183–84; Lee to Jackson, June 8, 1862, ibid., p. 187; Lee to Stuart, June 11, 1862, ibid., p. 192; Lee to Jackson, June 16, 1862, ibid., p. 194; Lee to Holmes, June 18, 1862, ibid., p. 195; Joseph L. Harsh, *Confederate Tide Rising:*

Robert E. Lee and the Making of Southern Strategy, 1861–1862 (Kent, OH: Kent State University Press, 1998), p. 78.

8. McClellan to Mary Ellen McClellan, June 22, 1862, *Papers of McClellan*, p. 305.

9. Sidney George Fisher, *A Philadelphia Perspective: The Diary of Sidney George Fisher*, edited by Nicholas B. Wainwright (Philadelphia: Historical Society of Pennsylvania, 1967), p. 428.

10. See Brian K. Burton, *Extraordinary Circumstances: The Seven Days Battles* (Bloomington, Indiana: Indiana University Press, 2001).

11. McClellan to Stanton, June 25, 1862, *Papers of McClellan*, pp. 309–10; Lincoln to McClellan, June 26, 1862, *CWAL*, 5:286; McClellan to Stanton, June 25, 1862, *Papers of McClellan*, p. 312.

12. McClellan to Stanton, June 26 (2 letters), 27, 28, 1862, *Papers of McClellan*, pp. 312–13, 317, 321, 323 and note.

13. McClellan to Lorenzo Thomas, July 1, 1862, ibid., p. 327.

14. Lincoln to Seward, June 28, 1862, *CWAL*, 5:292; Lincoln, Call for 300,000 Volunteers, July 1, 1862, ibid., 5:296–97.

15. Lincoln to McClellan, July 2, 1862, ibid., 5:301.

16. See, for example, Harsh, *Confederate Tide Rising*, pp. 84, 88–89, 180–81; on McClellan during and after Glendale, see Rafuse, *McClellan's War*, pp. 227–29.

17. Jones, *A Rebel War Clerk's Diary*, p. 86.

18. Lee to Davis, July 4, 6, 1863, *WPL*, pp. 208–9; McClellan to Lincoln, July 7, 1862, *Papers of McClellan*, 341; McClellan to Lincoln, July 7, 1862, ibid., p. 344.

19. Fisher, *A Philadelphia Perspective*, 429.

20. Lee to Mary Lee, July 9, 1862, *WPL*, p. 230.

21. Order Constituting the Army of Virginia, June 26, 1862, *CWAL*, 5:287.

22. Wallace J. Schutz and Walter N. Trenerry, *Abandoned by Lincoln: A Military Biography of General John Pope* (Urbana: University of Illinois Press, 1990), pp. 100–04; Peter Cozzens, *General John Pope: A Life for the Nation* (Urbana: University of Illinois Press, 2000), pp. 83–89.

23. Schutz and Trenerry, *Abandoned by Lincoln*, pp. 91–99; Cozzens, *Pope*, pp. 74–78.

24. Harsh, *Confederate Tide Rising*, pp. 107–10.

25. Lee to Davis, July 26, 1862, *WPL*, p. 238; Lee to Jackson, July 27, 1862, ibid., p. 239; Lee to Randolph, July 28, 1862, ibid., p. 241; Lee to Jackson, August 7, 1862, ibid., p. 248.

26. See John F. Marszalek, *Commander of All Lincoln's Armies: A Life of General Henry W. Halleck* (Cambridge, MA: Harvard University Press, 2004).

27. Marszalek, *Halleck*, pp. 137–38; McClellan to Samuel L. M. Barlow, July 23, 1862, *Papers of McClellan*, p. 369. One sign of McClellan's sense of reality was that he had not removed the third star from his shoulder straps as general-in-chief, although it had been months since he had held that responsibility. See McClellan to Mary Ellen McClellan, July 20, [1862], ibid., p. 367.

28. Marszalek, Halleck, pp. 138–41; Sears, McClellan, p. 235; McClellan to Halleck, July 26, 1862, *Papers of McClellan*, p. 372; McClellan to Samuel L. M. Barlow, July 30, 1862, ibid., pp. 376–77.

29. McClellan to Lincoln, July 14, 1862, *Papers of McClellan*, pp. 357–58; McClellan to Mary Ellen McClellan, July 15, [1862], ibid., p. 358.

30. Donald, *Lincoln*, p. 389.

31. McClellan to Halleck, August 4, 1862, *Papers of McClellan*, pp. 383–84.

32. John Hennessy, *Return to Bull Run: The Campaign and Battle of Second Manassas* (New York: Simon and Schuster, 1992), pp. 25–28.

33. Lee to George W. Randolph, August 14, 1862, *WPL*, p. 252.

34. Lee to Davis, September 3, 4, 5, 1863, *WPL*, pp. 292–96.

35. Lee to the People of Maryland, September 8, 1862, ibid., pp. 299–300; Lee to Davis, September 8, 1862, ibid., p. 301.

36. Welles, Diary, 1:105; McPherson, *Tried by War*, p. 121. McClellan's comment can be found in McClellan to Lincoln, August 29, 1862, *Papers of McClellan,* p. 416.

37. Burlingame and Ettlinger, *Inside Lincoln's White House*, p. 37.

38. Lee to Davis, September 9, 1862, *WPL*, p. 303; Halleck to Lincoln, September 12, 1862, Robert Todd Lincoln Papers, Library of Congress.

39. Daly, *Diary of a Union Lady*, p. 168; Strong, Diary, p. 254 (September 11, 1862).

40. See Stephen W. Sears, *Landscape Turned Red: The Battle of Antietam* (New Haven: Ticknor & Fields, 1983) and James M. McPherson, *Crossroads of Freedom: Antietam* (New York: Oxford University Press, 2002); McClellan quoted on the lost order, Sears, *McClellan*, p. 282.

41. See Gary W. Gallagher, "The Net Result of the Campaign Was in Our Favor," and Brooks D. Simpson, "General McClellan's Bodyguard," in Gary W. Gallagher, ed., *The Antietam Campaign* (Chapel Hill: University of North Carolina Press, 1999), chapters one and two.

42. George G. Meade to Margaret Meade, September 20, 1862, George Meade, *The Life and Letters of General George Gordon Meade* (New York: Scribners, 1913), 1:311 (hereafter *Letters of Meade*); Daly, *Diary of a Union Lady*, p. 174.

43. "Record of Dismissal of John J. Key," *CWAL*, 5:442–43.

44. McClellan to Mary McClellan, October 2, 1862, *Papers of McClellan*, p. 488; Lincoln to McClellan, October 13, 1862, *CWAL*, 5:460–61.

45. McPherson, *Tried by War*, p. 140.

46. Mary A. Livermore, *My Story of the War* (Scituate, MA: Digital Scanning, 2001 [1888]), p. 556.

47. Douglas S. Freeman, *R. E. Lee*, four volumes (New York: Charles Scribners' Sons, 1934–35), 2:415–20.

48. McPherson, *Tried by War*, p. 141; Freeman, Lee, 2:423–28.

49. Woodworth, *Davis & Lee at War*, pp. 197–98.

CHAPTER FOUR

1. Daniel E. Sutherland, *Fredericksburg & Chancellorsville: The Dare Mark Campaign* (Lincoln: University of Nebraska Press, 1998) offers a view of operations along the Rappahannock that unites these two campaigns.

2. Milo M. Quaife, ed., *From the Cannon's Mouth: The Civil War Letters of General Alpheus S. Williams* (Detroit: Wayne State University Press and Detroit Historical Society, 1959), pp. 150–51.

3. Lee to George W. Randolph, November 7, 1862, *WPL*, p. 328; Lee to G. W. C. Lee, November 10, 1862, ibid., p. 333.

4. McPherson, *Tried by War*, p. 143.

5. Lee to Randolph, November 17, 1862, *WPL*, p. 338; Lee to Jackson, November 19, 1862, ibid., p. 340; Lee to Davis, November 20, 1862, ibid., p. 341; Lee to Cooper, November 2, 1862, ibid., p. 342.

6. Marvel, *Burnside*, pp. 168–69.

7. Meade to Margaret Meade, November 22, 23, 1862, *Letters of Meade*, 1:330, 331.

8. On Fredericksburg, see George C. Rable, *Fredericksburg! Fredericksburg!* (Chapel Hill: University of North Carolina Press, 2002) and Francis A. O'Reilly, *The Fredericksburg Campaign: Winter War on the Rappahannock* (Baton Rouge: Louisiana State University Press, 2003).

9. Ethan S. Rafuse, *Robert E. Lee and the Fall of the Confederacy, 1863–1865* (Lanham: Powman & Littlefield, 2008), 22.

10. Lee to Mary Lee, December 16, 1862, *WPL*, p. 365.

11. Lee to Seddon, December 16, 1862, ibid., p. 363; Lee to Mary Lee, December 25, 1862, ibid., p. 380.

12. Lee to Seddon, January 10, 1863, *WPL*, pp. 388–89.

13. Lee to Seddon, January 10, 1863, ibid.

14. William O. Stoddard, *Inside the White House in War Times: Memoirs and Reports of Lincoln's Secretary* (Lincoln: University of Nebraska Press, 2000), p. 101; McPherson, *Tried by War*, p. 145.

15. Marvel, *Burnside*, pp. 202, 209.

16. Ibid., p. 209.

17. Lincoln to Halleck, January 1, 1863, *CWAL*, 6:31; Marszalek, *Halleck*, pp. 163–65.

18. Lincoln to Burnside, January 8, 1863, CWAL, 6:46; see ibid., 6:32–33, for the exchange with Halleck, and ibid., 6:47–48, for Halleck's letter to Burnside of January 7, 1863.

19. Lincoln to Hooker, January 26, 1863, ibid., 6:78–79.

20. Lee to Davis, January 13, 1863, *WPL*, p. 391.

21. Lee to Seddon, February 4, 1863, and Lee to Davis, February 5, 1863, ibid., pp. 397–99.

22. Lee to G.W.C. Lee, February 28, 1863, ibid., p. 411.

23. Lee to Longstreet, March 27, 1863, ibid., p. 417.

24. Lee to Seddon, April 9, 1863, ibid., p. 430.

25. Woodworth, *Davis and Lee at War*, pp. 218–21; Lee to Cooper, April 16, 1863, WPL, p. 434; Lee to Davis, April 16, 1863, ibid., p. 435.

26. *Quaife, From the Cannon's Mouth*, p. 176.

27. Lincoln, Memo of Hooker's Plan, [c. April 6–10, 1863], *CWAL*, 6:164–65.

28. For Chancellorsville, see Stephen W. Sears, *Chancellorsville* (Boston: Houghton Mifflin, 1996) and Ernest B. Furgurson, *Chancellorsville 1863: The Souls of the Brave* (New York: Knopf, 1992).

29. Woodworth, *Davis and Lee at War*, p. 224.

30. Donald, *Lincoln*, p. 436.

31. Rafuse, *Lee and the Fall of the Confederacy*, p. 37.

32. Meade to Margaret Meade, May 8, 1863, *Letters of Meade*, 1:372; Lincoln to Hooker, May 7, 1863, CWAL, 6:201.

33. Lincoln to Hooker, May 13, 14, 1863, *CWAL*, 6: 215, 217.

34. Lincoln to Hooker, May 14, 1863, ibid., 6:217.

35. McPherson, *Tried by War*, p. 178.

36. Halleck to Grant, March 20, 1863, *PUSG*, 7:401. Although Halleck claimed that the "eyes and hopes of the whole country" looked west to Grant's army, that seems wishful thinking.

CHAPTER FIVE

1. Woodworth, *Davis and Lee at War*, pp. 228–29; Lee to Seddon, May 10, 1863, *WPL*, p. 482; Lee to Davis, May 11, 1863, ibid., pp. 483–84

2. Lee to D. H. Hill, May 16, 1863, *WPL*, p. 485; Lee to Hood, May 21, 1863, ibid., p. 490.

3. Lee to Hood, May 21, 1863, ibid; Lee to Davis, May 30, 1863, ibid., pp. 495–96.

4. Lee to Davis, June 7, 1863, ibid., pp. 502–03; Lee to Seddon, June 8, 1863, ibid., pp. 504–05.

5. Lee to Davis, June 10, 1863, ibid., pp. 507–09.

6. Rafuse, *Lee and the Fall of the Confederacy*, 56.

7. Lincoln to Hooker, June 5, 1862, *CWAL*, 6:249; Stephen W. Sears, *Gettysburg* (Boston: Houghton Mifflin, 2002), p. 62.

8. Hooker to Lincoln, June 10, 1863, and Lincoln to Hooker, June 10, 1863, *CWAL*, 6:257–58; Lincoln to Hooker, June 13, 1863, ibid., 6:271; Lincoln to Hooker, June 14, 1863, ibid., 6:273; Welles, *Diary*, 1:328 (June 14, 1863).

9. Sears, *Gettysburg*, pp. 86–89. See also Steven E. Woodworth, *Beneath a Northern Sky: A Short History of the Gettysburg Campaign* (Lanham, MD: Rowman & Littlefield, 2008), chapters one and two, and Edwin B. Coddington, *The Gettysburg Campaign: A Study in Command* (New York: Charles Scribner's Sons, 1968), chapters one through nine, for the campaign prior to July 1.

10. Lee to Stuart, June 22, 23, 1863, *WPL*, pp. 523, 526; Lee to Davis, June 23, 1863, ibid., pp. 527–28. For the debate over the raid, see Eric J. Wittenberg and J. David Petruzzi, *Plenty of Blame to Go Around: Jeb Stuart's Controversial Ride to Gettysburg* (New York: Savas Beatie, 2006).

11. Welles, *Diary*, 1:344 (June 26, 1863).

12. Ibid., 1:348 (June 28, 1863); Lincoln to Alexander K. McClure, June 30, 1863, *CWAL*, 6:311; Lincoln to Joel Parker, June 30, 1863, ibid., 6:311.

13. See Sears, *Gettysburg*, chapters seven through fourteen; Woodworth, *Beneath a Northern Sky*, chapters three through nine; and Coddington, *The Gettysburg Campaign*, chapters eleven through nineteen.

14. For these and other questions concerning generalship at Gettysburg, see Brooks D. Simpson, "'If Properly Led': Command Relationships at Gettysburg," Steven E. Woodworth, ed., *Civil War Generals in Defeat* (Lawrence: University Press of Kansas, 1999), pp. 161–89.

15. On operations between July 4 and 14, see Kent Masterson Brown, *Retreat from Gettysburg: Lee, Logistics, and the Pennsylvania Campaign* (Chapel Hill: The University of North Carolina Press, 2005); Eric J. Wittenberg, J. David Petruzzi, and Michael F. Nugent, *One Continuous Fight: The Retreat from Gettysburg and the Pursuit of Lee's Army of Northern Virginia*, July 4–14, 1863 (New York: Savas–Beatie, 2008); Woodworth, *Beneath a Northern Sky*, chapter ten; Coddington, *The Gettysburg Campaign*, chapter twenty, and Sears, *Gettysburg*, chapter fourteen.

16. Sears, *Gettysburg*, 475.

17. Ibid., pp. 476–78.

18. Coddington, *The Gettysburg Campaign*, pp. 545–46.

19. Welles, *Diary*, 1:363–64.

20. Allan Nevins, ed., *A Diary of Battle: The Personal Journals of Colonel Charles S. Wainwright, 1861–1865* (New York: Harcourt, Brace & World, 1962), 259 (July 11, 1863).

21. Brooks D. Simpson, *Abraham Lincoln and the Gettysburg Campaign* (Gettysburg: Farnsworth Military Impressions, 1998), pp. 43–44.

22. Ibid., p. 45.

23. Ibid., pp. 46–48.

24. Ibid., pp. 48–49; Lincoln to Meade, July 14, 1863, *CWAL*, 6:327–28.

25. Lee to Mary Lee, July 15, 1863, *WPL*, p. 551; Lee to Margaret Stuart, July 26, 1863, ibid., p. 561.

26. Reed, *Combined Operations*, pp. 266–93; see also William H. Roberts, *Now for the Contest: Coastal and Oceanic Naval Operations in the Civil War* (Lincoln: University of Nebraska Press, 2004), chapter four.

27. Reed, *Combined Operations*, pp. 295–314.

28. Lee to Davis, June 7, 1863, *WPL*, p. 503; Lee to Samuel Jones, June 20, 1863, ibid., p. 523; Lee to Davis, June 23, 1863, ibid., pp. 527–28.

29. Lee to Davis, June 25, 1863 (two letters), ibid., pp. 530–33.

30. Coddington, *The Gettysburg Campaign*, pp. 100–2.

31. Lee to Longstreet, August 31, 1863, *WPL*, p. 594; Lee to Davis, September 6, 1863, ibid., p. 596.

32. Lee to Davis, September 11, 14, 23, 1863, ibid., pp. 599, 600–01, 602–03; Lee to Longstreet, September 25, 1863, ibid., pp. 604–05.

33. George R. Agassiz, ed., *Meade's Headquarters, 1863–1865: Letters of Colonel Theodore Lyman from the Wilderness to Appomattox* (Boston: Atlantic Monthy Press, 1922), p. 22.

34. Welles, *Diary*, 1:383 (July 26, 1863); Meade to Halleck, September 18, 1863, *CWAL*, 6:467–68.

35. Lincoln to Halleck, September 19, 1863, *CWAL*, 6:466–67.

36. Meade to Margaret Meade, September 30, 1863, *Letters of Meade*, 2:151.

37. Meade to wife, October 21, 1863, ibid., 2:154.

38. Meade to wife, October 23, 1863, ibid., 2:154; Welles, *Diary*, 1:473 (October 21, 1863).

39. Welles, *Diary*, 1:472 (October 16, 1863).

40. Ibid., 1:472–73 (October 20, 1863).

41. Meade to Margaret Meade, November 9, 1863, *Letters of Meade*, 2:155–56.

42. Meade to Margaret Meade, November 25, December 2, 1863, ibid., 2:156–58.

43. Lee to Davis, August 8, September 9, 1863, *WPL*, pp. 589, 597.

44. Welles, *Diary*, 1:472 (October 16, 1863).

CHAPTER SIX

1. Halleck to Grant, January 8, 1864, *PUSG*, 10:17–18; Grant to Halleck, January 19, 1864, ibid., 10:39–40; Comstock Diary, January 18, 1864, Cyrus B. Comstock Papers, Library of Congress.

2. Halleck to Grant, February 17, 1864, PUSG, 10:110–12; see Lincoln to William B. Franklin and William F. Smith, December 22, 1862, *CWAL*, 6:15.

3. See John J. Hennessy, "I Dread the Spring: The Army of the Potomac Prepares for the Overland Campaign," in Gary W. Gallagher, ed., *The Wilderness Campaign* (Chapel Hill: The University of North Carolina Press, 1997), chapter three.

4. Lee to Davis, February 3, 18, 1864, *WPL*, pp. 666–67, 675.

5. For the politics of Grant's promotion, see Brooks D. Simpson, *Ulysses S. Grant: Triumph over Adversity, 1822–1865* (Boston: Houghton Mifflin, 2000), chapter thirteen.

6. Ibid., chapter fourteen.

7. Lee to Davis, March 25, 30, 1864, *WPL*, pp. 682–84, 687–88; Lee to Longstreet, March 28, 1864, ibid., pp. 684–85; Lee to G. W. C. Lee, March 29, 1864, ibid., pp. 685–87.Lee to Davis, April 15, 1864, ibid., pp. 699–700.

8. In *Lincoln and His Generals* (New York: Knopf, 1952), T. Harry Williams claimed (page 304–5) that in his *Memoirs* Grant had invented a story of how Lincoln had proposed a plan of operations in Virginia. However, a reading of Grant's account shows that the plan Lincoln set forth resembled his earlier suggestion to Ambrose Burnside in November 1862. Williams mentioned that plan (page 198), but apparently forgot it in his haste to paint a portrait of Lincoln as a superior natural strategist to all his generals, including Grant.

9. Simpson, *Grant*, pp. 288–89; John Russell Young, *Around the World with General Grant*, 2 volumes (New York: The American News Company, 1879), 2:307.

10. For the Overland Campaign as a whole, see Mark Grimsley, *And Keep Moving On: The Virginia Campaign, May–June 1864* (Lincoln: University of Nebraska Press, 2002).

11. See Gordon Rhea, *The Battle of the Wilderness: May 5–6, 1864* (Baton Rouge: Louisiana State University Press, 1994).

12. See Gordon Rhea, *The Battles for Spotsylvania Court House and the Road to Yellow Tavern, May 7–12, 1864* (Baton Rouge: Louisiana State University Press, 1997); William D. Matter, *If It Takes All Summer: The Battle of Spotsylvania* (Chapel Hill: The University of North Carolina Press, 1988).

13. Horace Porter, *Campaigning with Grant* (New York: Century, 1897), pp. 69–70.

14. Strong, *Diary*, pp. 445–47, 449 (May 13, 15, 17, 18, 1864); Brooks D. Simpson, "Great Expectations: Ulysses S. Grant, the Northern Press, and the Opening of the Wilderness Campaign," in Gallagher, ed., *The Wilderness Campaign*, chapter one.

15. On the failures in the Valley and Bermuda Hundred, see Grimsley, *And Keep Moving On,* chapter four.

16. Michael Burlingame, ed., *Lincoln Observed: Civil War Dispatches of Noah Brooks* (Baltimore: Johns Hopkins University Press, 1998), p. 109; Donald B. Cole and John J. McDonough, eds., *Witness to the Young Republic: A Yankee's Journal, 1828–1870* (Hanover, NH: University Press of New England, 1989), p. 450 (May 22, 1864).

17. Simpson, *Grant,* pp. 314–15.

18. See Gordon C. Rhea, *To the North Anna River: Grant and Lee, May 13–25, 1864* (Baton Rouge: Louisiana State University Press, 2000).

19. Simpson, *Grant,* pp. 316–17.

20. See Gordon C. Rhea, *Cold Harbor: Grant and Lee, May 26–June 3, 1864* (Baton Rouge: Louisiana State University Press, 2002); Simpson, *Grant,* pp. 322–27.

21. Freeman, *R. E. Lee,* 3:398.

22. Ibid., 3:397–401.

23. See Noah Andre Trudeau, *The Last Citadel: Petersburg, Virginia, June 1864–April 1865* (Boston: Little, Brown, 1991), chapter three; John Horn, *The Petersburg Campaign, June 1864–April 1865* (Conshohocken, PA; Combined Books, 1993), chapters two and three.

24. Burlingame, *Lincoln Observed,* p. 113.

25. Lee to Davis, June 26, 29, July 10, 1864, *WPL,* pp. 807, 811, 817–18.

26. See Frank E. Vandiver, *Jubal's Raid: General Early's Attack Upon Washington in 1864* (Lincoln: University of Nebraska Press, 1992 [1960]).

27. Simpson, *Grant,* p. 355.

28. Cole and McDonough, *Witness to the Young Republic,* p. 453 (July 17, 1864).

29. Burlingame, *Lincoln Observed,* p. 127.

30. On the command problems Grant faced in the summer of 1864, see Brooks D. Simpson, "Ulysses S. Grant and the Problems of Command in 1864," Steven E. Woodworth, ed., *The Art of Command in the Civil War* (Lincoln: University of Nebraska Press, 1998), chapter six.

31. Simpson, *Grant,* pp. 360–67; see also Earl J. Hess, *Into the Crater: The Mine Attack at Petersburg* (Columbia: University of South Carolina Press, 2010) and Richard Slotkin, *No Quarter: The Battle of the Crater, 1864* (New York: Random House, 2009).

32. Simpson, *Grant,* pp. 367–69.

33. Strong, *Diary,* p. 470 (August 6, 1864), p. 478 (August 27, 1864).

34. Horn, *The Petersburg Campaign,* chapter six. In his letter accepting the nomination McClellan repudiated the peace plan in the Democratic platform. Sears, McClellan, pp. 375–77.

35. Lee to Davis, September 2, 1864, *WPL,* p. 848.

36. Grant to Sherman, September 10, 1864, *PUSG,* 12:144.

37. Simpson, *Grant,* pp. 378–79; see Jeffry D. Wert, *From Winchester to Cedar Creek: The Shenandoah Valley Campaign of 1864* (Mechanicsburg, PA: Stackpole Books, 1997), chapters one through five.

38. Grant to Butler, September 27, 1864, and Grant to Meade, September 27, 1864, *PUSG,* 12:219–21, 222–23; Grant to J. Russell Jones, October 4, 1864, ibid., 12:278. For a

detailed description of this operation, see Richard J. Sommers, *Richmond Redeemed: The Siege at Petersburg* (Garden City, NY: Doubleday, 1981).

39. Grant to Stanton, October 3, 1864, *PUSG*, 12:263; Grant to Butler, October 3, 1864, ibid., 12:266; Grant to Halleck, October 4, 1864, ibid., 12:272–73.

40. Wert, *From Winchester to Cedar Creek*, chapters ten through twelve.

41. Grant to Stanton, October 27, 1864, *PUSG*, 12:351–52; Simpson, *Grant*, pp. 386–88.

42. Lee to Davis, November 2, 1864, *WPL*, p. 868.

CHAPTER SEVEN

1. Simpson, *Grant*, pp. 382–84, 390–92.

2. Ibid., pp. 392–403.

3. Lee to Wade Hampton, [November 21, 1864], *WPL*, p. 871; Lee to William P. Miles, January 19, 1865, ibid., p. 885; Lee to James A. Seddon, January 27, 1865 and February 8, 1865, ibid., pp. 886–87, 890.

4. Brooks D. Simpson, *Let Us Have Peace: Ulysses S. Grant and the Politics of War and Reconstruction, 1861–1868* (Chapel Hill: University of North Carolina Press, 1991), pp. 72–74.

5. Brooks D. Simpson, "Facilitating Defeat: The Union High Command and the Collapse of the Confederacy," in Mark Grimsley and Brooks D. Simpson, eds., *The Collapse of the Confederacy* (Lincoln: University of Nebraska Press, 2001), pp. 89–91; Simpson. *Let Us Have Peace*, pp. 75–78.

6. Horn, *The Petersburg Campaign*, p. 209.

7. Lee to John C. Breckinridge, February 19, 1865, *WPL*, p. 904.

8. Lee to John C. Breckinridge, February 24, 1865, ibid., p. 916; Lee to Davis, March 10, 1865, ibid., p. 914.

9. Grant to Meade, March 3, 1865, *PUSG*, 14:95.

10. Lee to Breckinridge, March 9, 1865, *Wartime Papers of Lee*, p. 913; Lee to Davis, March 14, 1865, ibid., p. 915.

11. Lee to Longstreet, February 22, 1865, ibid., pp. 907–8.

12. Bruce Catton, *Grant Takes Command* (Boston: Little, Brown, 1968), p. 435.

13. Lee to Davis, March 27, 1865, *WPL*, p. 918.

14. Grant to Meade, March 3, 1865, *PUSG*, 14:95; Grant to Sheridan, March 14, 1865, ibid., 14:164; Grant to Sherman, March 16, 1865, ibid., 14:172–75; Grant to Sheridan, March 19, 1865, ibid., 14:182–13; Grant to Jesse R. Grant, March 19, 1865, ibid., 14:187.

15. Grant to Sherman, March 22, 1865, ibid., 14:203; Grant to Meade, March 24, 1865, ibid., 14:211–12.

16. Grant to Sheridan, March 28, 1865, ibid., 14:243–44; Grant to Sheridan, March 29, 1865, ibid., 14:253; Grant to Sheridan, March 30, 1865 (two letters), ibid., 14:269, 270; Bruce Catton, *A Stillness at Appomattox* (Garden City, NY: Doubleday, 1954), pp. 344–46.

17. Grant, anticipating trouble between Sheridan and Warren, had authorized the former to relieve the latter should it prove necessary. The impatient Sheridan judged that it was necessary, but a court of inquiry convened in the 1880s disagreed. At Five Forks Warren paid for his behavior throughout the Overland campaign. Had Grant not trusted Warren to do his job, it would

have been better to reassign him, an option Grant had explored but not pursued in February.

18. Lee to Davis, April 1, 1865, *WPL*, p. 922, Lee to Breckinridge, April 2, 1865, ibid., pp. 924–25; Lee to Davis, April 2, 1865, ibid., pp. 925–26, 927–28.

19. Rafuse, *Lee and the Fall of the Confederacy*, pp. 228–34.

20. Grant to Sherman, April 3, 1865, *PUSG*, 14:339.

21. Rafuse, *Lee and the Fall of the Confederacy*, pp. 234–35.

22. Grant to Sherman, April 5, 1864, *PUSG*, 14:352; Sheridan to Grant, April 6, 1865, ibid., 14:358; Grant to Lee, April 7, 1865, ibid., 14:361.

23. Lincoln to Grant, April 7, 1865, ibid., 14:358; Lee to Grant, April 7, 1865, ibid., 14:361.

24. Grant to Lee, April 8, 1865, and Lee to Grant, April 8, 1865, ibid., 14:367.

25. Freeman, *Lee,* 4:120. Much is made of the fact that after Lee had agreed to meet with Grant, he turned down a suggestion to have the army scatter in an effort to prolong the struggle through guerilla warfare. One should point out that the time for that option had come and gone by the morning of April 9, 1865. Moreover, the suggestion offered by artillerist Edward Porter Alexander was not to wage guerrilla war. Rather, he urged having the army scatter with men under orders to report to Johnston in North Carolina or to return to their home states to await orders from their respective governors. Lee's refusal to consider this request does him honor as a man and as a soldier, but it is not quite the same thing as rejecting a guerrilla war that he never considered. See Alexander, *Fighting for the Confederacy*, pp. 530–33.

AFTERWORD

1. John H. Brinton, *Personal Memoirs of John H. Brinton* (New York: The Neale Co., 191), p. 239; Carl von Clausewitz, *On War*, edited and translated by Michael Howard and Peter Paret (Princeton: Princeton University Press, 1976), p. 119.

BIBLIOGRAPHICAL ESSAY

The literature on the Eastern Theater in the American Civil War is vast. Many of the following titles influenced my thinking about the subject of this book; others appeared after I had already formed my ideas, but proved useful as evidence of current scholarship. Two volumes in particular, Brian Holden Reid's *America's Civil War: The Operational Battlefield, 1861–1863* (2008), and Donald Stoker's *The Grand Design: Strategy and the U.S. Civil War* (2010), reinforced my sense that much remained to be said about Civil War grand strategy, military strategy, and the operational art. They built on a foundation formed by Herman Hattaway and Archer Jones, *How the North Won the Civil War* (1982); Rowena Reed, *Combined Operations in the Civil War* (1978); Edward Hagerman, *The American Civil War and the Origins of Modern Warfare: Ideas, Organization, and Field Command* (1988); and Archer Jones, *Civil War Command and Strategy: The Process of Victory and Defeat* (1992). I had tested some of my own ideas previously in various writings, including *Abraham Lincoln, the Gettysburg Campaign, and the War in the East, 1861–1863* (1998) and *America's Civil War* (1996).

Several studies offer overviews of the war, its conduct, and the commanders. In *Lincoln and His Generals* (1952), T. Harry Williams spent much time on the Eastern Theater; James M. McPherson updates this perspective in *Tried by War: Abraham*

Lincoln as Commander in Chief (2008). For the Confederates, Gabor S. Boritt, *Jefferson Davis's Generals* (1999) has several chapters which look at the war in the East; its twin, *Lincoln's Generals* (1994) pays far more attention to the East than the West. In *Retreat to Victory: Confederate Strategy Reconsidered* (2001), Robert G. Tanner questions interpretations of Confederate strategy that embrace a defensive posture. Joseph L. *Harsh's Confederate Tide Rising: Robert E. Lee and the Making of Southern Strategy, 1861–1862* (1998) offers great insight into Lee's thinking, whereas Steven E. Woodworth, *Davis and Lee at War* (1995) explores Confederate war effort and military strategy in the Eastern Theater. Finally, in terms of the continuing debate between some scholars as to the relative importance of the war in the East and in the West, see Richard M. McMurry, *The Fourth Battle of Winchester: Toward a New Civil War Paradigm* (2002), an entertaining counterfactual exploration that argues for the primacy of the war in the West, an argument echoed in Steven E. Woodworth's suggestively titled *Decision in the Heartland: The Civil War in the West* (2008).

Nearly every prominent Civil War general has been the subject of at least one modern biography. An exception to this rule is Irvin McDowell, who continues to labor in obscurity. The first commander of the Army of the Potomac is far more fortunate: see Stephen W. Sears, *George B. McClellan: The Young Napoleon* (1988); Ethan S. Rafuse, *McClellan's War: The Failure of Moderation in the Struggle for the Union* (2005); and Stephen W. Sears, ed., *The Civil War Papers of George B. McClellan: Selected Correspondence, 1860–1865* (1989). Peter Cozzens, *General John Pope: A Life for the Nation* (2000), seeks to rescue its subject from being the butt of various jokes, while Wallace J. Schutz and Walter N. Trenerry, *Abandoned by Lincoln: A Military Biography of General John Pope* (1990) presents a more spirited defense. William Marvel, *Burnside* (1991), offers a far more favorable assessment of its subject than one usually finds in the literature, while Walter H. Hebert, *Fighting Joe Hooker* (1943) remains the only biography of the general who would be dictator. Although George G. Meade still lacks a major modern biography, one can learn much from Freeman Cleaves, *Meade of Gettysburg* (1960), Ethan S. Rafuse, *George Gordon Meade and the War in the East* (2003), and Richard Sauers, *Meade: Victor of Gettysburg* (2004). For Ulysses S. Grant, see Brooks D. Simpson, *Ulysses S. Grant: Triumph over Adversity, 1822–1865* (2000) and Bruce Catton, *Grant Takes Command* (1968), as well as the thirty-one volumes of John Y. Simon, et al., eds, *The Papers of Ulysses S. Grant* (1967–2009). As for subordinate commanders, one should consult Mark Snell, *From First to Last: The Life of William B. Franklin* (2002); David M. Jordan, *Winfield Scott Hancock: A Soldier's Life* (1988) and *"Happiness Is Not My Companion": The Life of General G. K. Warren* (2001); Roy Morris, Jr., *Sheridan: The Life and Wars of General Phil Sheridan* (1992); and Eric J. Wittenberg, *Little Phil: A Reassessment of the Civil War Leadership of Gen. Philip H. Sheridan* (2002). A suggestive overview of command issues in the Army of the Potomac is in Stephen R. Taaffe, *Commanding the Army of the Potomac* (2006);

Michael C. C. Adams offers an explanation of Union challenges in *Our Masters the Rebels: A Speculation on Union Military Failure in the East, 1861–1865* (1978).

Craig L. Symonds, *Joseph E. Johnston: A Civil War Biography* (1992) and T. Harry Williams, *P. G. T. Beauregard: Napoleon in Gray* (1955), look at the commanders of First Manassas. Robert E. Lee is the subject of Douglas Southall Freeman's massive four volume work, *R. E. Lee* (1934–35), with a shorter treatment in Emory M. Thomas, *Robert E. Lee: A Biography* (1995). I benefited much from Ethan S. Rafuse, *Robert E. Lee and the Fall of the Confederacy, 1863–1865* (2008); one should also read Clifford Dowdey and Louis H. Manarin, eds., *The Wartime Papers of Robert E. Lee* (1961) and Brian Holden Reid, *Robert E. Lee: Icon for a Nation* (2007). As for subordinate Confederate commanders, see James I. Robertson, *Stonewall Jackson: The Man, the Soldier, The Legend* (1997) and *General A. P. Hill: The Story of a Confederate Warrior* (1987); Jeffry D. Wert, *General James Longstreet: The Confederacy's Most Controversial Soldier* (1993) and *Cavalryman of the Lost Cause: A Biography of J. E. B. Stuart* (1998); Donald C. Pfanz, *Richard S. Ewell: A Soldier's Life* (1998); and Emory M. Thomas, *Bold Dragoon: The Life of J. E. B. Stuart* (1986). Gary Gallagher, ed., *Fighting for the Confederacy: The Personal Recollections of General Edward Porter Alexander* (1989) sheds much light on the war in the East from a Confederate perspective; Jay Luvaas, ed., *The Civil War: A Soldier's View* (1958) brings together the thoughtful writings of G. F. R. Henderson. A tremendous achievement, Douglas Southall Freeman's three-volume study, *Lee's Lieutenants* (1942–44), presents a compelling if not always convincing portrait of Confederate generalship in the Army of Northern Virginia.

When it comes to the major field armies involved in the fighting in the East, one turns to Bruce Catton's masterful trilogy, *Mr. Lincoln's Army* (1951), *Glory Road* (1952), and *A Stillness at Appomattox* (1953). A more modern treatment is Jeffry D. Wert, *The Sword of Lincoln: The Army of the Potomac* (2005). For the Army of the James, one should turn to Edward G. Longacre, *Army of Amateurs: General Benjamin F. Butler and the Army of the James, 1863–1865* (1997). In addition to Freeman, *Lee's Lieutenants*, one should consult Joseph T. Glatthaar, *General Lee's Army: From Victory to Collapse* (2008) and J. Tracy Power, *Lee's Miserables: Life in the Army of Northerner Virginia from the Wilderness to Appomattox* (1998) for accounts of the Army of Northern Virginia. For naval operations, in addition to Reed, see William H. Roberts, *Now for the Contest: Coastal and Oceanic Naval Operations in the Civil War* (2004).

The various battles and campaigns in the Eastern Theater during the American Civil War have been examined in a rather large number of studies, some offering exceedingly detailed descriptions of military actions and combat. What follows is at best an introduction to that extensive body of work.

For First Manassas, see William C. Davis, *Battle at Bull Run: A History of the First Major Campaign of the Civil War* (1977) and Ethan S. Rafuse, *A Single Grand Victory:*

The First Campaign and Battle of Manassas (2002). Peter Cozzens, *Shenandoah 1862: Stonewall Jackson's Valley Campaign* (2008) and Robert G. Tanner, *Stonewall in the Valley: Thomas J. "Stonewall" Jackson's Shenandoah Valley Campaign, Spring 1862* (1996) cover operations in the Shenandoah Valley in the spring of 1862. Stephen W. Sears, *To the Gates of Richmond: The Peninsula Campaign* (1992) and Brian K. Burton, *Extraordinary Circumstances: The Seven Days Battles* (2001) offer contrasting assessments of the first sustained Union drive toward Richmond, while Steven H. Newton, *Joseph E. Johnston and the Defense of Richmond* (1998) defends Johnston. Finally, John J. Hennessy in *Return to Bull Run: The Campaign and Battle of Second Manassas* (1993) presents the best study of one of Lee's greatest victories.

Explorations of the Maryland Campaign, including the battle of Antietam, are to be found in Stephen W. Sears, *Landscape Turned Red: The Battle of Antietam* (1983); Joseph L. Harsh, *Taken at the Flood: Robert E. Lee and Confederate Strategy in the Maryland Campaign of 1862* (1999); and Benjamin Franklin Cooling, *Counter-Thrust: From the Peninsula to the Antietam* (2007). James M. McPherson offers a broader overview in *Crossroads of Freedom: Antietam* (2002), while readers may choose from one of two editions of Ezra Carman's study of the campaign, the first edited by Joseph Pierro (2008); a second version, edited by Thomas G. Clemens, will appear in two volumes (the initial volume was published in 2010). George C. Rable, *Fredericksburg! Fredericksburg!* (2002) and Francis Augustín O'Reilly, *The Fredericksburg Campaign: Winter War on the Rappahannock* (2003) cover that December disaster. On Chancellorsville, see Ernest B. Furgurson, *Chancellorsville 1863: The Souls of the Brave* (1992) and Stephen W. Sears, *Chancellorsville* (1996), as well as the classic *The Campaign of Chancellorsville: A Strategic and Tactical Study* (1910) by John Bigelow, Jr. The campaigns of Burnside and Hooker are treated together in Daniel E. Sutherland, *Fredericksburg and Chancellorsville: The Dare Mark Campaign* (1998).

Many books exist on the battle of Gettysburg. To attempt to offer a list of the titles that have informed my thinking would overwhelm the reader. Edwin B. *Coddington, The Gettysburg Campaign: A Study in Command* (1968) remains a classic, but see also Stephen W. Sears, *Gettysburg* (2004); a concise treatment can be found in Steven E. Woodworth, *Beneath a Northern Sky: A Short History of the Gettysburg Campaign* (2003). Several of the essays in Gabor S. Boritt, ed., *The Gettysburg Nobody Knows* (1997) shed much-needed light on the battle's impact on the war. One learns much about an underexplored aspect of Lee's 1863 invasion in Eric J. Wittenberg, J. David Petruzzi, and Michael F. Nugent, *One Continuous Fight: The Retreat from Gettysburg and the Pursuit of Lee's Army of Northern Virginia, July 4–14, 1863* (2008) and Kent Masterson Brown, *Retreat from Gettysburg: Lee, Logistics, and the Pennsylvania Campaign* (2005).

For the Overland Campaign of 1864, one turns first to the work of Gordon Rhea, who in four volumes to date has taken readers to Cold Harbor: *The Battle of the Wilderness, May 5-6, 1864* (1994); *The Battles for Spotsylvania Court House and the Road to Yellow Tavern, May 7–12, 1864* (1997); *To the North Anna River: Grant and Lee, May 13–25, 1864* (2000); and *Cold Harbor: Grant and Lee, May 26–June 3, 1864* (2002). For a single-volume overview, one should consult Mark Grimsley, *And Keep Moving On: The Virginia Campaign, May–June 1864* (2002).

William Glenn Robertson, *Back Door to Richmond: The Bermuda Hundred Campaign, April–June 1864* (1987) and Herbert Schiller, *The Bermuda Hundred Campaign* (1988) explore Benjamin F. Butler's efforts in the spring of 1864. William C. Davis, *The Battle of New Market* (1975) and Charles Knight, *Valley Thunder: The Battle of New Market and the Opening of the Shenandoah Campaign, May 1864* (2010) examine the opening drive in the Shenandoah Valley, while the oft-ignored campaign in southwest Virginia is the subject of Richard R. Duncan, *Lee's Endangered Left: The Civil War in Western Virginia, Spring of 1864* (1998). Frank E. Vandiver, *Jubal's Raid: General Early's Famous Attack on Washington in 1864* (1960) and Benjamin Franklin Cooling, *Jubal Early's Raid on Washington, 1864* (1995) review that operation. The campaigns in the Shenandoah Valley are covered in Edward J. Stackpole, *Sheridan in the Shenandoah: Jubal Early's Nemesis* (1961); Jeffry D. Wert, *From Winchester to Cedar Creek: The Shenandoah Campaign of 1864* (1987); and Scott C. Patchan, *Shenandoah Summer: The 1864 Valley Campaign* (2007).

Surprisingly, the operations around Petersburg have not received the attention that they deserve. Noah Andre Trudeau's trilogy, *Bloody Roads South: The Wilderness to Cold Harbor, May–June 1864* (1989); *The Last Citadel: Petersburg, Virginia, June 1864–April 1865* (1991); and *Out of the Storm: The End of the Civil War, April–June 1865* (1994) tells the story from the crossing of the James to the surrenders in 1865. John Horn offers a concise treatment of *The Petersburg Campaign, June 1864–April 1865* (1993). For the crater, see Michael A. Cavanaugh and William Marvel, *The Battle of The Crater: "The Horrid Pit," June 25–August 6, 1864* (1989); Richard Slotkin, *No Quarter: The Battle of the Crater, 1864* (2009); and Earl J. Hess, *Into the Crater: The Mine Attack at Petersburg* (2010). A. Wilson Greene, *The Final Battles of the Petersburg Campaign: Breaking the Backbone of the Rebellion* (2008), covers the closing episodes of the campaign. For the Appomattox campaign, one might also consult Chris M. Calkins, *The Appomattox Campaign, March 29–April 9, 1865* (1997) and William Marvel, *Lee's Last Retreat: The Flight to Appomattox* (2002).

INDEX

Note: CSA, Confederate States Army; USA, United States Army; USN, United States Navy.

ABOUT THE AUTHOR

BROOKS D. SIMPSON received his BA degree from the University of Virginia (1979) and his MA and PhD degrees from the University of Wisconsin (1982, 1989). He taught at Wofford College for three years before joining the faculty at Arizona State University in 1990, where he is presently ASU Foundation Professor of History. In 1995 he was a Fulbright scholar at Leiden University, the Netherlands. His books include *Let Us Have Peace: Ulysses S. Grant and the Politics of War and Reconstruction, 1861–1868*; *American's Civil War*; *The Reconstruction Presidents*; and *Ulysses S. Grant: Triumph Over Adversity, 1822–1865*.